The Moral Philosophy of John Steinbeck

Edited by
Stephen K. George

The Scarecrow Press, Inc.
Lanham, Maryland • Toronto • Oxford
2005

SCARECROW PRESS, INC.

Published in the United States of America
by Scarecrow Press, Inc.
A wholly owned subsidiary of
The Rowman & Littlefield Publishing Group, Inc.
4501 Forbes Boulevard, Suite 200, Lanham, Maryland 20706
www.scarecrowpress.com

PO Box 317
Oxford
OX2 9RU, UK

British Library Cataloguing in Publication Information Available

Library of Congress Cataloging-in-Publication Data

The moral philosophy of John Steinbeck / edited by Stephen K. George.
    p. cm.
 Includes bibliographical references and index.
 ISBN 0-8108-5441-4 (pbk. : alk. paper)
 1. Steinbeck, John, 1902–1968—Ethics. 2. Moral conditions in literature. 3.
Ethics in literature. I. George, Stephen K., 1965–

PS3537.T3234Z755 2005
813'.52—dc22

                                      2004029876

Dedicated to David Annis, who helped start this journey;
Louisa, Emma, Margaret, and Elizabeth,
for guiding me along the way;
and
my wife, Rebecca,
whose virtue has been
my dearest companion

Contents

Foreword
Richard E. Hart   vii
Acknowledgments   ix
Introduction
Stephen K. George and *Luchen Li*   xi

Part I: Steinbeck and Moral Philosophy

John Steinbeck's lower-case utopia: Basic Human
Needs, a Duty to Share, and the Good Life
Patrick K. Dooley   3

John Steinbeck and the Morality of Roles: Lessons
for Business Ethics
Joseph Allegretti   21

John Steinbeck: An Ethics of Fiction
John H. Timmerman   33

"I Want to Make 'Em Happy": Utilitarian Philosophy
in Steinbeck's Fiction
John J. Han   41

The Existential Vacuum and Ethan Allen Hawley:
John Steinbeck's Moral Philosophy
Barbara A. Heavilin   49

Part II: Ethical Explorations of Steinbeck's Fiction

Moral Experience in *Of Mice and Men*: Challenges
and Reflection
Richard E. Hart   61

Of Death, Life, and Virtue in Steinbeck's *Of Mice and Men* and *The Grapes of Wrath*
  Allene M. Parker   73

Judging Elisa Allen: Reader Entrapment in "The Chrysanthemums"
  Terry Gorton   87

The Power of Strange Faces: Revisiting *The Grapes of Wrath* with the Postmodern Ethics of Emmanuel Levinas
  Michael D. Hansen   107

The Emotional Content of Cruelty: An Analysis of Kate in *East of Eden*
  Stephen K. George   131

"No Sanctuary": Reconsidering the Evil of Cathy Ames Trask
  Sarah Appleton Aguiar   145

Business, Sex, and Ethics in *The Wayward Bus*
  Joseph Allegretti   155

"The Disintegration of a Man": Moral Integrity in *The Winter of Our Discontent*
  Stephen K. George   169

Bibliography   183
Index   193
About the Contributors   197
About the Editor   201

Foreword

Philosophy, especially moral philosophy, has taken a decidedly "applied" turn over the past thirty years. Work in the realm of moral theory, the summum bonum of moral philosophy throughout its history, persists but is now complemented and extended by applications of ideas and principles of morality to areas such as medicine, business management, the environment, and journalism. Thirty years ago professional philosophers could scarcely get a return phone call from physicians with whom they wished to collaborate on problems of ethics in medicine. Today most medical schools offer, if not require, training in medical ethics. We now have professional journals, think tanks, Ph.D. programs, innumerable conferences, and a wealth of undergraduate and graduate courses in all areas of applied ethics. Philosophers, such as medical ethicists, even find themselves interviewed on radio or television for their views on controversial ethical dilemmas.

Another important "applied" development in philosophical ethics has been the exploration of morality and literature. Philosophers with an interest in aesthetics have always worked on the philosophical "theory of" literature. Witness, among others, Plato and Aristotle, Nietzsche, Sartre, and Camus. Contemporary inquirers include Richard Rorty, Martha Nussbaum, and Justus Buchler. But these figures have, as well, accentuated the ways in which moral issues and dilemmas are embodied within and uniquely articulated by works of literary art. We now recognize such categories as "philosophical fiction," dramas that wrestle with responsibility and principle, or poetry that inflames the moral imagination. Indeed, the late novelist John Gardner authored a notable, albeit controversial book, *On Moral Fiction*, in which he gave the interface between literature and morality full and varied treatment.

We know literature has the capacity to offer unique perspectives on and experiences of morality in connection with the human struggle to understand, do good, and achieve ideals. Such perspectives and experiences are not necessarily produced by or readily available to reason and argument. In this regard the writer does not develop or defend a particular ethical theory or principle; the fictional work is not the same as a philosophical argument. Rather, the work of literature examines, rotates perspectives, provokes, while allowing the reader to witness the dramatic context in its wholeness. The writer honestly shows and the reader collaborates with the writer—exploring questions of morality and experiencing the tension and uncertainty of moral conflict. The writer portrays. The audience experiences and judges.

In this regard John Steinbeck has not been rigorously examined or fully appreciated as a contributor to moral philosophy. Millions of readers worldwide admire his work while serious scholars, philosophers among them, have not paid sufficient attention. The present volume goes a long way toward correcting this glaring deficiency. Reading Steinbeck disabuses us of the notion that only religionists, social theorists, and philosophers deal constructively with morality. Writers—as well as painters, composers, photographers, and filmmakers—have much to offer anyone who cares about right and wrong, accountability and justice. The authors gathered here are a diverse group with respect to training and point of view. Some are experts on business, some literature scholars and teachers, some philosophers. Some disagree with one another, both theoretically and in the reading of particular Steinbeck texts. But collectively, they amply demonstrate that Steinbeck was not just a superb experimental stylist, social critic, and, in many ways, the conscience of America. He was, as well, a moral philosopher who probed deeper than nearly any other American writer the contours of individual and societal ethics. These essays portray Steinbeck—the continual searcher for truth and goodness—as both harshly critical, perhaps cynical at times, and unabashedly optimistic about the moral perfectibility of man. To his credit, Steinbeck trusted his readers to carry forth the moral burdens and challenges of his work. In turn, his readers, and the scholars who here testify, are treated to a virtual Steinbeckian gold mine of novel ideas, viewpoints, and provocations concerning what the ancient Greeks regarded as the never-ending pursuit of the good life and an improved society.

Richard E. Hart
Bloomfield College

Acknowledgments

This book had its genesis during my doctoral studies at Ball State University. My dissertation, *Of Vice and Men: A Virtue Ethics Study of John Steinbeck's* The Pearl, East of Eden, *and* The Winter of Our Discontent, was ably guided by department colleagues Bill Miller, Wade Jennings, and Bruce Hozeski, to whom I owe a debt of gratitude. However, my love of ethical applications to literature was most encouraged by the then chair of Ball State's Philosophy Department, David Annis. Without David's early guidance and encouragement, this book probably would never have come to be.

I am also indebted to my fine editorial board—English colleagues Richard Astro and Luchen Li and philosophy professors Richard Hart and Patrick Dooley—all of whom have gone over this work more than once, offering just the right mix of editorial insight and enthusiasm. Of these four colleagues and friends, Richard Hart has played an especially crucial role. I am indebted to him for a fine essay and foreword as well as for his early encouragement of this project.

I would also like to thank the Archives and Special Collections of Ball State University—in particular John Straw and Tetsumaro Hayashi—for their courtesy and helpfulness during my 2004 Burkhart Award visit. My own department chair, Kip Hartvigsen, and the English Department of Brigham Young University-Idaho have been untiringly supportive in providing materials and funds for editing this collection. Artist Brandon Dorman created a wonderful cover portrait of the author, and Jim Croasmun of BYU-Idaho's Instruction & Technology Department provided much needed assistance with formatting issues. Scarecrow Press and Stephen Ryan deserve much credit for believing in my proposal and for allowing four of its essays to appear first in volume 1, issue 2, of *The Steinbeck Review*. And, of course, where would *The Moral Philosophy of John Steinbeck* be without the many contributors and their philosophically provocative essays. My deepest thanks to all of them.

No acknowledgment is complete without thanking those nearest to you: my children Louisa, Emma, Margaret, Henry, Charles, and Elizabeth, and my wife Rebecca. As always, your support and encouragement cannot be measured.

Copyright Acknowledgments

Grateful acknowledgment is made to Viking Penguin, a division of Penguin Group (USA) Inc., and to The Penguin Group (UK) for permission to reprint from *The Grapes of Wrath* by John Steinbeck, copyright 1939, renewed copyright 1967 by John Steinbeck. Used by permission of Viking Penguin, a division of Penguin Group (USA) Inc.

Acknowledgment is also made for the following:

Stephen K. George's "'The Disintegration of a Man': Moral Integrity in *The Winter of Our Discontent*" from *Steinbeck Yearbook*, volume one, edited by Barbara A. Heavilin, with the permission of The Edwin Mellen Press.

John Timmerman's "John Steinbeck: An Ethics of Fiction" reprinted from *John Steinbeck: A Centennial Tribute*, edited by Stephen K. George. Copyright 2002 by Stephen K. George. Reproduced with permission of Greenwood Publishing Group, Inc., Westport, Connecticut.

John Steinbeck's cover photograph reproduced courtesy of Elaine Steinbeck and Ball State University Libraries, Archives and Special Collections, Muncie, Indiana. Steinbeck portrait created by Brandon Dorman (www.brandondorman.com) and courtesy of the editor. Photograph and artistic reproduction used with the permission of the Steinbeck Heritage Foundation.

Introduction

> For a novelist is a rearranger of nature so that it makes an understandable pattern, and a novelist is also a teacher, but a novelist is primarily a man and subject to all of a man's faults and virtues, fears and braveries. . . . And because he is usually a moral man in attention and honest in approach, he sets things down as truly as he can. . . . A novel may be said to be the man who writes it.
>
> —John Steinbeck, Letter to Elizabeth Otis and Chase Horton, April 26, 1957

Of all the famous modernist writers—Hemingway, Faulkner, Eliot, Lawrence, Fitzgerald—John Steinbeck stands apart for his serious interest and background in moral philosophy. His personal reading list of books owned or borrowed numbers some three dozen religious and philosophic works, including *The Dialogues of Plato*, the *Tao Teh Ching*, Kant's *Critique of Pure Reason*, Spinoza's *Ethics*, the *Discourses* of Epictetus, and the Bible.[1] Along with Ed Ricketts, Steinbeck produced a major work of ecological philosophy, *The Sea of Cortez*, which according to Richard Astro captures "his philosophy of life,"[2] specifically the author's preoccupation with ethical relations among ourselves and with the natural world around us. If anything, Steinbeck's interest in ethics increased in his later years, when many of his works—*The Wayward Bus*, *East of Eden*, *The Winter of Our Discontent*, *Travels with Charley*—shift from a somewhat detached social criticism to an intense focus on human virtue and vice, the question of evil, and the moral state of America. Still, the author's highest duty, as indicated above, was to honesty in his craft and truth in his fiction. Millions of readers across the world today believe he fulfilled that duty.

In his last book, *America and Americans*, John Steinbeck observes that "[e]thics, morals, codes of conduct, are the stern rules which in the past we needed to survive—as individuals, as groups, as nations."[3] Given the continued threats to our society and world from the immoral behavior of political leaders and celebrities, embezzlement by corporate CEOs, and atrocities of international terrorists, such moral boundaries seem more relevant today than ever. With the clarity of a gifted novelist grounded in ethical ideas and theory, Steinbeck deftly explores the moral contortions of individuals, social groups, and nations. For example, *The Grapes of Wrath* and *In Dubious Battle* question the government's ability to deal with poverty, natural disaster, and labor disputes; *The Winter of Our Discontent* exposes how distorted values can corrupt business professionals and government officials; *Once There Was A War* and *The Moon Is Down* reveal the psychological and moral challenges faced by soldiers; *East of Eden* explores the interdependency of good and evil while inviting the reader to make her own choice; *Tortilla Flat* and *Cannery Row* probe the negotiation of values between mainstream America and its subcultures; and *To A God Unknown* and *Sea of Cortez* dissect the ongoing struggle between humankind and the natural world. The ethical scope and complexity of Steinbeck's canon, from beginning to end, is impressive.

More importantly, a search for truth that allowed for ambiguity, paradox, and revision is the essence of both philosophical reasoning and Steinbeck, much of whose inquiry as a thinker-artist can be categorized into two areas: personal and societal ethics. Within personal ethics the author examines such traditional concepts as friendship, loyalty, heroism, and integrity through the various moral conflicts within his fiction: George's execution of Lennie in *Of Mice and Men*, Adam Trask's forgiveness of Caleb in the closing pages of *East Of Eden*, Ethan Hawley's struggle to return the family talisman and its promise of moral clarity to his daughter Ellen in *Winter*. Often these depictions of individual morality are rooted in western religion, particularly Christianity, with many of his best-known works employing biblical themes, syntax, tone, and imagery. Yet Steinbeck, always skeptical of organized religion, made these depictions unique by blending traditional religious precepts with Eastern philosophy, pagan myth, and his own holistic worldview. To some degree, Steinbeck's fictive religions—Jim Casy's Emersonian Christianity, Mack and the boy's spiritual pragmatism—are the means by which human beings may redeem corrupted institutions while making ethical sense of the brutal social and natural forces around them. Decades before the current consensus on environmental ethics, John Steinbeck understood the interconnectedness of humanity with all things organic and inorganic.

The author's exploration of societal ethics is no less prescient. Long before the term "Enron" became synonymous with corporate greed, Steinbeck writes, "In America we have developed the Corporation Man. His life, his family, his future—as well as his loyalty—lie with his corporation. . . . His position in the pyramid of management is exactly defined by the size of his salary and his bonuses."[4] The ethical implications of equating one's identity and worth with business position and success are explored fictively in *The Wayward Bus*'s Elliot Pritchard, *The Winter of Our Discontent*'s Mr. Baker and Ethan Hawley, and (in contrast) *Cannery Row*'s Doc and Mack and the boys, where Steinbeck concludes that the virtues we admire—kindness, honesty, and compassion—lead only to failure in our economic system, while those we detest—greed, egotism, meanness—bring business success. As Americans we "admire the quality of the first" but "love the produce of the second."[5]

Further explorations of societal ethics run the gamut from politics and war to gender and racial relations. Significantly, Steinbeck's fiction often poses the values of other ethnic groups and subcultures—Paisanos, Mexican Indians, Chinese immigrants, vagrants, prostitutes—as both contrastive and corrective to mainstream culture. And contrary to most of the contemporary depictions of these groups, the author's many Oriental, Paisano, and Mexican characters (Lee of *East of Eden*, Danny of *Tortilla Flat*, Kino and Juana of *The Pearl*) are strong and stereotype-defying, with ways of life and philosophies often far more virtuous than those of their Caucasian counterparts. These ethnic groups fascinated Steinbeck in part because they represented a moral vision that he longed to grasp and strived to capture in his fiction. The Steinbeck canon as a whole implicitly argues that ethical relationships between peoples and cultures are impossible without compassion for the "other" and an appreciation of his ways of thinking about and experiencing the world.

The essays contained within this volume seek to aid in this appreciation by offering perspectives first on what Steinbeck's own moral philosophy entails and second on how that philosophy plays out in the laboratory of the writer's fiction. For Patrick Dooley, the author's worldview fits nicely within an Aristotelian framework of virtue, work, and the good life. For Joseph Allegretti, Steinbeck's philosophy is particularly relevant to the field of business ethics. John Timmerman divides his study into intrinsic and extrinsic ethics, ultimately arguing that Steinbeck's ethics of fiction is deontological or duty-based. In contrast, John Han finds a strong utilitarian or consequentialist underpinning to Steinbeck's fiction, from *Tortilla Flat* to *East of Eden*. Barbara Heavilin concludes Part I by asking us to reflect on what Steinbeck would make of current existential and nihilistic ethics.

In part II the ethical interplay of Steinbeck's fictional world is explored from a variety of perspectives. Richard Hart begins by making a strong case for the moral power of "lived experience"—specifically racism and sexism—in what may be the author's most banned book, *Of Mice and Men*. Allene Parker and Stephen George approach four major Steinbeck works—*Of Mice and Men*, *The Grapes of Wrath*, *East of Eden*, and *Winter*—from the now flourishing field of Aristotelian or virtue ethics, specifically examining courage, compassion, cruelty, and moral integrity as exhibited by the novels' characters. Terry Gorton provides a unique reading of Steinbeck's most anthologized story, "The Chrysanthemums," and asks us to reconsider the ethical challenges it still prompts from readers seventy years later. Michael Hansen applies the philosophical perspective of one of the most influential of postmodern ethical critics, Emmanuel Levinas, to what is arguably the author's most ethical work, *The Grapes of Wrath*. And Sarah Aguiar and Joseph Allegretti invite readers to reevaluate the evil of Cathy Trask and the moral insightfulness of *The Wayward Bus*, respectively, with both authors offering provocative new readings.

Implicit in all of these essays is the idea that Steinbeck's moral philosophy is ultimately rooted in what is contemporarily known as narrative ethics, or the ability to tell a story in such a way that the experience itself has the potential to make the reader better for the time spent with the book. Although literature rarely poses directly as an attempt to represent universal truths and values, it does explore the possibilities and consequences of specific human thoughts, emotions, and actions in a rich narrative form. As argued by philosophy/literary critics from Aristotle to Wayne Booth, the narrative act should ideally serve an ethical end, specifically a searching out (rather than a positing) of universal truths and values. John Steinbeck, one of American literature's most versatile and gifted storytellers, was unabashedly such a searcher. As the author writes in *East of Eden*, "We have only one story. All novels, all poetry, are built on the never-ending contest in ourselves of good and evil."[6] Steinbeck's narrative world always has a high moral purpose. His ability to depict the violence, injustice, and despair of fully wrought fictive creations—Lennie Small, Ma Joad, Cal Trask, Ethan Hawley—evokes the highest levels of moral thought and feeling.

Further, unlike some of his literary contemporaries, Steinbeck's fiction and nonfiction almost always evidences a confidence in humanity's ability to find its way through the moral challenges of the self as well as those within religion, business, war, politics, and ethnic conflict. He finds beauty and virtue in Americans and non-Americans alike, and he implicitly extends this virtuousness to his readership. Believing that the function of fiction is to foster moral and spiritual growth by exposing "our many grievous faults . . . for the purpose of improvement,"[7] John Steinbeck nevertheless leaves us with our own choice as we, the participating reader, witness George executing a trusting Lennie, Rose of Sharon breastfeeding a starving man, and Cannery Row's Doc wiping his eyes upon reading "Black Marigolds." Steinbeck truly believes that all people, even someone as deformed as Cathy Trask, have a choice, that "[p]eople are not basically immoral. . . . They want to be moral but it takes a little courage."[8] With his portrayals of humanity's many degradations balanced precariously with a hope for our species' perfectibility, John Steinbeck's canon offers an array of characters that has influenced not only our culture but also many of our deepest beliefs concerning our moral responsibilities to our fellow beings, society, and the natural world. If indeed a "novel may be said to be the man who writes it,"[9] then the critical explorations that follow should reveal as much about John Steinbeck the man as they do his enduring moral philosophy.

Stephen K. George
Brigham Young University-Idaho

Luchen Li
Kettering University

Notes

1. Robert J. DeMott, *Steinbeck's Reading: A Catalogue of Books Owned and Borrowed* (New York: Garland Publishing, 1984), 14, 38, 64, 67, 91, 104.

2. Richard Astro, "Introduction," *The Log from the Sea of Cortez* (New York: Penguin, 1995), vii.

3. John Steinbeck, *America and Americans and Selected Nonfiction*, eds. Susan Shillinglaw and Jackson Benson (New York: Viking Penguin, 2002), 398.

4. Ibid., 358.

5. John Steinbeck, *Cannery Row* (New York: Penguin, 1994), 135.

6. John Steinbeck, *East of Eden* (New York: Penguin, 1992), 415.

7. Steinbeck, *America and Americans*, 173.

8. Thomas Fensch, ed., *Conversations with John Steinbeck* (Jackson: University Press of Mississippi, 1988), 74.

9. This insight into Steinbeck's creative and moral process was selected from a personal letter to his friend Chase Horton and literary agent Elizabeth Otis, whom Elaine Steinbeck described (in a letter to Tetsumaro Hayashi) as "far and away the most important influence in my husband's literary career." The entire collection is housed as the "John Steinbeck Correspondence with Elizabeth Otis and Chase Horton, 1956-1965," in the Archives and Special Collections of Bracken Library, Ball State University (Muncie, IN), and numbers over a hundred letters and other items.

Part I: Steinbeck and Moral Philosophy

John Steinbeck's lower-case utopia: Basic Human Needs, a Duty to Share, and the Good Life

PATRICK K. DOOLEY
St. Bonaventure University

Should the *Biography Channel* remake its program on the life and works of John Steinbeck, perhaps the new version's theme song ought to be Aaron Copland's "Fanfare to the Common Man." In great measure, Steinbeck won the Nobel Prize on account of a legendary ability to understand people, especially ordinary folks. Indeed, unnoticed and ignored, forgettable and seemingly unexceptional common men and women populate his works. With the possible exceptions of weddings and funerals, few of Steinbeck's protagonists get dressed up; his heroes are blue-collar or no-collar. His simpatico fondness for ordinary Americans also extends to middle or lower class Norwegians, Mexicans, Russians, and French. Note the eager anticipation in his May 27, 1952 letter to Elizabeth Otis (his literary agent) describing his stay with a lower-middle class French farm family:

> We are going to stay with the Frenchman in his house which he says has a toilet but no water. He says we can stay at an hotel—but I would rather stay with him. He has three daughters and he says—"They have many friends who I hope will not bother you." This is a great thing for me. I will be able to see French lower middle class farm life as I could not in any other way. I don't know how long I will stay but I will surely stay until I get a good sense of people, thinking and way of life. It is a wonderful chance.[1]

One could dip into virtually any chapter of any of Steinbeck's books to find a celebration of the modest aspirations of average men and women who seek to win for themselves, by way of work and democratic participation, a decent life. But they aspire not to win it for themselves; Steinbeck repeatedly stresses that whenever ordinary folks satisfy their basic needs, their next impulse is to share their goods with their marginalized fellows. This is especially true in his first two powerful, if gritty, novels, *Of Mice and Men* and *The Grapes of Wrath*. In these two works Steinbeck's picture of the good life amounts to an unspectacular lower-case utopia of work, family, and home. So, too, do most of his middle and later works, including *Travels with Charley: In Search of America* and *America and Americans*. But in these last two volumes, along with the ordinary contentment that was the rule in his earlier studies, Steinbeck worries, for he senses in his native land a discontent that he links with too much ease and too many things. In what follows, we will take a close look at Steinbeck's account of a generation of striving and sharing Americans in the 1930s, and then, two generations later, some of their comfortable and jaded descendents. While the first cohort is happy or believes they will soon be able to gain happiness, the second group is sated but nevertheless dissatisfied.

To consider this argument, putting Steinbeck's diagnosis in an Aristotelian framework is helpful. In his *The Nicomachean Ethics,* Aristotle argues that a "good" (morally good, that is) person is also a happy person. Or reading his argument from the other direction, he contends that a happy person is a good (a well-developed, that is) person.[2] For Aristotle, then—and I would contend that this holds true for Steinbeck, as well—genuine moral goodness, genuine human happiness, and genuine human development are three ways to describe the same thing: a well-lived and fulfilling human life in a good society. Conversely, a disordered society cannot facilitate happiness, goodness, or development. The short answer to the difference between a good and a disordered society (and the happy or discontented humans who live in each) has to do with needs and wants. For Aristotle, needs reside in invariant structures in human nature; wants, whether benign or malignant, are person-dependent and culture-specific add-ons. Accordingly, I will argue that in the limited aspirations in *Of Mice and Men* and *The Grapes of Wrath*, Steinbeck's lower-case utopians pay attention to their own and the needs of others, while the distopians he encounters in *Travels with Charley* and *America and Americans* are driven by excessive, sometimes specious wants.

Steinbeck's lower-case utopians

The bindle stiffs in *Of Mice and Men* live in bunkhouses and hire out for work by the week. Even those who stay for a whole planting or harvest season eventually move on to their next job: "Guys like us," George explains to Lennie, "that work on ranches, are the loneliest guys in the world. They got no family. They don't belong no place. . . . They ain't got nothing to look ahead to." But he goes on to tell Lennie, "With us it ain't like that. We got a future." Since they have a "family" in each other, they dream of a home and a future where they will have "a little house and a couple of acres . . . an' live off the fatta the lan'."[3] They both deeply want to believe that they can make this elusive, yet mesmerizingly tangible fantasy happen for them. Surely they will have the happiness of having such rudimentary desires fulfilled. Henry David Thoreau argues that the algorithm for happiness and contentment is to reduce one's wants to basic needs (for Thoreau: food, fuel, shelter, and clothes)[4] that can be readily satisfied. George and Lennie's fantasy future is likewise minimalist. They want to own a little place, do their own work, and raise their own crops. This dream is so real to them that they are convinced that as soon as they raise the funds, they will only need to buy an already established, up-and-running small farm. George tells Lennie and Old Candy, a first-time listener, how it will be:

> "Well, it's ten acres. . . . Got a little win-mill. Got a little shack on it, an' a chicken run. Got a kitchen, orchard, cherries, apples, peaches, 'cots, nuts, got a few berries. They's a place for alfalfa and plenty of water to flood it. They's a pig pen. . . . All kin's a vegetables in the garden and if we want a little whisky we can sell a few eggs or something or milk. We'd jus live there. We'd belong there. There wouldn't be no more runnin' round the country and gettin' fed by a Jap cook. No sir, we'd have our own place where we belonged and not sleep in no bunk house."[5]

Old Candy has $300 in the bank; with each of their monthly wages, in four short weeks the men will have the $450 needed to make the fantasy future a real one. The black stable buck, Crooks, is also drawn in, though he had heard many others describe similar dreams: "'I never seen a guy really do it,' he said. 'I seen guys nearly crazy with loneliness for the land, but ever' time a whore house or a blackjack game took what it takes.'" Still, Crooks also wants to be part of this "family": "If you . . . guys would want a hand to work for nothing—just his keep, why I'd come an' lend a hand. I ain't so crippled that I can't work like a son-of-a-bitch if I want to."[6]

Of course, Lennie's run-in with Curley's wife ruins it all. But Old Candy and (one supposes) Crooks, though newcomers to the George and Lennie version of "the old words," already had that fantasy future indelibly imprinted on their dream-consciousness. Looking at the dead body of Curley's wife, Candy mourns:

> "I could of hoed in the garden and washed dishes for them guys." He paused, and then went on in a singsong. And he repeated *the old words*: "If they was a circus or a baseball game . . . we would of went to her . . . jus' said 'ta hell with work,' an' went to her. Never ast nobody's say so. An' they'd of been a pig and chickens . . . an' in the winter . . . the little fat stove . . . an' the rain comin'. . . . an' us jus' settin' there."[7]

The dream future of George and Lennie and Old Candy and Crooks, ever only a mere possibility, vanishes.

But in contrast to these dashed dreams, the hope for a decent life and a low-key happiness depicted in *The Grapes of Wrath* has probability on its side. This is because it has the crucial ingredient missing in the lower-case utopia in *Of Mice and Men*: the energy and momentum of loyalty to family.

Whereas Thoreau's Walden Pond "experiment in living deliberately" had him freely reduce his wants to his needs, the Joads and those they encounter on

their westward errand had brutally diminished lives forcefully thrust upon them
by drought and depleted farm land and/or by the bottom line economics of distant corporations or faceless banks that "tractored all the tenants off a the lan'."[8]
Since many of the California pilgrims struggle to meet the most basic needs of
food, fuel, shelter, and transportation, a duty-to-share ethic emerges in *The
Grapes of Wrath*, as when Tom's first night out of prison finds him and Jim
Casy at the abandoned Joad home place with Muley Graves. Tom asks, "What
you gonna eat, Muley? How you been gettin' your dinner?" Muley then takes
two cottontails and a jackrabbit out of his sack. Casy wonders, "You sharin'
with us, Muley Graves?" Whereupon Steinbeck gives his initial account of a
duty-to-share (whenever basic needs are unmet) ethic: "Muley fidgeted in em-
barrassment. 'I ain't got no choice in the matter.' He stopped on the ungracious
sound of his words. 'That ain't like I mean it. That ain't, I mean'—he stum-
bled—'what I mean, if a fella's got somepin to eat and an' another fella's hungry—why, the first fella ain't got no choice.'"[9] Tellingly, Steinbeck's Okies
describe a number of moral obligations as "got to's."

Vital, and therefore most pressing, obligations cannot be ignored, for they
minister to essential matters: hunger and shelter, heath and sickness, birth and
death. The first day on the road, even before they have left Oklahoma, Grampa
has a stroke. Though they have just met the Wilsons at a makeshift roadside
camp, their new neighbors immediately loan their tent to shelter Grampa. When
Pa is told this, he compliments the Wilsons on their "generosity." Note that both
Ivy and Sairy Wilson counter that although thanks might be appropriate for optional moral actions ("should do"), this is a case of a strict obligation ("must
do"): "Pa called, 'Mr. Wilson! . . . We're thankful to you folks.' 'We're proud to
help,' said Wilson. 'We're beholden to you,' said Pa. 'There's no beholden in a
time of dying,' said Wilson, and Sairy echoed him, 'Never no beholden.'"[10]

Further, important moral duties to the deceased and to the living trump legal
obligations. Neither the Wilsons nor the Joads have difficulty ignoring the law
that requires a coroner and an undertaker. Their reasoning is straightforward:
following the law will cost $40 and "We got to get to California 'fore our money
gives out." They simply wash Grampa's body, wrap it in a quilt-shroud, and
bury it along with a note sealed in a Mason jar: "This here is William James
Joad, dyed of a stroke, old, old man. His fokes bured him becaws they got no
money to pay for funerls."[11] Steinbeck, speaking through Pa and Casey, is clear
about duties and rights and about the priority of moral obligations over legal
ones: "'Sometimes the law can't be foller'd no way,' said Pa. 'Not in decency,
anyways. They's lots of times you can't. . . . Sometimes a fella got to sift the
law. I'm sayin' now I got a right to bury my own pa. Anybody got somepin to
say?' The preacher rose high on his elbow, 'Law changes,' he said, 'but got to's
go on. You got the right to do what you got to do.'" After Grampa is lowered in
the grave, each man threw in a shovel full of dirt. Note Steinbeck's perspica-
cious commentary: "When all had taken their *duty* and their *right*, Pa attacked
the mound of loose dirt and hurriedly filled the hole."[12]

Both duties and rights are complicatedly mixed as the Joads turn to fixing the Wilson's car. From one point of view, the loan of the tent to minister to the dying Grampa has created a reciprocal obligation. Even though both the Wilsons insist that "no beholden" is due, Al says, "'I'll fix your car—me and Tom will.' And Al looked proud that he could return the family's obligation. 'We could use some help.' Wilson admitted the retiring of the obligation." Each family's responses to the other widen the circle of family. The Joads will fix the Wilson's car and the two families will join up: "An' me an' Al both knows about a car, so we could keep that car a-rollin. We'd keep together on the road an' it'd be good for ever'body." Both Wilsons protest that they might become burdens. Ma Joad, Steinbeck's usual moral spokesperson in *The Grapes of Wrath,* comments, "'You won't be no burden. Each'll help each, an' we'll all git to California. Sairy Wilson he'ped lay Grampa out,' and she stopped. The relationship was plain."[13]

Though the relationship was forged by obligations that had to be followed, the deeper message of the Wilsons's and Joads's responses to several "got to's" is that humans are at their ethical best—and thereby most fulfilled—when they help each other. For instance, Sairy had earlier waved off Ma's offer to replace the quilt used as Grampa's shroud: "You shouldn' talk like that. We're proud to help, I ain't felt so—safe in a long time. People needs—to help." And at the chapter's end when Sairy reiterates her concern about becoming a burden to the group, Ma offers similar counsel: "We gonna see you get through. You said yourself, you can't let help go unwanted."[14] Both women clearly understand and respond to Steinbeck's duty-to-share ethic that resolutely insists that basic human needs must be neither ignored nor left unmet.

Down to their last forty dollars, the Joads enter California finding neither a Promised Land nor a Utopia but Hovervilles. The first night as Ma makes stew, fifteen hungry children crowd near her cooking fire. "Ma looked up from her work, 'You want to get ast to eat huh? . . . Didn' none of these there have no breakfast?'"[15] Though it greatly distresses her, Ma must modify her allegiance to a duty-to-share ethic. She can no longer respond to the imperatives of an objective and relationship-neutral formalist morality that regards all persons, be they family or friends, fellow countrymen or foreigners, as equally deserving. When she calls her family to supper she knows she must somehow juggle her obligation to care for her family with her outreach to the needy:

Ma said helplessly, "I dunno what to do. I got to feed the fambly. What'm I gonna do with these here?" The children stood stiffly and looked at her. Their faces were blank, rigid, and their eyes went mechanically from the pot to the tin plate she held. . . . Ma ladled stew into tin plates, very little stew, and she laid the plates on the ground. "I can't send 'em away," she said. "I don' know what to do. Take your plates inside. I'll let 'em have what's lef'". . . . Ma shook her head, "I dunno what to do. I can't rob the fambly. I got to feed the fambly."[16]

Ma's solution to the "us vs. them" dilemma, giving primary attention to her family's need and responding to others to the extent that she can, is unappreciated by the mother of one of the hungry children she had fed. A "strong, broad woman" appeared at the Joad tent:

> Ma looked questioningly at her, "Can I he'p you in any way?"
> The woman set her hand on her hips, "You kin he'p me by mindin' your own children an' lettin' mine alone. . . . My little fella come back smellin' of stew. You give it to 'im. He tol' me. Don' you go a-boastin' an' braggin' 'bout havin' stew."
> "Set down," Ma said. "That was 'bout the las' stew we're gonn have till we get work. S'pose you was cookin' a stew an' a bunch of little fellas stood aroun' moonin,' what'd you do? We didn't have enough, but you can't keep it when they look at ya like that."[17]

In her answer to the angry mother, Ma's defense of her generosity appeals, then, to both duty and sentiment.[18] Unfortunately, when needs outstrip resources, these morally praiseworthy motives are bound to painfully and unavoidably conflict.

One strategy that Ma uses to lessen the conflict is to have the family take their plates of stew inside the tent. Uncle John, seeing the hungry children, loses his appetite: "I ain't hungry . . . I'd still see 'em inside the tent."[19] Tom and Ma understand that in this case sentiments must be blunted and duty responded to, and so they insist that Uncle John eat his supper. Earlier, in Steinbeck's wonderful chapter 17, he describes how the families who happen to camp together for a night are forged into a community wherein both duties and rights are encoded first into rules and then into laws, including a law about eating in the presence of the hungry: "And as the worlds moved westward, rules became laws, although no one told the families. It is unlawful to foul near the camp; it is unlawful in any way to foul the drinking water; it is unlawful to eat good rich food near one who is hungry, unless he is asked to share."[20]

In the last third of *The Grapes of Wrath* the Joads face many situations where the duty-to-share ethic—now modified to "respond to family needs first, and others if possible"—is put to the test. However clear this modified maxim might be in theory, it is cumbersome in practice, for who counts as family and when is there enough to share with non-family members?

The Joad family is one of the first to get to Tulare for the cotton picking season. For the first time they are members of the migrant gentry as they settle into a boxcar: "those who had the boxcars were old-timers, and in a way aristocrats." But even though the Joad family is now reduced to seven—Grampa and Granma have died, Noah has left, Connie has deserted, Casy has been incarcerated, and Tom has become a fugitive—they are still entitled to half of a railroad car. The Wainwrights share the other end, with a canvas tarpaulin hung in the middle. Gradually, however, the Joad-Wainwright distinction blurs as they share work, rides, and meals. And then, when the heavy winter rains come, the canvas divider is taken down to cover the truck engine, and "the two families in the car were one." The two families were uniting in any case due to the onset of Rose of Sharon's time to deliver. After a night of pain, her child is stillborn as a "blue shriveled little mummy."[21] Ma, nearly as exhausted as Rose of Sharon, is unwilling to let Mrs. Wainwright spell her. Their conversation rehearses now familiar refrains: the "no-need to be beholden" comments about burying Grampa and the "anyone would do the same thing" account of sharing the stew:

> Ma fanned the air slowly with her cardboard. "You been frien'ly," she said. "We thank you."
> The stout woman smiled. "No need to thank. Ever'body's in the same wagon.[22] S'pose we was down. You'd give us a han'."
> "Yes," Ma said, "we would."
> "Or anybody."
> "Or anybody. Use'ta be the fambly was first. It ain't so now. It's anybody. Worse off we get, the more we got to do."[23]

So far we have looked at Steinbeck's account of the moral obligation connected with a strict duty ("must do") to share in the face of vital needs such as food and shelter, birth and death, and in dire circumstances, a primary and sometimes even exclusive obligation to family. Steinbeck's moral reflections also range over optional ("should do") moral matters; especially touching are his depictions of the generosity of ordinary people.

Among Steinbeck's commonplace saints are the good-hearted cook, Al, the waitress, Mae, and the truckers who frequent the roadside café so compellingly described in chapter 15. Their patrons are rich couples in big cars (Mae calls them "shitheels"), truck drivers, and families in overloaded, unreliable cars and makeshift truck campers. As two truckers discuss with Mae and Al the exodus of down-and-out families, a father and two young tow-headed boys enter the café to buy a loaf of bread (and maybe some candy for the boys). The family budget is eleven cents. "His humility was insistent" as the father pleads his case: "'We got to make a dime do all of us'. . . . Mae said, 'You can't get no loaf a bread for a dime. We only got fifteen-cent loafs.' From behind her Al growled. 'God Almighty, Mae, give 'em bread.' 'We'll run out 'fore the bread truck comes.' 'Run out, then, goddam it,' said Al." Perhaps it is Al's generosity that is the leaven that first inspires Mae. She lies that the peppermint sticks that the boys want are two for a penny (they're a nickel apiece). Responding to her cue, the truckers who had planned to spend a quarter each ("Fifteen cents for pie an' coffee an' a dime for Mae") walked out the door leaving twice as much. Mae calls to Al, "'Look there.' She pointed at the coins beside the cups—two half-dollars. Al walked near and looked, and then he went back to his work. 'Truck drivers,' Mae said reverently, 'an' after them shitheels.'"[24]

Two other scenes of uncommon generosity come to mind: the Wallace family in the Weedpatch government camp and the clerk in the peach company's store for migrant workers. Tom meets the Wallace family, who are flush, at least for now: "We been eatin' good for twelve days now. Never missed a meal in twelve days—none of us. Workin' an' gettin' our pay an' eatin." They have the wherewithal to share and so they do, giving Tom breakfast—"We got plenty— thank God!"—and inviting him to come with them to see if he can work, too. Though the Wallaces well understand that the work they have found will not last, they still share their good fortune. Apparently they will turn to helping others before they satisfy the rest of their wardrobe wants:

> "You got work now," Tom suggested.
> "Yea, but it ain't gonna las' long. Workin' for a nice fella. Got a little place. Works 'longside of us. But, hell—it ain't gonna las' no time."
> Tom said, "Why in hell you gonna git me on? I'll make it shorter. What you cuttin' your own throat for?"
> Timothy shook his head slowly. "I dunno. Got no sense, I guess. We figgered to get us each a hat. Can't do it, I guess."[25]

A couple of weeks later, the Joads reluctantly leave the government camp in search of work. The first day out the whole family is hired on to pick peaches and after several hours of work Ma gets a chit for one dollar while the rest of the family keeps picking. In the "price for this and that" give-and-take between Ma and the company store clerk, he is flippant and she is earnest:

> "Any reason you got to make fun? That help you any? . . . "Who owns this here store?"
> "Hooper Ranches, Incorporated, ma'am."
> "An' they set the prices?"
> "Yes, ma'am."
> She looked up, smiling a little. "Ever'body comes in talks like me, is mad?"
> He hesitated for a moment. "Yes, ma'am."
> "An' that's why you make fun?"
> "What cha mean?"
> "Doin' a dirty thing like this. Shames ya, don't it? Got to act flip, huh?" Her voice was gentle. The clerk watched her, fascinated. He didn't answer.

Her dollar credit used for staples, Ma remembered that Tom has twice asked for sugar for his coffee. Surely by now, she says, the rest of the family has earned much more than the ten cents for sugar:

> "You let me have some sugar an' I'll bring the slip in later."
> "I can't do it, ma'am. That's the rule. No slip, no groceries. The manager, he talks about that all the time. No, I can't do it. No I can't. They'd catch me. They always catch fellas. Always. I can't."
> "For a dime?"
> "For anything, ma'am."[26]

Then softened by Ma's empathy for his plight, "He looked pleadingly at her and then his face lost its fear. He took ten cents from his pocket and rang it up in the cash register. . . . 'There you are,' he said. 'Now it's all right. You bring in your slip an' I'll get my dime back.'" Ma, chastened by his compassion, replies, "Thanks to you . . . I'm learnin' one thing good. . . . Learnin' it all the time, ever' day. If you're in trouble or hurt or need—go to poor people. They're the only ones that'll help—the only ones."[27]

In short, the ethical message of *The Grapes of Wrath* is invigorated by numerous instances of the generosity of ordinary, decent people. Steinbeck teaches by way of anecdotes as well as by general moral maxims. As to the first, recall that the book begins with a trucker who blinks at the Oklahoma City Transport Company's policy of "No Riders" to give Tom a lift. As to the second, among the "rules become laws" explicated in chapter 17 one finds rights: "the right of privacy in the tent; the right to keep the past black hidden in the heart; the right to talk and to listen; the right to refuse help or to accept, to offer help or to decline it. . . ," and duties: "And when a baby died a pile of silver coins grew at the door flap, for a baby must be well buried, since it had nothing else in life. An old man may be left in a potter's field, but not a baby."[28]

Surprisingly, while generosity is celebrated as a cardinal virtue, charity is usually shunned by haves and have-nots as a vice in Steinbeck's moral scheme, particularly when it amounts to a breach of justice. Not all the haves in *The Grapes of Wrath* are seen as heartless, greedy capitalists, though distant, faceless corporations are said to practice a "curious, ritualized thievery." On the other hand, family-owned, small businesses are commended as engaging in "trade," a commerce that is based on an equity transaction between buyer and seller. From the seller's point of view, charity is going beyond a fair trade: "We' runnin' a business," the used car salesman explains, "not a charity ward."[29] From the buyer's point of view, receiving more than is just is *suffering* charity. In the café scene discussed above, the father does not want a fifteen cent loaf of bread for ten cents. The trade he wants to negotiate with Mae is that she sell him ten cents worth, else, as he says, "That'd be robbin' you, ma'am."[30]

Earlier in the story, Pa describes a similar equity between buyer and seller: "We done it clean. . . . There can't be no blame be laid on us. We never took nothin' we couldn't pay; we never suffered no man's charity."[31] Later, the ladies' committee explains that in the Weedpatch Government camp's arrangements, the offer of temporary credit cannot be considered charity. As Jessie tells Mrs. Joyce:

> "You jes' waltz right over t' the Weedpatch store an' get you some grocteries. The camp got twenty dollars' credit there. . . . An' you can pay it back to the Central Committee when you git work. . . . Mis' Joyce. . . . How come you let your girls git hungry?"
> "We ain't never took no charity," Mrs. Joyce said.
> "This ain't no charity, an' you know it," Jessie raged. "We had all that out. They ain't no charity in this here camp. We won't have no charity."[32]

The difference between suffering charity versus accepting temporary help is work. In the former, one's dignity is crushed because no repayment is required yet the cost is the assumption of superiority and an air of condescension. In the Ladies' Camp Committee conversation, Anne Littlefield explains:

> "If a body's ever took charity, it makes a burn that don't come out. This ain't charity, but if you ever took it, you don't forget it. . . . Las' winter; an' we was a-starvin'—me and Pa an' the little fellas. An' it was a-rainin'. Fella tol' us to go the Salvation Army. . . . We was hungry—they made us crawl for our dinner. They took our dignity. . . . I ain't never seen my man beat before, but them—them Salvation Army done it to 'im."[33]

Above all the key to human dignity, according to Steinbeck, is work. The Okies, after all, seek to be migrant *workers*. As long as they can find work, even low-paying jobs, and are able to provide for themselves, no matter how tattered their clothes or dilapidated their cars, they retain dignity and self-worth. As Pa explains, "No, we ain't got no money. . . . But they's plenty of us to work, an' we're all good men. Get good wages out there an' we'll pull 'em together. We'll make out."[34] Accordingly, the credit available from the Weedpatch Central Committee is a loan, not a gift. In addition, though the sanitary facilities, good order, and security are the conspicuous attributes of the government camps, an equally crucial and longer lasting contribution is the respect granted to each new member followed by the expectation that each adult will become involved in the democratic processes of camp life.[35] In other words, the camps facilitate the conditions wherein the migrants can reclaim their accustomed roles as working and autonomous adults. Mr. Thomas, who had hired the Wallaces and Tom to dig the irrigation ditch, understands the difference that the camp makes: "You fellas live in that government camp, don't you? . . . The people [there] make their own laws. . . . Those folks in the camp are getting used to being treated like humans."[36]

Ma, who had finally begun to lose hope and had stopped looking toward the future, is strongly bolstered by the dignity accorded her when the camp manager, Jim Rawley, graciously drank the cup of coffee she offered him their first morning in Weedpatch: "she looked for motive on his face, and found nothing but friendliness. . . . 'Why I feel like people again.'"[37] After the visit by the Ladies' Committee, she begins to dream again as she hopes for work for the menfolk so they can stay at the government camp. She looks forward to the time when there might be enough money to buy a little stove, some used bed springs, and a bigger tent. Work, of course, is her first wish, for it is the necessary prerequisite for all other elements of a decent life. In fact, every lower-case utopia described in *The Grapes of Wrath* begins with the baseline of work—if necessary work for hire, but eventually culminating in working one's own place. Tom's famous "I'll be there" litany as he and Ma part includes, "I'll be in the way kids laugh when they're hungry an' they know supper's ready. An' when our folks eat the stuff they raise an' live in the houses they build." Tom's mentor

Casy had earlier offered a similar vision of the good life for all humans: "These here folks want to live decent and bring up their kids decent. An' when they're old they wanta set in the door an' watch the downing sun. An' when they're young they wanta dance an' sing and lay together. They wanta eat an' get drunk and work. An' that's it—they want jus' fling their goddam muscles aroun' an' get tired."[38]

Occasionally, the lower-case utopias in *The Grapes of Wrath* contain a short list of higher aspirations, usually based on a calendar picture of California. When Pa was asked if he was glad to be going west, he said, "Well—sure. . . . 'Course it'll be all different out there—plenty work, an' ever'thing nice an' green, an' little white houses an' oranges growing' aroun'." The other frequent add-on appeals to one of the central tenets of the American dream: the conviction that more education will mean a better job leading to a brighter future. Education for all, first for the children: "Won't have no cold in the winter. Kids won't freeze on the way to school. I'm gonna take care my kids don't miss no more school. I can read good, but it ain't no pleasure to me like a fella that's used to it."[39] And then night school and correspondence courses for the adults. Recall the trucker who gave Tom a lift at the beginning of the novel: "Why I'm thinkin' of takin' one of them correspondence school courses. Mechanical engineering. It's easy. Just study a few easy lessons at home. I'm thinkin' of it. Then I won't drive no truck. Then I can tell other guys to drive trucks." For Connie, "study at home, maybe radio" or "'bout tractors"; for Al, "Diesel engines." Tom, Al, Connie, Rose of Sharon, and the rest of the family firmly believe that education will bring them "nice clean work and a future" with leisure and discretionary funds for luxuries like restaurant meals and movies.[40]

Of course, such "luxuries" were soon commonplace for the emerging middle class in America. Some twenty years later when Steinbeck made his own westward journey, he found many Americans routinely satisfying, and even surpassing, their basic needs. Yet it seemed many of them were discontented. On one of his first days in *Travels with Charley*, Steinbeck bought milk from a Massachusetts dairy farmer and asked to camp under an apple tree. He notes, "The dairy man had a Ph.D. in mathematics, and he must have had some training in philosophy. He liked what he was doing and he didn't want to be somewhere else—one of the very few contented people I met in my whole journey."[41] What we will now examine are Steinbeck's reasons for being leery about whether material satisfaction can be equated with a good and happy life.

Steinbeck in Search of America, 1962 and 1966

America survived the dirty thirties, the Great Depression, and World War II—but was it a better society? Steinbeck's hunch was that though Americans were materially better off, an emotional and spiritual impoverishment lurked. At the beginning of his 1962 journalistic travelogue, *Travels with Charley in Search of*

America, he notes that he had to be careful to not let his hypothesis taint what he could learn about America from his travels and "interviews" of ordinary people:

> So it was that I determined to look again, to try to rediscover this monster land. Otherwise, in writing, I could not tell the small diagnostic truths which are the foundation of the larger truth. One sharp difficulty presented itself . . . my name had become reasonably well known. . . . This being so, my trip demanded that I leave my name and my identity at home. I had to be peripatetic eyes and ears, a kind of moving gelatin plate. I could not sign hotel registers, meet people I knew, interview others, or even ask searching questions.

To his surprise, however, "in over ten thousand miles, in thirty-four states, . . . [he] was not recognized even once."[42]

His comment about the Massachusetts diary farmer noted above notwithstanding, he met many people living good lives and at peace with themselves and with their neighbors. Interestingly, and perhaps significantly, the first people to earn his imprimatur were potato pickers in Maine. Like the Joads in California, they were "migrant-crop picking people" but they were not Americans. Steinbeck's admiration for the clan of Canucks was not on account of their being Canadians, but because of their pride in doing basic work: "Here in Maine a great many . . . French Canadians . . . came over the border for the harvest season. . . . We Americans bring in mercenaries to do our hard and humble work. I hope we may not be overwhelmed one day by peoples not too proud or too lazy or too soft to bend to the earth and pick up the things we eat." Steinbeck treasured the Canadians because of their hardiness, loyalty to family, and enjoyment in working together: "This clan, having put their own small farm to bed for the winter in the Province of Quebec, came over the line to make a small nest egg. They even carried a little feeling of holiday with them almost like the hops- and strawberry-pickers from London and the Midland cities of England." After their supper they joined Steinbeck in the cabin of his Rocinante for beer, pop, and then "a bottle of very old and reverend brandy brought along for weddings, frostbite, and heart attacks." He left the campground early the next morning without repeating the good-byes of the evening before: "I never saw them again. But I like them."[43]

Many other ordinary Americans "interviewed" at truck stops, restaurants, campgrounds, Mom and Pop motels, and filling stations confirmed Steinbeck's faith in the soundness of America and the decency of Americans. Surely, though, no one more impressed him than a service station owner, "a giant with a scarred face and an evil white eye," who went several extra miles to get replacements for his blown rear tires. It was raining and it was Sunday and the size of heavy-duty tires he needed was rare. But Steinbeck's "evil saint" made several calls and twisted several arms and within four hours he had his tires. Steinbeck observes, "And if ever my faith in the essential saintliness of humans becomes tattered, I shall think of that evil-looking man. . . . I could have knelt in the mud and kissed the man's hands but I didn't. I tipped him rather royally and he said, 'you didn't ought to do that.'"[44] And so on that rainy Sunday, Oregon's evil-looking saint suffered Steinbeck's charity.

However, Steinbeck's first days in Oregon had not been encouraging. His first night he met a disconsolate, self-pitying twenty-year-old who had studied to be a hairstylist and wanted to move to New York City but couldn't muster the willpower to break free of his father's business of a restaurant and cluster of cabins just over the Idaho border. The following day Steinbeck and Charley had to put up with an inept, alcoholic veterinarian, with Steinbeck concluding, "It wasn't that this veterinary didn't like animals. I think he didn't like himself, and when that is so the subject usually must find an area for dislike outside himself. Else he would have to admit to his self-contempt."[45]

These two sad and failed Oregonians set the stage for Steinbeck's diagnosis of what seems to ail America—destruction and waste in the name of growth and progress. Steinbeck is appalled with the "new" cities of the 1950s and 1960s:

> American cities are like badger holes, ringed with trash—all of them—surrounded by piles of wrecked and rusting automobiles, and almost smothered with rubbish. . . . The mountains of things we throw away are much greater than the things we use. In this, if in no other way, we can see the wild and reckless exuberance of our production, and waste seems to be the index.[46]

He is unable to recognize the old Seattle in the city he drives through: "This Seattle was not something changed that I once knew. It was a new thing. Set down there not knowing it was Seattle, I could not have told where I was. Everywhere frantic growth, a carcinomatous growth . . . I wonder why progress looks so much like destruction." And if Washington's cities are a disgrace, Steinbeck's native California towns are so distasteful to him that he begins to question his competence as an observer and judge: "I have never resisted change, even when it has been called progress, and yet I felt resentment toward the strangers swamping what I thought of as my country with noise and clutter and the inevitable rings of junk." Unsure of himself, he wonders whether his "flurry of nostalgic spite" might be doing the West, his family, and old friends a deep disservice: "My return caused only confusion and uneasiness . . . [so] my departure was flight."[47]

As Steinbeck turns back east and starts his return home to Long Island, he takes stock of his project: "It would be pleasant to be able to say of my travels with Charley, 'I went out to find the truth about my country and I found it.' And then it would be such a simple matter to set down my findings and lean back comfortably with a fine sense of having discovered truths and taught them to my readers. I wish it were that easy." He goes on to reflect upon the reliability of his perceptions and assessments, especially the negative ones on America and Americans: "From start to finish I found no strangers. If I had, I might be able to report them more objectively. But these are my people and this is my country. If I found matters to criticize and to deplore, they were tendencies equally present in myself." Much of his equilibrium was recovered by his drive through the desert wildernesses of Arizona and New Mexico where the impact of *homo Americanus* was negligible. Then, too, his confidence was restored when he found a competent and compassionate young veterinarian who correctly diagnosed and treated Charley's prostatitis: "the ailment never came back. There's absolutely nothing to take the place of a good man."[48]

Eager to get home, Steinbeck still took a side trip to visit the Deep South. He went to New Orleans to investigate the Cheerleaders who gathered every school day to hurl invectives at several small black children whom a court order had allowed to attend a white school. Steinbeck's account of the ugliness of the racism he witnessed is the most disturbing and unforgettable part of his whole travelogue. He got close enough to see bigotry firsthand:

> The papers had printed that the jibes and cheers were cruel and sometimes obscene, and so they were. . . . No newspaper had printed the words these women shouted. It was indicated that they were indelicate, some even said obscene. On television the sound track was made to blur or had crowd noises cut in to cover. But now I hear the words, bestial and filthy and degenerate. In a long and unprotected life I have seen and heard the vomiting of demoniac humans before. Why then did these screams fill me with a shocked and sickened sorrow?[49]

Steinbeck offers two answers: the speeches were not spontaneous but "tried and memorized and carefully rehearsed" and, more damning, the daily crowd that the Cheerleaders attracted was a responsive, participatory chorus of admiring racists, "blowsy women" with the "demented cruelty of egocentric children. . . . *They were crazy actors playing to a crazy audience.*"[50]

For several days thereafter, Steinbeck mentally pondered and processed in conversation with passersby, hitchhikers, and café patrons the searing impact that the Cheerleaders (and their audience) had had on him. In a rare editorial aside he explains why he gives so much attention to racism in the Deep South and in the country in general:

> With all the polls and opinion posts, with newspapers more opinion than news so that we no longer know one from the other, I want to be very clear about one thing. I have not intended to present, nor do I think I have presented, any kind of cross-section so that the reader can say, "He thinks he has presented a true picture of the South." I don't. I've only told what a few people said to me and what I saw. I don't know whether they were typical or whether any conclusion can be drawn.[51]

Sociological adequacy and reliable sampling techniques notwithstanding, Steinbeck insists on the deep meaning and far-reaching importance of what he had experienced. There are no caveats in his conclusions: "I *know* it is a troubled place and a people caught in a jam. And I *know* that the solution when it arrives will not be easy or simple."[52]

The ending Steinbeck originally proposed for *Travels with Charley* was an "Appendix: L'Envoi" that described John's and Elaine's attendance at the January 1961 inauguration of John F. Kennedy.[53] Five years later, when Steinbeck continued his search in his final book, *America and Americans,* he found a country much changed by the assassinations of John F. Kennedy, Robert F. Kennedy, and Martin Luther King Jr., as well as by the election of Lyndon Johnson and the passage of ground-breaking civil rights legislation. By 1966 race had moved closer to the center of attention in America, so in his fourth chapter of *America and Americans,* "Created Equal," Steinbeck takes up the Negro problem. Interestingly, he recasts the problem of race in terms of a lower-case utopia wherein satisfying basic human needs is the key to both happiness and moral goodness:

> In the constant pressure of the Negro causes, some thoughtless people ask, "What are they after? What do they want?" It's very simple. They want exactly the same things other Americans want—peace, comfort, security and love. The human wants everything he can conceive of and, as through education and understanding his concepts grow broader, he will want more and different things—perhaps even better things.[54]

While conceding that every human wants "more and different things," Steinbeck interjects his concern with the word "perhaps." So even if most Americans assume that the quest for more and different things automatically means "better things," Steinbeck continues to have serious doubts.

In *America and Americans* Steinbeck at times rails like an Old Testament prophet as he persistently focuses on the disease of plenty and the hazard of leisure that he sees eroding the American spirit. Are we becoming, he asks,

> . . . a national kennel of animals with no purpose and no direction? For a million years we had a purpose—simple survival—the finding, planting, gathering, or killing of food to keep us alive, of shelter to prevent freezing. This was a strong incentive. Add to it defense against all kinds of enemies and you have our species' history. But now we have food and shelter and transportation and the more terrible hazard of leisure. I strongly suspect that our moral and spiritual disintegration grows out of our lack of experience with plenty.[55]

In his ninth chapter, "America and the Future," the tone of his summary indictment is shrill and strident: America is on the "verge of moral and hence nervous collapse." Inasmuch as his confidence in social renewal rests on any society's facing up to its problems, Steinbeck diagnoses America's malady with unflinching candor: "Now we face the danger which in the past has been most destructive to the human: success—plenty, comfort, and ever-increasing leisure. No dynamic people has ever survived these dangers. If the anaesthetic of satisfaction were added to our hazards, we would not have a chance of survival—as Americans." Still, he ends his book on a hopeful note. America's best impulses, Steinbeck concludes, "will serve us in the future as they have in the past to clarify and to strengthen our process. We have failed sometimes, taken wrong paths, paused for renewal, filled our bellies and licked our wounds; but we have never slipped back—never."[56]

Conclusion

Were it possible, I would like to press Steinbeck on his optimism about America's future. Will American society be renewed and become a good society? Will it be a society that promotes human development? Will persons in that society be genuinely happy? We began with Aristotle's linkage of moral goodness, happiness, and human development. In a stunning passage near the beginning of *Journal of a Novel: The East of Eden Letters,* Steinbeck expertly recapitulates Aristotle's theory of virtue: "I am assailed with virtue—a feeling toward virtue but without virtue's self. Define virtue! It is that quality of character which is pleasant and desirable to its owner and which makes him perform acts of which he can be proud and with which he can be pleased."[57] If asked which acts are the ones "of which he can be proud and . . . pleased," I believe Steinbeck would appeal to his paradigmatic moral framework: a lower-case utopia that ministers to the basic human needs of hunger and shelter, health and sickness, birth and death, for all people.

The satisfaction of almost all these basic needs is compressed, in literary form, into the unforgettable act of compassion at the end of *The Grapes of Wrath.* For Aristotle, performing morally good actions brings fulfillment and happiness, both of which Rose of Sharon experiences in her virtuous response to the starving man in the "rain-soaked barn":

> Rose of Sharon loosened one side of the blanket and bared her breast. "You got to," she said. She squirmed closer and pulled his head close. "There!" she said. "There." Her hand moved behind his head and supported it. Her fingers moved gently in his hair. She looked up and across the barn, and her lips came together and smiled mysteriously.[58]

Rose of Sharon's smile becomes much less mysterious once we appreciate Steinbeck's understanding that an ethical response to a basic human need brings not only happiness but is the basis for a good life. It is in this response of virtue that America's promising future lies.

Notes

1. Elaine Steinbeck and Robert Wallsten, eds. *Steinbeck: A Life in Letters* (New York: Penguin, 1989), 447.
2. See *The Nicomachean Ethics,* Book One, especially chapters 4, 7, 9, and 13 for Aristotle's argument linking moral goodness with human development and happiness.
3. John Steinbeck, *Of Mice and Men* (New York: Penguin, 1994), 15.
4. See Thoreau's *Walden,* especially his first chapter, "Economy," and his "Conclusion," for his case for reducing wants to needs.
5. Steinbeck, *Of Mice and Men,* 55-56.
6. Ibid., 75.

7. Ibid, 93: emphasis added.

8. John Steinbeck, *The Grapes of Wrath* (New York: Penguin, 1992), 64.

9. Ibid., 66.

10. Ibid., 189-90.

11. Ibid., 191-94.

12. Ibid., 190-91, 197: emphasis added.

13. Ibid., 190, 202.

14. Ibid., 192, 203.

15. Ibid., 344-45.

16. Ibid., 350-51.

17. Ibid., 352-53.

18. Arguably the best treatment on the conflict between sentiment and duty is Jonathan Bennett's essay, "The Conscience of Huckleberry Finn," published in *Philosophy*, Volume 49, 1974. Another source is Arthur Miller's "Steinbeck" in both *John Steinbeck: Centennial Reflections By American Writers* (Shillinglaw) and *John Steinbeck: A Centennial Tribute* (George). Specifically, Miller notes "the struggle within . . . [Steinbeck] between an overflowing sympathy for suffering, a veritable embrace of those in pain, and a hard-headed grasp of moral dilemmas from which, with all the good will in the world, there is no escape."

19. Steinbeck, *The Grapes of Wrath*, 351.

20. Ibid., 266.

21. Ibid., 558-59, 593, 603.

22. Of course, Mrs. Wainwright would say "in the same wagon" instead of "in the same boat," for a wainwright is a builder or repairer of wagons!

23. Steinbeck, *The Grapes of Wrath*, 606.

24. Ibid., 214, 217, 220.

25. Ibid., 396-97, 400-401.

26. Ibid., 512-13.

27. Ibid., 513-14.

28. Ibid., 265-66.

29. Ibid., 89, 211.

30. Ibid., 218.

31. Ibid., 190.

32. Ibid., 431.

33. Ibid., 432.

34. Ibid., 257.

35. Steinbeck's contentions on dignity and democratic participation are best articulated in his *Harvest Gypsies* essays; on this point see my essay "Human Dignity, the Need for Community, and 'The Duty of the Writer to Lift Up': John Steinbeck's Philosophy" published in *Steinbeck Studies*, Volume 15, 2002.

36. Steinbeck, *The Grapes of Wrath*, 403-4.

37. Ibid., 416, 420.

38. Ibid., 341, 572; note also the philosophy of work articulated in chapter 14 of *The Grapes of Wrath*: "The last clear definite function of man—muscles aching to work, minds aching to create beyond the single need—this is man. To build a wall, to build a house, a dam, and in the wall and house and dam to put something of Manself, and to Manself take back something of the wall, the house, the dam; to take hard muscles from the lifting, to take the clear lines and form from conceiving. For man, unlike any other

thing organic or inorganic in the universe, grows beyond his work, walks up the stairs of his concepts, emerges ahead of his accomplishments."

39. Steinbeck, *The Grapes of Wrath*, 149, 271-72.

40. Ibid., 16, 224, 248, 343.

41. John Steinbeck, *Travels with Charley in Search of America* (New York: Penguin, 2002), 22.

42. Ibid., 5-6.

43. Ibid., 50, 53-55.

44. Ibid., 141-42.

45. Ibid., 136.

46. Ibid., 22.

47. Ibid., 138, 148, 156-57.

48. Ibid., 159, 179.

49. Ibid., 195.

50. Ibid., 195-96: emphasis added.

51. Ibid., 206-7.

52. Ibid., 207: emphasis added.

53. This piece is printed for the first time in the 2002 Penguin Books "Centennial Edition" of *Travels with Charley*.

54. John Steinbeck, *America and Americans and Selected Nonfiction*, eds. Susan Shillinglaw and Jackson Benson (New York: Viking, 2002), 353.

55. Ibid., 396.

56. Ibid., 397, 403-4.

57. John Steinbeck, *Journal of a Novel: The* East of Eden *Letters* (New York: Penguin, 1969), 22.

58. Steinbeck, *The Grapes of Wrath*, 619.

John Steinbeck and the Morality of Roles: Lessons for Business Ethics

JOSEPH ALLEGRETTI
Siena College

John Steinbeck may seem like an unlikely resource for business ethics in the 21st century. After all, Steinbeck is often characterized as a proletarian writer whose best work dispassionately dissected the lives of the uprooted and homeless during the Great Depression. What does *In Dubious Battle* have to say about today's labor-management struggles that are fought not with guns and knives but with legal briefs and media pronouncements? What do George and Lennie from *Of Mice and Men* have in common with the homeless and the unemployed who scramble for survival in sprawling urban centers like New York or Los Angeles? What can *The Grapes of Wrath* contribute to current debates about agribusiness and genetically engineered vegetables? Isn't Steinbeck's focus on rural life and itinerant workers hopelessly irrelevant to the contemporary world of insider trading, multinational corporations, and internet commerce?

This view of Steinbeck asks too much and too little of him. It is too much to expect Steinbeck to provide answers to the specific ethical problems that afflict business today. But neither can Sophocles or Shakespeare provide direct guidance to the businessperson trying to decide whether to misstate corporate earnings, dump toxic substances in a river, or sell an unsafe product. This does not mean that Steinbeck is irrelevant to the world of business and business ethics. As McAdams and Koppensteiner observe, "Ordinarily, literature will not provide *solutions* to specific problems, but we believe that it is a useful ingredient in the process of *strengthening moral reasoning* about those problems."[1] Stories "strengthen moral reasoning" not by providing a detailed philosophical analysis of moral problems but by showing people struggling with moral choices and presenting alternative perspectives. As I have argued elsewhere, "Stories enflesh and make real the cold hard facts of a moral problem or dilemma. They help us to understand—in a way that codes and case law cannot—why a person does what she does, at what cost, and for what reasons."[2]

When we experience great works of literature, our life story intersects with the story we are reading. Psychiatrist Robert Coles puts it well: "Novels and stories are renderings of life; they can not only keep us company, but admonish us, point us in new directions, or give us the courage to stay a given course. They can offer us kinsmen, kinswomen, comrades, advisers—offer us other eyes through which we might see, other ears with which we might make soundings." At its best, literature furnishes us with "a moment of recognition, of serious pause, of tough-self scrutiny."[3]

This is how Steinbeck can contribute to business ethics students and to businesspersons seeking moral guidance. As an illustration, let us consider the lessons for business and business ethics from Steinbeck's most famous novel, *The Grapes of Wrath.*

Losing the Person in the Role

Many standard textbooks in business ethics adopt a similar approach to their topic: early in the book, ethical theories such as utilitarianism and deontology are explained, and these theories are then employed to analyze real and hypo-thetical case studies about the environment, consumer safety, job discrimination, and the like.[4] The focus is on knowing and applying philosophical principles to make decisions. Little attention is paid to the *contexts* in which decisions are made. Few of the major textbooks, for example, analyze in any detail the extent to which an employee's *role* within a corporation affects her approach to ethical issues.[5] But as Michael Hardimon reminds us, by "signing on for a role, we promise to carry out the duties of the role, the tasks that the role requires."[6] Our roles alter our moral universe. Trevino and Nelson explain:

> Roles can reduce a person's sense of his or her individuality by focusing atten-tion on the role and the expectations that accompany it. It doesn't really matter who fills the role. It's the role requirements that are important. This focus on the role reduces the individual's awareness of the self as an independent indi-vidual who is personally responsible for an outcome.[7]

Roles, then, can diminish an employee's sense of personal responsibility for her actions. As a result, she may find herself engaging in conduct that she would ordinarily condemn as immoral. When this happens, role morality overrides personal morality.

I know of no more dramatic and forceful presentation of role morality than Steinbeck's discussion of the tractor men in chapter 5 of *The Grapes of Wrath.*[8] Chapter 5 is one of the interchapters in which Steinbeck "universalizes" his story by expanding his narrative eye beyond the Joad family.[9] The chapter is divided into three parts. In the first part, the owners and their agents come onto the dry and unproductive land being farmed by their sharecropping tenants. They bring terrible news: the tenants and their families must pack up and leave immediately. In the second part, the owners send in tractors to plow up the lands, destroy the fences and buildings that sit there, and drive off the tenants. In the final part, one of the tenant farmers confronts a tractor driver and the driver defends his actions. The several sections of chapter 5 are linked by their focus on the way moral responsibility is diffused and diluted by the roles people play.

In the first part of chapter 5, the owners or their agents come onto the land. Steinbeck writes, "Some of the owner men were kind because they hated what they had to do, and some of them were angry because they hated to be cruel, and some of them were cold because they had long ago found out that one could not be an owner unless one were cold. And all of them were caught in something larger than themselves." The personalities of the owners change—some become kind, some become cruel—as they wrestle with nagging moral doubts about their actions. They subdue these doubts by convincing themselves that they have no choice but to dispossess their tenants. It's not their fault—it's the bank, it's the company, that is responsible. This bank, this company, is something inhuman, amoral, a machine. More than that, the owners call it a "monster" that needs money like humans need air. Banks and companies "don't breathe air, don't eat side-meat. They breathe profits; they eat the interest on money. If they don't get it, they die the way you die without air, without side-meat. It's a sad thing, but it is so. It is just so."[10]

The tenant farmers plead for more time, just one more year, but to no avail. The sharecropping system is dead and finished, say the owners. The banks will hire a few men to grow cotton, pay them a wage, and take the crop for as long as they can until they kill off the land. The tenant farmers must leave immediately. And as the farmers plead their case, the owners do little more than repeat a litany of denial:

> It's not us, it's the bank. . . .
> We're sorry. It's not us. It's the monster. The bank isn't like a man. . . .
> The bank is something more than men, I tell you. It's the monster. Men made it, but they can't control it. . . .
> No. The bank, the monster owns it. You'll have to go. . . .
> We're sorry, said the owner men. The bank, the fifty-thousand-acre owner can't be responsible.[11]

This abdication of personal moral responsibility is addressed directly in the second portion of chapter 5 when the tractor men arrive to plow under the fields and evict the tenant farmers. The men on the tractors have relinquished their humanity and become things, machines, objects of destruction. Their very appearance reveals their loss of humanity: "The man sitting in the iron seat did not look like a man; gloved, goggled, rubber dust mask over nose and mouth, he was a part of the monster, a robot in the seat." Goggled and muzzled, the tractor men cannot feel or smell the land and have lost all connection to it: "If a seed dropped did not germinate, it was nothing. If the young thrusting plant withered in drought or drowned in a flood of rain, it was no more to the driver than to the tractor."[12] Scholars sometimes bemoan the loss of personal responsibility that comes from being a small cog in a great machine,[13] but few writers have captured this loss of moral agency so acutely and vividly.

In the final part of chapter 5, Steinbeck recounts a conversation between one of the tractor men and a tenant farmer:

> "Why, you're Joe Davis's boy!"
> "Sure," the driver said.
> "Well, what you doing this kind of work for—against your own people?"
> "Three dollars a day. I got damn sick of creeping for my dinner—and not getting it. I got a wife and kids. We got to eat. Three dollars a day, and it comes every day."
> "That's right," the tenant said. "But for your three dollars a day fifteen or twenty families can't eat at all. Nearly a hundred people have to go out and wander on the roads for your three dollars a day. Is that right?"
> And the driver said, "Can't think of that. Got to think of my own kids. Three dollars a day, and it comes every day. Times are changing, mister, don't you know? Can't make a living on the land unless you got two, five, ten thousand acres and a tractor. . . . You try to get three dollars a day someplace. That's the only way."[14]

Joe Davis's son is not evil-spirited or mean, but he has a job to do, a role to play. In the language of philosopher Richard Wasserstrom, the tractor man sees himself as an "amoral technician" whose only duty is to do what his job requires, no questions asked.[15] When he is at home he may be kind and compassionate, but when he is at work he embraces the "dog-eat-dog" mentality and the "I'm-only-following-the-rules" excuse.

In desperation a tenant farmer threatens to kill the tractor driver. But what good will that do? As the driver points out, "And look—suppose you kill me? They'll just hang you, but long before you're hung there'll be another guy on the tractor, and he'll bump the house down. You're not killing the right guy." The frustrated farmer asks, "Who gave you orders? I'll go after him. He's the one to kill." But that won't work either. The tractor men get their orders from the bank, the bank gets its orders from a president and board of directors, the directors get their orders from someone or something back East. The chain of command extends back indefinitely, with the bewildered driver himself concluding, "I don't know. Maybe there's nobody to shoot. Maybe the thing isn't men at all."[16]

Only the "system" seems responsible. But who, then, is really responsible? Is anyone responsible at all? As Thomas Carson explains:

> The farmer is adamantly defending the view that individuals or groups of individuals are always responsible for corporate actions. . . . He contends that some individual human being (or some group of human beings) is responsible for evicting him from his home and he is determined to kill whoever it is that is responsible. The bulldozer driver questions whether there is any individual person (or group of persons) who is responsible for evicting the farmer. He rejects

various attempts by the farmer to hold particular individuals responsible for his eviction.[17]

Steinbeck is doing more in this passage than presenting competing sides in a moral debate. The debate between the farmer and the driver raises an important point for business and one too often overlooked by business ethicists— *organizations have a life of their own.* Individuals make up a company, but a company has its own culture, values, and morality. This corporate ethos encourages certain behavior and discourages other behavior. The corporate culture at Enron, for example, focused on obtaining short-term profits and driving up the stock price. There was a "win-at-all-costs" mentality. Employees who raised doubts about the way deals were structured and recorded were punished, while those who went along with the corporate culture were lavishly rewarded.[18] The corporate ethos, then, can act like a cloak to obscure the moral responsibility of the individuals who make up the company. As Trevino and Nelson explain, in "organizations the individual often becomes disconnected from the consequences of his or her actions and doesn't feel personally responsible for them. Responsibility becomes diffused. No individual feels the need to take personal responsibility, so in the end no one does, and unethical behavior is more likely."[19] "It's not us, it's the bank," say the owners. *It's not my fault. I was only following orders. I was only doing my job.* Steinbeck's story of the tractor men shows how membership in a group can create a kind of moral blindness that ultimately leads to a loss of moral agency.

Those familiar with Steinbeck's work will not be surprised by his criticism of the way group morality can overpower personal morality. Steinbeck was intrigued by the concept of the "phalanx" or group man. In 1933 he wrote to a friend: "The fascinating thing to me is the way the group has a soul, a drive, an intent, an end, a method, a reaction and a set of tropisms which in no way resembles the same things possessed by the men who make up the group."[20] As the character Doc says in *In Dubious Battle,* "A man in a group isn't himself at all; he's a cell in an organism that isn't like him any more than the cells in your body are like you."[21] Men and women who join a group "have thus surrendered their identities and wills to the collective will of the mass."[22] Personal morality dissolves all too easily in the group.

Steinbeck's portrayal of the tractor men is as contemporary as this morning's business headlines. The tractor men are no different from the corporate executive who breaks the law because her boss tells her to, the stockbroker who makes a killing by illegal insider trading because everyone else is doing it, the accountant who shreds documents to protect a client, or the research scientist who fudges data because further tests could cost the company profits. In each case, the role has gobbled up the person.

Transcending Roles and Role Morality

Chapter 5 ends with a tenant farmer and his family watching helplessly as a tractor man demolishes their house. The message seems to be that ordinary men and women are powerless against the forces of mechanization, bureaucratization, and corporate mentality. Our last image of the tractor man reminds us of the price he has paid for his "three dollars a day": "And the driver was goggled and a rubber mask covered his nose and mouth."[23] He has traded his humanity for a paycheck.

The real question is not whether the tractor men (or the banks, for that matter) are acting ethically or unethically by dispossessing the tenant farmers. The real question is whether they even recognize that their actions raise a moral issue. Steinbeck raises the question whether it is possible to move from moral blindness to moral awareness. Is there any way to escape the moral tunnel vision that too often accompanies a role? Most business ethicists are silent on this point. Even Trevino and Nelson, whose business ethics textbook is one of the few to discuss role morality in any detail, do little more than caution managers to "consider the extent to which organizational roles encourage either ethical or unethical behavior."[24]

Michael Hardimon, however, makes a helpful suggestion. The problem, explains Hardimon, is not that people accept or identify with their roles. The problem is that role identification can lead to "the loss of self within the role."[25] A role can be transformed into a "mask" that denies one's essential humanity and moral responsibility, for "The risk of wearing a mask is that the I, the self behind the mask, will be lost."[26] In order to guard against the loss of the self, workers need to cultivate a healthy detachment from their roles. They need to remember that they are more than the roles they play—they retain "duties that are independent of one's role, duties that apply to people generally."[27]

Employers, of course, have an important part to play here. A company can either encourage or discourage an exaggerated sense of role identification on the part of its workers. A company that is truly committed to moral reflection can take several concrete steps—for example, it can provide ethics training for workers and supervisors, adopt a clear ethics policy, establish procedures for employees to raise ethical questions and report ethical lapses, incorporate ethics into reward systems for workers and managers, and so on.

Here again Steinbeck has something valuable to contribute to business ethics. His concern, however, is not with the corporation's efforts to create an ethical climate—it is both broader and narrower than that. Steinbeck's response to the problem of excessive role identification and the loss of personal responsibility proceeds at two levels—the macro level of society and the micro level of the individual worker. At the macro level, Steinbeck is calling for the transformation of the business world and economy. If all persons could find good paying and meaningful work in organizations that respect and reward moral conduct, then employees would no longer feel a need to hide behind their roles to avoid responsibility for their actions. *The Grapes of Wrath* can be read as an appeal for the creation of a more just and compassionate economy—an economy where the son of Joe Davis will not have to choose between dispossessing his neighbors or earning enough to feed his children.

Steinbeck also suggests a second way to counter the morally deadening effects of a role. This way is more personal, less dramatic, but perhaps equally radical. Employees can begin to see themselves and what they do in a new light, a transformation beautifully described in chapter 26 of *The Grapes of Wrath*. In this chapter the Joads are picking peaches and living at a company-owned camp. When Ma goes to buy food at the company store, she encounters a clerk who seems to epitomize a narrow role morality. Even his physical description reveals his cramped moral sensibilities: he is a "tiny man," "completely bald," whose nose is "long and thin, and curved like a bird's beak." When Ma notes how expensive his prices are compared to the costs in town, the clerk offers no sympathy. His tone is sharp and condescending. Finally, Ma confronts him directly:

> "You own this here store?"
> "No, I jus' work here."
> "Any reason you got to make fun? That help you any?" She regarded her shiny wrinkled hands. The little man was silent. "Who owns this here store?"
> "Hooper Ranches, Incorporated, ma'am."
> "An' they set the prices?"
> "Yes, ma'am."
> She looked up, smiling a little. "Ever'body comes in talks like me, is mad?"
> He hesitated for a moment. "Yes, ma'am."
> "An' that's why you make fun?"
> "What cha mean?"
> "Doin' a dirty thing like this. Shames ya, don't it? Got to act flip, huh?" Her voice was gentle. The clerk watched her, fascinated. He didn't answer.[28]

The clerk grows silent as if waiting for something to happen. When Ma asks him how he came to take this job, his reply echoes the voice of the tractor man in chapter 5: "'A fella got to eat,' he began; and then, belligerently, 'A fella got a right to eat.'" Ma's response cuts like a knife: "What fella?" she asks.[29] The clerk's first response states a biological fact ("A fella got to eat"), but his second response makes a moral claim ("A fella got a right to eat"). Ma accepts this moral claim but widens it. By asking "What fella?" she is really proclaiming "All people." The clerk has a moral right to eat, but so does Ma, her family, and all human beings. The clerk's snide and sarcastic exterior falls away as Ma's criticism strikes home. He drops his belittling tone and begins to address Ma with respect, acknowledging their common humanity—they are both human beings struggling to survive in a hostile world.

As Ma gets ready to leave with her meager purchases, she remembers that she has no sugar for coffee. Her family is out working in the fields; surely she can have the sugar now and pay him the ten cents when they finish for the day. At first the clerk refuses. "The little man looked away—took his eyes as far from Ma as he could. 'I can't do it,' he said softly. 'That's the rule. I can't. I'd get in trouble. I'd get canned.'" Once again he tries to escape into his role. But now a surprising thing happens. The clerk looks at Ma and "then his face lost its fear." He takes ten cents from his own pocket and pays for the sugar. "'There you are,' he said. 'Now it's all right. You bring in your slip an' I'll get my dime back.'"[30]

For Ma, the lesson of this encounter is, "If you're in trouble or hurt or need—go to poor people. They're the only ones that'll help—the only ones."[31] But there is another lesson here, one equally important. Trapped by the confines of his role, worried about his own livelihood, the store clerk is like the tractor man from chapter 5—his moral universe is limited to his own self-interest. In chapter 5, however, the characters are all abstract and impersonal; there are owners, banks, tractor men, and tenant farmers. Here in chapter 26 the clerk comes face to face with Ma Joad, a real woman of character, commitment, and fierce love. He is no longer a faceless clerk dealing with a nameless customer. He is a human being encountering another human being. In that one-to-one relationship, he changes.[32]

The transformation of the store clerk is the small-scale parallel of the transformation of the Joad family. As *The Grapes of Wrath* opens, the Joads care for little beyond the welfare of their own family. But as they journey westward and their nuclear family begins to disintegrate, they slowly begin to undergo a transformation of consciousness. As Louis Owens explains:

> From the outset of the migration to California . . . the family begins to change as the nuclear family that Ma holds so dear begins to fragment and the Joads begin to become part of a larger "organization of the unconsciousness." The first step in this gradual change is the family's inclusion of Casy in the council and on the journey. The final steps are Tom's dedication of his life to all men and Rose of Sharon's breast-feeding of the starving stranger. Between these two ends, Steinbeck makes it clear that the Joads have become part of something much larger than themselves.[33]

In the same way, it is the personal encounter with another suffering human being that empowers the clerk to move beyond the limits of his role. Empathy liberates him—he now realizes that he is part of something larger than himself.

Steinbeck's lesson for business ethics is simple but profound. Roles can restrict our moral universe. They can function as moral blinders. But roles depend for their power upon the willingness of an employee to see herself in the third person: as a store clerk, a banker, a lawyer, or an accountant. When we see ourselves in the third person, we ask, "What does my job demand of me? What is a clerk, banker, lawyer, or accountant supposed to do?" Our role provides the answer—do what the role expects of you, whether the behavior conforms or conflicts with your own values. But as soon as a store clerk, or any worker, begins to relate to others not as a worker but as a human being, the demands of our common humanity eclipse the duties of role. The worker no longer brushes aside moral issues by claiming, "I was only doing my job" or "I had no choice." Instead, the question now becomes: "Who am *I* and what should *I* do?" Asking such a question can transform persons, the companies in which they work, and the culture at large.

At the end of *The Grapes of Wrath*, says Warren French, the Joads' "education is complete; they have transcended familial prejudices. What happens to them now depends upon the ability of the rest of society to learn the lesson that the Joads have learned."[34] In the same way, the store clerk in chapter 26 has learned the lessons of empathy and accountability that allow him to transcend his role and take responsibility for his actions. Steinbeck leaves us with a question and a challenge: How can we create and nurture business policies and practices that make such moments of transcendence possible?

Future Agenda

The Grapes of Wrath has much to contribute to the discipline of business ethics. But Steinbeck's significance for the business world is not confined to that book. Once we acknowledge Steinbeck's relevance for the world of work and business ethics, the possibilities for further study multiply rapidly. Consider just a few:

- An exploration of how individual morality is submerged and lost within a group or institution, focusing on *In Dubious Battle*.
- An analysis of society's obligations to the unemployed and the marginalized, using *Of Mice and Men*.
- A study of the self-defeating nature of greed, relying on *The Pearl*.
- An examination of what constitutes good, productive, and creative work by focusing on the character of Doc from *Cannery Row* and *Sweet Thursday*.
- An examination of the "the superficial conventions of a society ruled by business and advertising,"[35] with *The Wayward Bus* as the central text.
- A study of the complex relationship between moral goodness and wealth, relying on *East of Eden*.
- A case study of moral corruption, self-deception, and betrayal, using *The Winter of Our Discontent*, the Steinbeck novel that deals most directly with questions of business and business ethics.

Doubtless there are other subjects that could be explored in these and other works of Steinbeck. But clearly the author will not be irrelevant to the world of business until issues of choice, responsibility, and character become irrelevant. Until that distant moment, business ethics needs John Steinbeck.

Notes

1. Tony McAdams and Roswitha Koppensteiner, "The Manager Seeking Virtue: Lessons from Literature," *Journal of Business Ethics* 11 (1992): 630.

2. Joseph G. Allegretti, "Can Legal Ethics Be Christian?" in *Christian Perspectives on Legal Thought*, ed. Michael W. McConnell, Robert F. Cochran, Jr., and Angela C. Carmella (New Haven: Yale University Press, 2001), 462.

3. Robert Coles, *The Call of Stories: Teaching and the Moral Imagination* (Boston: Houghton Mifflin, 1989), 159-60.

4. See, e.g., Beauchamp & Bowie; Ferrell, Fraedrich & Ferrell; Velasquez.

5. Trevino and Nelson is a notable exception (see note 7).

6. Michael O. Hardimon, "Role Obligations," in *Morality and the Market: Ethics and Virtue in the Conduct of Business*, ed. Eugene Heath (New York: McGraw-Hill, 2002), 397.

7. Linda K. Trevino and Katherine A. Nelson, *Managing Business Ethics: Straight Talk About How To Do It Right*, 2nd ed. (New York: John Wiley & Sons, 1999), 160.

8. Two business ethics articles that mention chapter 5 of *The Grapes of Wrath* are Kennedy and Lawton ("Business Ethics in Fiction," 1992) and Carson ("Corporate Moral Agency: A Case from Literature," 1994), both from the *Journal of Business Ethics*. Neither employs the approach that I use here.

9. John H. Timmerman, *John Steinbeck's Fiction: The Aesthetics of the Road Taken* (Norman: University of Oklahoma Press, 1986), 107.

10. John Steinbeck, *The Grapes of Wrath* (New York: Penguin, 1992), 42-43.

11. Ibid., 45-46; Louis Owens notes in The Grapes of Wrath: *Trouble in the Promised Land* that the absence of quotation marks around the statements of the owners highlights their impersonality (30).

12. Steinbeck, *The Grapes of Wrath*, 48.

13. See, for example, Trevino & Nelson (166-69).

14. Steinbeck, *The Grapes of Wrath*, 50.

15. Richard Wasserstrom, "Lawyers as Professionals: Some Moral Issues," *Human Rights* 5 (1975), 5-6.

16. Steinbeck, *The Grapes of Wrath*, 52.

17. Thomas L. Carson, "Corporate Moral Agency: A Case from Literature," *Journal of Business Ethics* 13 (1994), 155.

18. Ronald R. Sims and Johannes Brinkman, "Enron Ethics (Or: Culture Matters More than Codes)," *Journal of Business Ethics* 45 (2003), 243-56.

19. Trevino and Nelson, 166.

20. Elaine Steinbeck and Robert Wallsten, eds., *Steinbeck: A Life in Letters* (New York: Penguin, 1989), 76.

21. John Steinbeck, *In Dubious Battle* (New York: Penguin, 1992), 150-51.

22. Louis Owens, The Grapes of Wrath: *Trouble in the Promised Land* (New York: Twayne, 1996), 65.

23. Steinbeck, *The Grapes of Wrath*, 52-53.

24. Trevino and Nelson, 163.

25. Hardimon, 399.

26. Joseph Allegretti, "Shooting Elephants, Serving Clients: An Essay on George Orwell and the Lawyer-Client Relationship," *Creighton Law Review* 27 (1993), 23.

27. Hardimon, 399.

28. Steinbeck, *The Grapes of Wrath*, 509-10, 512.

29. Ibid., 512.

30. Ibid., 513.

31. Ibid., 513-14.

32. Owens, 67; see Hansen's essay in *The Moral Philosophy of John Steinbeck* for a Levinasian analysis of "face to face" relationships in this novel.

33. Ibid.; Owens also notes on the previous page that the phrase "organization of the unconsciousness" comes from Steinbeck's *The Log from the Sea of Cortez*.

34. Warren French, *John Steinbeck*, 2nd ed. rev. (Boston: Twayne, 1975), 98.

35. Peter Lisca, *The Wide World of John Steinbeck*, new ed. (New York: Gordian Press, 1981), 240.

John Steinbeck: An Ethics of Fiction

JOHN H. TIMMERMAN
Calvin College

> Ethics, morals, codes of conduct, are the stern rules which in the past we
> needed to survive.
>
> *—America and Americans*

That John Steinbeck was, throughout his career, an ethical writer—concerned
with right and wrong choices and the consequences of those choices—is a common assumption. Yet relatively little has been done with the assumption in understanding the aesthetic nature of ethics in his work. When ethical contexts do
occur, they often come obliquely: the role of conflict and paradox, the relevance
of biblical/religious allusions, individual freedom and cultural oppression, and
the like. To a large degree, the divergence of such issues into simple "topics" in
Steinbeck studies is due to an inadequate language and consequent framework,
philosophically and literarily, for understanding Steinbeck as an ethical writer.
My aim in these few pages is to suggest that elementary, ethical lexicon and to
provide a framework of ethics and art that might lead to some future directions
of study.

In a special issue of *PMLA* (January 1999) devoted to the topic "Ethics and
Literary Study," general coordinator Lawrence Buell observed in his introduction that "Ethics has gained new resonance in literary studies during the past half
dozen years, even if it has not—at least yet—become the paradigm-defining
concept that textuality was for the 1970s and historicism was for the 1980s."
Consequently, Buell points out that "As with any groundswell, particularly when
the central term of reference already belongs to common usage, the challenge of
pinning down what counts as ethics intensifies as more people lay claim to it."[1]
If, as Buell notes, the study of ethics and literature is impeded by the lack of a
common set of terms, the particular instance of our concern with Steinbeck is

further complicated by those later works in which he postulates his own ethical claims.

The last decade of Steinbeck's life is often referred to as his "moral phase," marked by his infatuation with the chivalric code of *Morte d'Arthur*, his sudden and intense writing of *The Winter of Our Discontent* from March to May 1960, and his reflections in *America and Americans*, a prose retelling of *Winter* where he overtly addresses the moral contortions he perceives in America. Throughout such works he espouses a sort of "moral manhood." The glory of Camelot as a shimmering beacon of moral rectitude in a world blasted and darkened by moral perfidy grew in his mind as an analogy to America. Reflecting on the disparity between the Arthurian age and his own, Steinbeck wrote to Elia Kazan in 1959 that "The values have got crossed up. Courtesy is confused with weakness and emotion with sentimentality."[2] Obviously the statement begs the question, what, exactly, "crossed up" our values? *Winter* and *America and Americans* provide an answer, but that answer may be conveniently summarized in Steinbeck's letter to Adlai Stevenson on November 5, 1959, in which he excoriated American greed: "Having too many THINGS they spend their hours and money on the couch searching for a soul."[3] In *America and Americans*, Steinbeck voiced it as "We are poisoned with things."[4]

Whatever the degree of truth in Steinbeck's moral speculations and outrage, and of course it also appears in such antecedent works as *Cannery Row*, they are in themselves of little help in constructing an ethics of literature. In fact, I include them here precisely because moral statement is often confused with ethics. A pronouncement of what is morally right or wrong in an author's perception may be important to understanding an author's beliefs and may bear relevance to the thematic structure of a work, but it fails to encompass the literary nature of the work itself. Let me be more specific here on certain traits commonly misunderstood as qualities of ethical literature and Steinbeck's specific responses or alternatives to them.

In order to bring shape to Steinbeck's ethics of fiction, it is helpful to separate our approach into two parts. The first of these I will call Intrinsic Ethics; that is, what qualities inhere in the work itself to guide our understanding of the ethical positioning of the work. Such elements, for example, might include the motivations of a character to action, the action taken, and the consequences of that action. The second approach we may call Extrinsic Ethics; that is, how the author presents the work to the reader. Here a host of authorial choices enter: How much of the story to give over to metaphor, or even ambiguity, for the reader to resolve? What degree of intimacy is delivered by the narrative point of view? In this case, then, the work itself functions as metaphor, involving the reader in solutions and conclusions to which the author points rather than directs.

It should be obvious, furthermore, that we are in error if we construe Steinbeck's fiction as allegory. Even in those works packed most densely with symbolism (i.e., *The Pearl*, *East of Eden*) Steinbeck never confines the reader to the strict parameters of allegory where every symbol on narrative level A, for example, has to point to or fit into a meaning on level B. Symbolism, in Steinbeck's literary artistry, is mythic, identified with human experience, tradition, aspirations, and significance. Thereby Elisa Allen's "planter's hands" represent not only her gift of gardening, but also her creative artistry itself. Furthermore, her gardening gloves represent not only protection of those gifted hands, but also the repression of her femininity and creativity by culturally expected roles of the female. Steinbeck structures symbolism as signs stirring the reader's imagination and conclusions. Consequently, the very richness of his fiction lies in the multivariant, and sometimes opposing, interpretations that readers construct.

Intrinsic Ethics

A number of twentieth-century ethical systems might be entertained here, each with some degree of relevance to Steinbeck's fiction. Although rationalist ethics, which posited that the human mind itself was the guide to right and reasonable actions, had been fairly well shredded by early twentieth-century modernism, remnants certainly remained. As such they were subject to Steinbeck's unremitting scorn and attack as "the system," or as *Cannery Row* has it, "civilization." Contrary to Rationalism, then, an existential ethics might seem fitting, particularly when one considers the carefree Mack and the boys. But in their case, the ethical properties are actually self-interested rather than pursuing "authenticity" as Heidegger and Sartre had it, or "good faith" as de Beauvoir put it. Their rejection of and escape from civilization grants a degree of individual freedom but fails to measure the consequences or engage society with any redemptive value.

Apart from *The Grapes of Wrath*, few examples of disinterested ethics occur in Steinbeck's fiction. One could make a good case for Steinbeck holding to a social ethics, particularly as it has been redefined by recent philosophy as how one "holds," or brings a right attitude to, others in a social context. Many of Steinbeck's novels are clearly driven by a social conscience. For the sake of narrowing the argument here, however, consider a distinction between theological and deontological ethics, since they most frequently come to bear upon symbolic readings.

Perhaps the foremost, and most easily dismissed, of the misunderstandings regarding Steinbeck's ethics arises from the rippling current of biblical/religious allusions that flows through his novels. In *To a God Unknown*, they occur in such turgid and convoluted succession as to render the novel merely opaque. In such works as *The Grapes of Wrath* and *East of Eden*, they form deliberate substructures (by Steinbeck's own admission) that guide our understanding of the whole. Yet, as I have argued elsewhere, such allusions are artistic tools for Steinbeck and not at all evidence of personal belief.[5] Rather, we must disavow a theological ethics in Steinbeck's work. Theological ethics takes its name from the perspective of religion, which offers an interpretation of the nature of God and such God-human-nature relationships as sin, evil, goodness, and salvation. The defining nature of such relationships focuses upon some transcendent but always immanent source. This ethics begins with a faith act: that there is a divine being who has encoded standards of right and wrong behavior, who has revealed them to humanity, and who expects humanity to walk in those standards for relational ends between divinity and humanity.

While little sense of a theological ethics is manifested in Steinbeck's work, an acute sense of right and wrong behavior does appear. That is to say, Tom Joad picks up Jim Casy's fallen banner because he believes he "ought to." Instead of a theological ethics, Steinbeck most frequently positions us at a deontological ethics.[6] Instead of asking the familiar ethical question of what is the right or wrong choice, deontological ethics asks where one obtains a sense of rightness or wrongness itself. Is it simply a utilitarian pattern (what would bring about the most good for the most people) or a cultural norm? If one feels that certain acts are right (compassion for the needy) and certain others are wrong (genocide of a needy people), how do we know we ought to do one and not the other? To extend the issue, why do we see the genocidal tyrant as an aberration of some moral quality, not just doing wrong but being evil? Deontological ethics begins with an investigation of where the "oughtness" behind right and wrong human actions originates.

The modern shaping of deontological ethics occurred in Immanuel Kant's *The Critique of Practical Reason*, a response to his own *Pure Reason* which shaped his epistemology by marrying reason and experience but left no room for shaping ethical values. In *Critique* Kant argued that every human has a sense of "oughtness," or what he calls the "Categorical Imperative," the "thou ought." Humanity needs this to make sense and order out of life, to validate an ethical existence. Therefore, Kant postulates these universals derived from his Categorical Imperative: that everyone has freedom to seek the universal; that everyone has a soul that is free and that seeks; and that this soul has an underlying cause that is God. The cause of human knowledge in ethical choices, unlike Pure Reason, lies outside of the natural world.

For the deontologist ethical values are not merely good suggestions; they are obligations morally required of us. The right act, then, is to say this ought to be done. But how do we know that? One option derives from H. A. Pritchard's 1909 essay, "Does Moral Philosophy Rest on a Mistake?" in which he argues that we apprehend what we ought to do intuitively. We can see immediately or intuitively that certain actions are right without having to examine these acts as utilitarian. The source of "oughtness," then, is intuition, an innate quality of human nature itself. One can see the correspondence between Pritchard's and Kant's views but also sense that each leaves a problem. If this sense of oughtness originates in human nature, then the "right thing" is not always clear, which is where we find the majority of Steinbeck's characters ethically positioned. In response to Kant and Pritchard, however, others attempt to correct the intrinsic ambiguity by the standard of "disinterestedness." We are to be interested in the consequences of our actions upon others; we are disinterested in that we refuse to allow personal interests to outweigh the good of others.

It should be manifestly clear, albeit not directly articulated by Steinbeck, that his is a deontological ethics. In fact, his sense of intuited "oughtness" strikes a chord already in *The Sea of Cortez*, his otherwise futile attempt to adapt marine biology as a matrix for human action. Nonetheless, he writes there, "For the ocean, deep and black in the depths, is like the low dark levels of our minds in which the dream symbols incubate and sometimes rise up to sight like Old Man of the Sea." The "dream symbols" here are precisely those myths or stories by which we hold fellow humanity. Or again, "There is tied up to the most primitive and powerful racial or collective instinct a rhythm sense or 'memory' which affects everything. . . ."[7] But this voice—preconscious or whatever—is also, in the fiction, a markedly disinterested voice. The clearest expression of this, beyond question, is through Ma Joad and her belief in the "family of man." Self-interest, the quality of the landowners, Ma offsets and rejects by sacrificial living. No special rules govern Ma's behavior. She does it, even to directing Rose of Sharon to the starving man, because it ought to be done.

We discover first, then, that instead of taking biblical/religious allusions as the measure of Steinbeck's moral beliefs we see them functioning metaphorically and anagogically in the work. Furthermore, instead of a theological ethics expressed by a divine being to humanity, we find a deontological ethics of humanity responding to a sense of intuited oughtness. Beyond question, Steinbeck explored the nooks and crevices of human nature, bringing the hidden to light, exposing lies and fabrications, and exploring the costs of pursuing dreams. Such qualities in and of themselves might warrant the appellation of a "moral writer." But it was not Steinbeck's aim to reduce these investigations to a set of axiomatic truths or didactic principles.

Extrinsic Ethics

If the first area of investigation treated the ethical means by which characters discern good and evil in the novels, the second area, Extrinsic Ethics, treats the way the stories of these characters are offered to the audience. Steinbeck testified often, and throughout his career, that his primary aim as a writer was to tell a story. The stories varied as he felt compelled to tell them. He was unpopular with critics because he was unpredictable. When *In Dubious Battle* was perceived as a Marxist screed, he surprised everyone by writing the quiet little tragedy *Of Mice and Men*. He wrote the bright and rollicking *Tortilla Flat* during a brief interlude while composing the shadowed landscape of *The Long Valley*. Yet in ethical as well as in critical appraisal we are left with the question, to what ends are the stories told? If we have rejected an allegorical reading of Steinbeck's fiction, neither do we expect an Aristotelian argument of truthful ends and right actions. Nonetheless, story as such requires a teleology; the very nature of story narrative initiates a progression toward certain ends.

In a particularly helpful study of the ends and purposes of story, "The End of Literature: Reflections on Literature and Ethics," Clarence Walhout works out a careful synthesis between teleology and ethics in literature. Walhout defines *teleology* in terms altogether applicable to Steinbeck: "Teleology does not require an Aristotelian conception of an ideal or universal *telos* or end or goal. It does not even require that the *telos* be a certain or determinate good. It does imply, however, that living in time entails some sense of purposeful movement toward desired goals."[8] Such a view circumvents the common understanding of teleology as a fixed or transcendent goal, and thereby outside of human endeavor.[9]

Assuming then that teleology is the pursuit of ends or goals enacted in one's life—and consequently also in one's art—how does this belief affect what we make of ethics in literature? Again, Walhout expands his view in a way that also might apply directly to Steinbeck:

> Though universal truths and values may be important for the study of literature, the primary purpose of literature is not to convey or represent such truths or values but to explore the possibilities and consequences of specific human actions and thoughts in a narrative situation. Whatever we may mean by universal truths and values in literature, they are qualities that serve the end of literature and are not themselves the end. The end is the narration of actions that have ethical significance. . . . Actions that are narrated in literature are often taken as illustrations of universal truths and values rather than as what they are—the uncertain and often stumbling efforts of characters to find a way to act in a confusing world.[10]

Thereby, as Walhout points out, literature dramatizes for the reader the conflicts and choices universal to the human condition. Literature may be described as a searching out, rather than a positing, of universal truths or values.[11]

If such may be judged to hold for Steinbeck, it bears certain implications for his Extrinsic Ethics. A sense of teleology that is ongoing draws a reader into possibilities the author holds forth. Into a narrative the author provides conflicts and choices that the reader works through, thereby placing his or her own personhood into the possible resolutions or effects of those conflicts and choices. The reader participates in the story. While symbolism may guide possible choices, it is not structured in an exclusively determinative way to admit one choice only; for example, consider the conflicting meanings and choices provided by the symbolic gem in *The Pearl*. In arriving at an ethical position, then, both artist and reader necessarily work through the ambiguity that grants freedom of choice. To be sure, often the work ends in a tension of unresolved options. This is precisely the point to which Steinbeck often leads the reader (again, consider Pepé in "Flight"). Nonetheless, that very act of pondering conflicting values, of weighing alternatives, and of abandoning untenable responses constitutes an ethical act.

We see, then, that in terms of the intrinsic qualities of the narrative, Steinbeck's artistry is suggestive rather than declarative. Through the use of such constructs as metaphor, symbolism, and character action, he poses conflicts for the reader. Moreover, in terms of extrinsic qualities, he leaves many such conflicts and ambiguities for the reader to resolve. The author tells the story; the reader determines to what teleological ends the story is told. Steinbeck's call to the reader, fundamentally, is to come with me and follow this narrative road on a process of self-discovery. On that road the reader confronts a host of metaphorical and symbolic qualities, many of which emanate from biblical/religious sources. But here too, rather than determinative as a theological ethics, such sources are a call to a reflective plane of deontological ethics, requiring the reader's determination of what ought to be done. For John Steinbeck the reader is an essential participant in both the narrative as well as the ethical understanding of the work.

Notes

1. Lawrence Buell, "In Pursuit of Ethics," *PMLA* 114 (1999): 7.

2. Elaine Steinbeck and Robert Wallsten, eds. *Steinbeck: A Life in Letters* (New York: Penguin, 1975), 631.

3. Ibid., 652.

4. John Steinbeck, *America and Americans* (New York: Viking, 1966), 172.

5. See "John Steinbeck's Use of the Bible: A Descriptive Bibliography of the Critical Tradition," *Steinbeck Quarterly* 21 (Winter/Spring 1988): 24-39.

6. My summary of deontological ethics here is necessarily brief. Several of the best introductions to the philosophy include Nancy Davis' "Contemporary Deontology," Charles Fried's *Right and Wrong*, and John Rawls' *A Theory of Justice*.

7. John Steinbeck, *Sea of Cortez* (New York: Viking, 1941), 31, 34.

8. Clarence Walhout, "The End of Literature: Reflections on Literature and Ethics, *Christianity and Literature* 47 (1998): 459; see also Jeffrey Stout, who in *Ethics after Babel: The Languages of Morals and Their Discontents*, similarly argues that the *telos* need not be "a fixed conception of the good, derived once and for all from a philosophical view of the human essence" (237). For Stout, the *telos* is only worthwhile if it is in fact attainable in human affairs.

9. As I have pointed out elsewhere, Steinbeck's convoluted theory of "non-teleological thinking," as espoused in *The Log from the Sea of Cortez* and several letters, is in fact philosophically teleological thinking. (See *John Steinbeck's Fiction*, pages 16-23 and 158-59.) Steinbeck's fear was of ironclad moral systems that denied individual freedom. His "non-teleological thinking" comports nearly perfectly with Walhout's analysis.

10. Walhout, 461.

11. In *The Company We Keep: An Ethics of Fiction*, Wayne C. Booth contends that "[e]very appraisal of narrative is implicitly a comparison between the always complex experience we have had in its presence and what we have known before" (71).

"I Want to Make 'Em Happy": Utilitarian Philosophy in Steinbeck's Fiction

JOHN J. HAN
Missouri Baptist University

Since Steinbeck's first novel, *Cup of Gold*, was published in 1929, much has been written about his moral vision. Frederick I. Carpenter and Arnold L. Goldsmith, for example, see him as a Transcendentalist philosopher. Martin Shockley contends that Steinbeck's philosophy is fundamentally Christian although his religious vision is more in line with Unitarianism and the transcendentalist philosophy of Ralph Waldo Emerson and Walt Whitman than with orthodox Christianity. Chester E. Eisinger finds Jeffersonian agrarianism in Steinbeck's fiction. Freeman Champney, among others, considers Steinbeck a pro-communist based on a sociological reading of works such as *In Dubious Battle*, *Of Mice and Men*, and *The Grapes of Wrath*. Charles C. Walcutt and Alfred Kazin view Steinbeck as a naturalist whose ideology is informed by evolutionary theory. According to Joseph Fontenrose, however, Steinbeck is a romanticist, "an heir of the Romantic movement." Although Steinbeck is generally considered a realist or naturalist, Fontenrose observes, these are "mere labels."[1] John Timmerman's "John Steinbeck: An Ethics of Fiction" calls Steinbeck a deontological moralist whose work manifests "an acute sense of right and wrong behavior."[2] Others have labeled him a humanist, primitivist, crypto-Nazi, mystic, or pragmatist.

One area Steinbeck critics have ignored, however, is the utilitarian philosophy in his fiction. Although he never identified any specific moral theory as his own, he lived in a culture heavily influenced by utilitarianism. Utilitarians, also called consequentialists, hold that moral rightness must be determined by that which will bring about well-being for the greatest number, with any means justified by a generally beneficial consequence. That is, consequences must benefit the majority. Jeremy Bentham, a quantitative utilitarian, contended that moral conduct had little to do with pleasing God, but rather with the end result of providing the greatest happiness for the greatest number of people, and John Stuart Mill, a qualitative utilitarian, maintained that actions are right "in proportion as they tend to promote happiness, wrong as they tend to produce the reverse of happiness." Happiness is linked to "pleasure, and the absence of pain"; unhappiness to "pain, and the privation of pleasure."[3] "Act" utilitarianism, also called extreme or direct utilitarianism, maintains that an action should be considered moral or immoral based on how much happiness it will produce for the greatest number in a specific circumstance—with a specific action having no intrinsic moral character apart from its results in a specific circumstance. In contrast, "rule" utilitarianism, also called restricted or indirect utilitarianism, maintains that what is ethical is to follow a behavioral code that produces the best consequences if generally followed. An examination of Steinbeck's fiction shows that he is largely utilitarian, especially act utilitarian, in his moral philosophy.

Tortilla Flat is known as a humorous tale recounting the adventures of a group of pleasure-seeking paisanos. However, the work is more than a comic novella. As he wrote to his agent, Mavis McIntosh, Steinbeck intended in this work to explore the paisanos' "strong but different philosophic-moral system"—a system fundamentally utilitarian.[4] Throughout Tortilla Flat, the paisanos—Danny and his friends—pursue happiness, the supreme virtue of utilitarian morality. Such utilitarian words as "happy," "happily," "happiness," and "pleasure" occur repeatedly. Early in the work, Danny anticipates a "happy" life with his friends in the house inherited from his late grandfather.[5] Pilon, one of his friends, also thinks, "We will live happily."[6] Danny and Pilon, "well-fed, warm, and happy, sat in the rocking chairs and gently teetered back and forth."[7] For Pilon, dusk is a time of sweetness which announces the arrival of "the evening of pleasure and conversation."[8] Indeed, for Danny and his friends, who live in accordance with a utilitarian code of conduct (pursue happiness/pleasure and avoid misery/pain), there is "no bar to happiness."[9]

Even crimes are justified in Tortilla Flat because most of them are victimless and eventually benefit the dispossessed at the expense of the smaller number of haves. Chapter 1, "How Danny, home from the wars, found himself an heir, and how he swore to protect the helpless," has a hero who supposedly has great respect for the law but who commits crime without feeling guilty. After stealing ham, eggs, a lamb chop, and a fly swatter from a restaurant, Danny feels no remorse, and is thus, "on the surface" at least, "guiltless."[10] Before he steals a Plymouth Rock rooster, Pilon addresses the fowl, justifying his theft: "Here you play in the street, little chicken. Some day an automobile will run over you; and if it kills you, that will be the best that can happen. It may only break your leg or your wing. Then all of your life you will drag along in misery. Life is too hard for you, little bird." When he kills the rooster, there is "no cry of pain" because it dies "peacefully, or at least, quietly."[11]

These paisanos are similar to Robin Hood, the righteous outlaw from English legend who stole from the rich in order to give to the poor. From the perspective of utilitarian ethics, their thievery can be morally justified because taking wealth from a few rich people to redistribute among the poor produces a greater balance of pleasure (or happiness) over pain. A stealer's motives may be impure, but the results arising out of the crime are in themselves good—at least until any bad consequences arise.[12] Interestingly, Steinbeck never condemns the paisanos for their crimes, his 1937 foreword to the Modern Library edition of *Tortilla Flat* making it clear that he sympathizes with the paisanos and their philosophy: "When this book was written, it did not occur to me that paisanos were curious or quaint, dispossessed or underdoggish. They are people whom I know and like, people who merge successfully with their habitat. In men this is called philosophy, and it is a fine thing."[13] As Joseph Henry Jackson observes, "Steinbeck's paisanos were people for whom he held a deep affection that is transmitted to the reader, which is one way, and a wise one, to go about helping people to understand their fellow men."[14]

In Dubious Battle, a fictional account of a farm workers' strike in California, likewise depicts characters who have unknowingly embraced the principle of utility. The communist Mac desires to build an economically equal society—one that presumably would benefit the majority of people—through all possible means, including violence. A labor leader, he is a scrupulous strategist who pulls the strings for Jim, London, Mr. Anderson, and others. He believes that an individual may be manipulated and sacrificed to benefit the masses. He lures Mr. Anderson into allowing the strikers to camp on his orchard, although he knows that Mr. Anderson will probably be harmed by his action. Mac justifies his use of Joy's death by turning to the principle of utility:

He happens to be the one that's sacrificed for the men. Somebody has to break if the whole bunch is going to get out of the slaughter-house. We can't think about the hurts of one man. It's necessary, Doc. . . . Don't you get lost in a lot of sentimental foolishness. There's an end to be gained; it's a real end, hasn't anything to do with people losing respect. It's people getting bread into their guts. It's *real*, not any of your high-falutin ideas.[15]

Jim, Mac's loyal disciple, also believes that ends justify means. When Mac insists that he open Joy's casket, Doc Burton retorts, "Fun with dead bodies, huh?" Jim steps in and speaks for Mac: "We've got to use every means, Doc. We've got to use every weapon."[16] In another conversation with Doc Burton, who questions the manipulative tactics adopted by Mac and Jim, Jim replies, "Y'ought to think only of the end, Doc. Out of all this struggle a good thing is going to grow. That makes it worthwhile."[17]

In his January 15, 1935, letter to George Albee, Steinbeck noted that *In Dubious Battle* was not a protest novel:

I'm not interested in strike as means of raising men's wages, and I'm not interested in ranting about justice and oppression, mere outcroppings which indicate the condition. . . . The book is brutal. I wanted to be merely a recording consciousness, judging nothing, simply putting down the thing. . . . It is not controversial enough to draw the support of either the labor or the capital side although either may draw controversial conclusions from it, I suppose.[18]

Despite this disclaimer, *In Dubious Battle* was received by the reading public as a protest novel, which was justifiable because no work of fiction is free from ideology. In the novel, Steinbeck allows his characters—particularly the labor leaders, the fruit growers, and Doc Burton—to critique each other freely. Although Doc Burton is generally regarded as Steinbeck's mouthpiece, the author never condemns Mac and Jim for their radical social philosophy, allowing the two communists to defend their utilitarian position convincingly.[19]

Of Mice and Men (1937), a novella on male friendship, also has strong utilitarian undertones. It ends with George's killing his beloved friend, Lennie, to prevent him from being savagely lynched by Curley and his company. George's execution of Lennie is justified because of its eventually beneficial consequences for the majority of people. He kills Lennie out of pity or out of duty, not out of anger—assuring him immediately before the execution that he is not angry with him and never has been. While the deontologist argues that the intentional killing of innocent people is always wrong in principle, the utilitarian may argue that mercy killing is justified because it benefits both the victim and the society in general. Lennie is about to become the victim of a murderous lynch mob—and thus must be killed, George believes, for his own good. As John Ditsky points out, the situation is "quite hopeless," and Lennie's death represents "a matter of cold hard necessity imposing itself upon the frail hopes of man."[20]

Moreover, Lennie's death is foreshadowed by the mercy killing of Candy's ancient dog. The unmistakable thematic parallel between the dog and Lennie is implied in Carlson's argument for killing the smelly old pet, which he views pragmatically as no good to himself or to anyone else. Slim, the skinner, concurs with Carlson, taking the argument a step further: "I wisht somebody'd shoot me if I get old an' a cripple."[21] Candy, the owner of the dog, is unable to refute Carlson and Slim's argument that revolves around two principles—mercy and happiness for the greatest number of people. Killing the dog will release it from pain and, at the same time, relieve the men of his smelly presence in the bunkhouse. Similarly, George complains about a life with Lennie that prevents him from frequenting the brothels and getting drunk as often as he would like. But though his shooting of Lennie serves the utilitarian purposes of ridding himself of a cumbersome burden and society of a potential menace, George still kills out of compassion, not as an executioner. George's immediate motive for executing Lennie, then, is based on this compassion as well as the deontological moral principle of duty to your friend. Lennie is going to suffer anyway, so George feels morally compelled to help Lennie die quickly and in a more dignified way. However, such motives, while crucial to an ethical understanding of both George and the novel, are irrelevant in utilitarian philosophy, where only the consequences are considered.

In *The Grapes of Wrath* Jim Casy is an ex-preacher who questions the existence of God and seems to reject deontological concepts such as sin and living by principle. To him, a religion that cannot meet the needs of people—that cannot bring its followers overall well-being—is useless. He wants to "love people" and to bring them happiness.[22] Although Jim is a Christ-figure who tragically dies a martyr's death, he is a utilitarian in the sense that he sacrifices his own happiness for the sake of the general good. As a utilitarian, Jim seeks pleasure, hoping to find happiness by working side by side in the fields with the migrant workers. He also promotes pleasure for others, hoping to fulfill the dreams of the downtrodden: "These here folks want to live decent and bring up their kids decent. An' when they're old they wanta set in the door an' watch the downing sun. An' when they're young they wanta dance an' sing an' lay together. They wanta eat an' get drunk and work."[23] Later Steinbeck describes the migrant workers themselves finding happiness in storytelling and music, enjoying the company of their fellow travelers when they stopped for the night. Steinbeck, as narrator, never condemns such pleasure seeking because, according to his moral philosophy, humans inherently seek pleasure, as well as goodness, fairness, and justice. In this sense, one might say, *The Grapes of Wrath* promotes both deontological *and* utilitarian ethics. But the utilitarian strain within this novel, especially in the character of Jim Casy, is unmistakable.

Moreover, Steinbeck's utilitarian ethic is not limited to the early works of fiction discussed above. He also embraces the principle of majority good in *Cannery Row, East of Eden*, and *Sweet Thursday*. In the opening paragraph of *Cannery Row*, a man calls the inhabitants of Cannery Row "whores, pimps, gamblers, and sons of bitches." The narrator observes that if this man had "looked through another peephole he might have said, 'Saints and angels and martyrs and holy men,' and he would have meant the same thing." Rather than a clear deontological right or wrong, Steinbeck emphasizes the dependence of the group—saints and sinners—on each other for happiness, finding beauty as well as squalor in Cannery Row, a place that is "a poem, a stink, a grating noise, a quality of light, a tone, a habit, a nostalgia, a dream."[24] In *East of Eden*, Samuel Hamilton displays his utilitarian disposition while talking with Adam and Lee about the biblical story of Cain and Abel. When Lee says that he does not know the details of the story, the joyous Samuel declares, "I'm having enjoyment. And I made a promise to myself that I would not consider enjoyment a sin. I take a pleasure in inquiring into things. I've never been content to pass a stone without looking under it."[25] Although Mack and the boys in *Sweet Thursday* are felons, their pleasure seeking is fundamentally harmless and understandable. Therefore, the author observes sympathetically, "Their association with larceny, fraud, loitering, illegal congregation, and conspiracy on all levels was not only accepted, but to a certain extent had become a matter of pride to the inhabitants of Cannery Row."[26]

Perhaps the question of whether Steinbeck is a deontologist or a utilitarian/consequentialist is insignificant to the writer himself because he was not a philosopher, but a writer whose main task was simply to tell a story. Steinbeck refused to be conveniently labeled for his fiction, as is shown in a letter to Elizabeth Otis in which he stated that he would accept no tags of any kind. Steinbeck was frustrated and puzzled, too, by critics who seemed to read too much into his fiction, complaining to Elizabeth Otis about critical reviews of *Tortilla Flat* that took the book seriously. Regarding *Of Mice and Men*, he complained that even before its publication "there has been a lot of nonsense written about it."[27] Steinbeck's deeply held distrust of literary critics is also conveyed in his essay "A Letter on Criticism," written in response to the invitation of *The Colorado Quarterly*. Here Steinbeck declares that literary criticism "is a kind of ill tempered parlour game in which nobody gets kissed" and objects strongly to "its classification and pickling."[28]

While Steinbeck's cynical comments are understandable, they should be taken with a grain of salt given that no writer creates in an intellectual vacuum. One of the long-held traditions of literature has been to influence morality (whether the author admits it or not) and to investigate philosophical issues, and, therefore, it is essential to interpret literature within a philosophical context.[29] It is nearly impossible to fully understand what a work means without investigating the author's moral-philosophical assumptions. Steinbeck's moral philosophy is in part deontological; acting out of duty and according to moral principles meant a great deal to him. At the same time, utilitarian ideas are unmistakably present in his fiction. Steinbeck was a product of his time, and intellectual influences on him—some of which conflict with each other—were multiple.

The pervasiveness of utilitarian thinking in Steinbeck's fiction is not surprising because utilitarianism, alongside romanticism and Puritanism, has always been an integral part of the American mind. The Romantic Movement, which arose in Europe toward the end of the eighteenth century, stressed individuality, originality, and subjective experience. It triggered the French Revolution and then the American Revolution. Romantic sentiments still affect the American psyche, which jealously guards its independent spirit. Puritanism, a Protestant theology focused on the sovereignty of God and moral rigor, has sustained American evangelicalism. It was a driving force behind the Great Awakenings, the religious/political movements in the eighteenth and nineteenth centuries. In *The Four Great Awakenings and the Future of Egalitarianism*, Robert W. Fogel observes that the United States is experiencing a fourth Great Awakening, which he argues began in 1950. The enormous popularity of such books as the *Left Behind* series and such televangelists as Benny Hinn is a reflection of the current Great Awakening. Although Puritanism is a Calvinistic theology, its doctrines of the sovereignty of God and total depravity of human beings—together with its emphases on moral uprightness and the aversion to social pleasures and indulgences—inform evangelicals of diverse stripes.

Evangelical Christian circles today often denounce the pursuit of happiness as a non-Christian goal, but the utilitarian ideal of happiness has also blended with Christian theology on American soil. While the Declaration of Independence identifies the Judeo-Christian God as the Creator, it recognizes "Life, Liberty, and the Pursuit of Happiness" as unalienable rights. The Preamble of the Constitution also upholds the principle of utility by declaring that the Constitution is designed to "promote the general welfare" of America's citizens. In an open, representative democracy, we try to produce the best results for the majority. The utilitarian/consequentialist elements of American Christianity are evident also in the gospel of health and wealth popularized by such preachers as Norman Vincent Peale, Oral Roberts, Robert H. Schuller, and Joyce Meyer. Therefore, to view Steinbeck as in part a utilitarian philosopher is to view him as a fundamentally American writer who reflects the ethos of his culture and times. Although John Steinbeck's moral vision is not always coherent or totally consistent, elements of a utilitarian ethic are clearly embedded in his fiction from beginning to end.

Notes

1. Joseph Fontenrose, *John Steinbeck: An Introduction and Interpretation* (New York: Holt, Rinehart and Winston, 1963), 90; one may reasonably counter-argue that *romanticist*, a term Fontenrose attaches to Steinbeck, is also a mere label.

2. John Timmerman, "John Steinbeck: An Ethics of Fiction," in *John Steinbeck: A Centennial Tribute*, ed. Stephen K. George (Westport, Conn.: Praeger, 2002), 102.

3. Jeremy Bentham and John Stuart Mill, *The Utilitarians.* (Garden City, N.Y.: Anchor Press, 1973), 407; defining the term *happiness* is a great philosophical difficulty. The term originates in the Greek *eudaimonia*, which many ancient Greek philosophers considered as the end or goal of the ethical life. For example, Aristotle identified happiness primarily with self-actualization. Another group of Greek thinkers, the Epicureans, equated happiness with individual pleasure or self-interest. John Stuart Mill attempted to combine these two traditions of thought about happiness.

4. Elaine Steinbeck and Robert Wallsten, eds. *Steinbeck: A Life in Letters* (New York: Viking Press, 1975), 77.

5. John Steinbeck, *The Short Novels of John Steinbeck*: Tortilla Flat, The Red Pony, Of Mice and Men, The Moon Is Down, Cannery Row, The Pearl (New York: Viking, 1953), 8.

6. Ibid., 9.

7. Ibid., 10.

8. Ibid., 17.

9. Ibid., 28.

10. Ibid., 6.

11. Ibid., 10.

12. Bentham's radical idea of utility is modified later by Mill, who contends that not all pleasures have equal values. According to Mill, higher forms of happiness (those related to intelligence, education, physical health, and the like) are inherently preferable to lower forms of happiness (those related to sensual indulgence, selfishness, ignorance, etc.).

13. John Steinbeck, "Foreword," *Tortilla Flat* (New York: Modern Library, 1937).

14. Joseph Henry Jackson, "Introduction," *The Short Novels of John Steinbeck:* Tortilla Flat, The Red Pony, Of Mice and Men, The Moon Is Down, Cannery Row, The Pearl, by John Steinbeck (New York: Viking, 1953), viii-ix.

15. John Steinbeck, *In Dubious Battle* (New York: Modern Library, 1936), 201; we should note that Steinbeck's idea of group action changes over the years.

16. Ibid, 204.

17. Ibid., 253.

18. Steinbeck and Wallsten, 98-99.

19. *In Dubious Battle* displays Steinbeck's conflicting attitude toward utilitarianism. On the one hand, through the characters Mac and Jim, he insinuates that hurting a small number of people can be justified when it consequentially benefits the majority of people. On the other hand, sympathetic with Doc Burton, Steinbeck shows how cold and cruel the idea of utility can be.

20. John Ditsky, "Ritual Murder in Steinbeck's Dramas," *Steinbeck Quarterly* 11 (1978), 73.

21. Steinbeck, *The Short Novels of John Steinbeck*, 178.

22. John Steinbeck, *The Grapes of Wrath* (New York: Viking Press, 1939), 24.

23. Ibid., 259-60.

24. Steinbeck, *The Short Novels of John Steinbeck*, 273.

25. John Steinbeck, *East of Eden* (New York: Penguin, 1952), 306.

26. John Steinbeck, *Sweet Thursday* (New York: Viking Press, 1954), 13.

27. Steinbeck and Wallsten, 135.

28. E. W. Tedlock, Jr. and C. V. Wicker, eds. *Steinbeck and His Critics: A Record of Twenty-Five Years* (Albuquerque: University of New Mexico Press, 1957), 52-53.

29. Wilfred L. Guerin, et al. *A Handbook of Critical Approaches to Literature.* 4th ed. (New York: Oxford University Press, 1999), 25; numerous writers and critics— Homer, Aristophanes, Horace, Sir Philip Sidney, Samuel Johnson, Percy Bysshe Shelley, Matthew Arnold, and Leo Tolstoy, among others—have discussed the didactic role of literature. Of course, those who embrace the Aristotelian concept of the autonomy of literature or the theory of "Art for Art's Sake" will vigorously deny that they try to teach morality through their works. It would be virtually impossible, however, to separate literature from morality. The political and moral implications of a literary work seem to be a particular concern for many postmodern critics such as Jacques Derrida, Emmanuel Levinas, Alasdair C. MacIntyre, Wayne Booth, Martha Nussbaum, and Jürgen Habermas.

The Existential Vacuum and Ethan Allen Hawley: John Steinbeck's Moral Philosophy

BARBARA A. HEAVILIN
Taylor University

> Every age has its own collective neurosis. . . . The existential vacuum which is the mass neurosis of the present time can be described as a private and personal form of nihilism; for nihilism can be defined as the contention that being has no meaning.[1]

> —Viktor E. Frankl in *Man's Search for Meaning*

Steinbeck's acumen in seeing into the heart of things extends, surprisingly, to an understanding of what it means to be an older woman or a widow in the United States. In *America and Americans* he observes that in the United States there is

> a great over-supply of widows. We have found no use for this great supply of aging women. . . . By far the greater part find only a low-keyed social life without much pleasure or satisfaction—and that with other women exactly like themselves. Dorothy Parker wrote a play about them—a heartbreaking play. I see them in New York, in the delicatessens buying a quarter of a pound of sausage, a small dab of cheese, a minuscule plate of potato salad for their suppers. But luncheon seems to be a widow's meal, and they congregate in restaurants . . . where they talk together and look around brightly for *acquaintances* and for *something to do.*[2]

Here the smallness of the portions parallels the smallness of lives. The plight of these women lacking in pleasure, satisfaction, connections, and meaningful work, is a veritable portrait of what Viktor Frankl, the Jewish psychiatrist who survived imprisonment in the Nazi death camps during World War II, defines as "the existential vacuum," which "manifests itself mainly in a state of boredom."[3] Steinbeck's portrayal of this national malaise extends to include men and youth as well: "The young dread to grow up, the grown dread growing old, and the old are in a panic about sickness and uselessness."[4]

Both Steinbeck and Frankl believe that this self-absorption is a national sickness. Steinbeck observes that "year after year, thousands of families, having accumulated a nest egg through hard, *monotonous, boring* work, go back to the country and try with *puzzled failure* to re-create a self-sufficient island against the creeping, *groping assembly-line conformity* which *troubles* and *fascinates* them at the same time."[5] Frankl, too, points to conformity as a symptom of a modern malaise that has come about because there is no longer any "instinct" that tells human beings what they *have to do* and "no tradition" to tell them what they "*ought to do*." No longer ruled either by necessity or by conscience, they now either wish "to do what other people do (conformism)," or they "do what other people wish (totalitarianism)."[6] Pointing to the result of monotony and boredom that is the hallmark of this troublesome and fascinating assembly line that has come to define life in modern-day America, Frankl maintains:

> now we can understand Schopenhauer when he said that mankind was apparently doomed to vacillate eternally between the two extremes of *distress* and *boredom*. And these problems are growing increasingly crucial, for progressive automation will probably lead to an enormous increase in the *leisure hours* available to the average worker. The pity of it is that many of these will not know what to do with all their newly acquired free time.[7]

Both novelist and psychiatrist, then, describe the same social phenomenon.

Like Frankl, Steinbeck finds the roots of the ailment in the problems associated with increasing leisure time:

> As for the use of leisure, we are due to feel that pressure more and more as automation and increase of population force more and more leisure on us; and so far, in human history, leisure has caused us to get into destructive and unsatisfactory trouble. Unless some valuable direction can be devised and trained for in America, *leisure may well be our new disease, dangerous and incurable.*[8]

Neither Steinbeck nor Frankl, however, is a nihilist. Neither leaves the human condition, particularly the current American condition, in a state of abject and total hopelessness. Both agree that the condition is serious, even life-threatening, but Frankl's logotherapy and Steinbeck's fiction offer some strikingly similar "directions" for escaping and overcoming this societal malignancy. What Frankl diagnoses as "the existential vacuum"—a psychic emptiness brought on by a lack of a sense of meaning—is clearly manifested, for example, in Steinbeck's depiction of Ethan Allen Hawley in *The Winter of Our Discontent*. Like Frankl, Steinbeck offers a cure that coincides with the psychiatrist's observation that there are three ways to discover "meaning in life." First, there is meaning in work well done. Second, there is meaning in life's experiences and relationships. Third, there is meaning in a person's attitude towards unavoidable suffering. The last two of these "ways" need further explanation:

The second way of finding a meaning in life is by experiencing something—such as goodness, truth, and beauty—by experiencing nature or culture or, last but not least, by experiencing another human being in his very uniqueness—by loving him. . . . We must never forget that we may also find meaning in life even when confronted by a hopeless situation, when facing a fate that cannot be changed. For what then matters is to bear witness to the uniquely human potential at its best, which is to transform a personal tragedy into a triumph, to turn one's predicament into a human achievement. When we are no longer able to change a situation, . . . we are challenged to change ourselves.[9]

Hawley's existential vacuum almost destroys him: he fails to accomplish anything worthwhile; and he fails to achieve goodness, truth, beauty, and love. But out of near tragedy, he triumphs over self-absorption to discover meaning in a renewed love of family—both those in this world and those who have gone before him to "the other side of home where the lights are given."[10]

The "existential vacuum" is characterized by a frustrated lack of meaning for which some people compensate by seeking power, money, or pleasure—often with the "sexual libido" becoming "rampant."[11] In this vacuum the self is not actualized, even though they may seek inside themselves for meaning. For, according to Frankl, only by focusing outside of oneself and by arriving at a sense of responsibility to a Creator, to life, or to others can a person achieve a sense of selfhood, identity, connections to others, and, ultimately, of reality and meaning. Trapped inside of himself, Ethan manifests the emptiness and lack of meaning in life that characterize the existential vacuum.

Toying with the Freudian concept of the *id*, an unconscious over which we have no control, Ethan contemplates the recesses of his own mind. When he finds time to face a problem, he discovers that some dark jury without faces "in the dark and desolate caves" of his mind has already decided the verdict. He luxuriates in this image, cherishing this area of his psyche that is a "secret and sleepless area" like a deep, dark pool that spawns forms, few of which ever reach the consciousness. This is the arena of poets, he thinks to himself, finding an endless attraction to this inner landscape over which he has no control. But it is not finally in the mysteries of these psychic depths that human beings achieve a sense of the meaning of life. That accomplishment, Frankl insists, they must find *outside* of themselves.

In striving to find meaning and to achieve a sense of selfhood, therefore, Ethan looks in the wrong place—inside himself. But he also seeks to find in his house and family name a means of identity, reality, and actualization. Sitting at tea with Mary and the Bakers, he tells them of his "dreadful dream" in which Danny Taylor is melting away into nothingness, remarking, "I feel I should be my brother Danny's keeper." The general consensus among the three listeners is that Danny is a disgrace to the Taylor family name, that he will probably die a drunk, and that it would be an act of kindness to institutionalize him so that he could be cared for.[12] Sitting there in the Baker living room, Ethan thinks of himself and Danny and of the important connections of family, house, and name: "Hawley was more than a family. It was a house. And that was why poor Danny held onto Taylor Meadow. Without it, no family—and soon not even a name. By tone and inflection and desire, the three sitting there had canceled him."[13]

Ethan ponders the importance of a family home and history to enable people to realize that they actually exist. This material connection, he believes, is a connection to reality. Without it, people are simply canceled. People do not talk person to person but "house to house." Although he resents the group's "removal from real of Danny Taylor," he is powerless to keep it from happening.[14] For Ethan's own sense of reality is tied up with these three: family, house, name. Without them, he feels that he, like Danny, would be canceled out and become a nonentity.

More sinister than a sense of reality dependent upon family, house, and family name is Ethan's arrival at the conviction that the acquisition of money is the only way to hold on to these three. In a carefully reasoned argument, he convinces himself that modern people are like a rancher with no land, an army officer with no troops, a horseman with no horse. In such a condition, he reasons, people cannot survive. He rationalizes that this is the reason for his own change in morality. Whereas money itself has never been a primary goal, he thinks, it is essential in maintaining the rank in society with which he is comfortable. Again, he maintains that it is in the realm of the *id*—the place over which he has no conscious control—that this decision has been made. It has been made *for* him, but not *by* him, "in the dark place below . . . thinking level," and it "emerged not as a thought but as a conviction."[15]

Note the persuasiveness of this argument that maintains that his very survival and well-being are dependent upon the acquisition of money. By implication, this "conviction" has a basis in a moral conscience because of concern for his family's status and well-being; thus Ethan deceives himself because, as in the medieval play *Everyman*, his money and goods are finally hollow. They fail to deliver what they promise, leaving him empty and spiritually impoverished.

At a dinner and card-reading session with Margie Young-Hunt in his home, he is forewarned about being violated and possessed by the desire for riches. Earlier, Margie has predicted Ethan's acquisition of wealth, and in this session she affirms that prediction. Uncomfortable and ill at ease with the whole arrangement, Ethan envisions what is happening to him psychically, morally, and spiritually. And again he sees himself as out of control, passive, acted upon, but not acting, changed by an outside force that smacks of possession. He views himself as composed of "a mass of gauges and dials and registers," few of which he can read at all and those not with any degree of accuracy. Then he feels actual physical pain, searing and tearing, beginning in his bowels and moving upward to the ribs. He next hears a loud wind and feels himself driven like a ship without sails during a terrible sea storm. He even tastes the saltiness of the seawater and feels the dining room heaving as though it were a ship. He recognizes all of these sensations as warning signs, screaming danger. In a state of shock, he doubles over as he walks behind Margie's and Mary's chairs at the table. But the experience passes quickly, and he goes on as if nothing had happened, understanding now, however, why some people used to believe in devil possession. He certainly does not believe in possession, Ethan assures himself. He feels instead that he has been violated and has made peace with the violator.[16] Thus making "peace with the invader," Ethan, the Every American, succumbs to the corruption of the love of money—a moral corruption that is a chief hallmark of his times and his country. Frankl describes this corruption by money as means to power as one of "the various masks and disguises under which the existential vacuum appears."[17] To begin with, Ethan's attempts to overcome this vacuity are futile, for he fails to accomplish anything worthwhile.

Ethan's failure of accomplishment is accompanied by an unidentified longing. With an undeveloped, immature sense of self, he shores himself around with things gathered from what he calls "the world's attic." Since, as Frankl puts it, "No tradition tells him what he ought to do," he longs nostalgically for the moorings of the past:[18]

> I guess we're all, or most of us, the wards of that nineteenth-century science which denied existence to anything it could not measure or explain. The things we couldn't explain went right on but surely not with our blessing. We did not see what we couldn't explain, and meanwhile a great part of the world was abandoned to children, insane people, fools, and mystics, who were more interested in what is than in why it is. So many old and lovely things are stored in the world's attic, because we don't want them around us and we don't dare throw them out.[19]

Without those values that can be neither measured nor explained—that have been tossed away as nonexistent—he lacks a sense of purpose, and the work by which he earns a living provides neither satisfaction nor meaning.

From the outset his inability to achieve success or accomplish a satisfactory goal is apparent. A Harvard graduate, he returns to New Baytown to establish himself in his home community under the shield of the highly respected family name of Hawley ("wholly" or "holy" perhaps played on here since pride in the name itself is so closely tied to his sense of identity and worth). Here he runs his own inherited establishment, a neighborhood grocery store. He fails at this task, however, loses the store, and is reduced to the status of clerk in the business his family had previously owned. Both he and his family feel shamed by this reduction in circumstances. Ethan knows that "Mary wants to be proud" once more, and he believes that only money can fulfill her longing for material goods and social prestige.[20]

Nor does he accomplish the task of head of a family with any high degree of satisfaction. Although he loves his wife, Mary, his relationship to her is often tentative and shallow. He calls her names that she appropriately labels as "silly," doesn't really listen to her or take her seriously, often going to a private and secret "Place," a cave-like enclosure with a seaward view near the remnants of the Hawley dock. In this womb-like space he escapes his mundane world and avoids the intimacy of sharing, engaging rather in self-absorption and solip-

sism—a passive experience that he likens to a sheet being hung on the line to
dry. Had he ever bothered to ask her the questions he asked himself, their relationship may have reached a higher plane: "Does anyone ever know even the
outer fringes of another?" he muses. "What are you like in there? Mary—do you
hear? Who are you in there?"[21] Bothered by his taciturnity, Mary counters these
unasked questions with an echo of Eliot's *Waste Land*: "I never know what you
are thinking." Concerning his children he is likewise "silly," making no real
connection with them, asking Mary facetiously whether he "can . . . beat the
children a little to celebrate the day before Resurrection? I promise to break no
bones."[22]

Ironically, in view of his emotional detachment from his wife and children,
he regularly communes with Aunt Deborah and Old Cap'n, family members
now deceased. He remembers well their training and admonitions—an upbringing designed to ground him in family tradition and to enable him to uphold the
good Hawley name. Old Cap'n, Ethan maintained, had taught him about ships,
and life, and death so that he would know who he was inside and out. His Aunt
Deborah had grounded him in the scriptures so that Holy Week is so much of a
reality that he suffers through the hours of Christ's agony and is relieved when
the time has passed, and His suffering is over.

Yet, he is a failure as a Hawley as well. True, Old Cap'n and Aunt Deborah
have left their imprint on him, but he believes himself incapable of accomplish-
ing anything more than serving as a clerk in the grocery store that he had once
owned. Nor does the moral fortitude exemplified in Aunt Deborah's piety and
devotion hold him steady. For although he suffers through the events commemo-
rated by Holy Week that she had made real for him, this empathy does not prevent him from contributing to a childhood friend's downfall, meticulously planning a bank robbery, and betraying his boss Marullo by revealing to immigration
officials that he had entered the country illegally decades ago. Blinded by desire
for success and security, he puts aside his moral sense and moorings, believing
that he can take up his morality again once he has the riches essential to carry on
the Hawley tradition. He has not only failed to accomplish anything of moment,
then, but he has also laid aside his integrity.

Frankl's second way of finding meaning in life is by the experience of
goodness, truth, beauty, and love. Ethan's pathetic attempts in these areas take
him into the world of the grotesque—an askew and twisted parody of the real
that reveals a dwarfed, immature soul that is nonetheless sympathetic because he
represents the wounded, fallen human condition. Schooled in a living Christianity by Aunt Deborah and convinced of the basic morality of his forebears, Ethan
at first considers himself to be a good, moral person. Recognizing and rationalizing the change in moral bearings that he observes in himself, he blames them on
"Mary's wish [not to be poor anymore], Allen's desires [for money and material
possessions], Ellen's anger [over her family's poverty], and Mr. Baker's help."[23]

Continuing his rationalizations, he tries to absolve himself of responsibility for his own contemplated wrongdoings by looking at the town's businessmen—indulging himself in the fallacious, adolescent, everyone-is-doing-it plea:

> They abolished part of the Decalogue and kept the rest. And when one of our successful men had what he needed or wanted, he reassumed his virtue as easily as changing his shirt, and for all one could see, he took no hurt from his derelictions, always assuming that he didn't get caught. . . . [B]usiness is a kind of war. . . . Why not . . . make it all-out war in pursuit of peace? . . . To be alive at all is to have scars.[24]

Concealed in the half truth that life itself leaves a person wounded and scarred, Ethan attempts to make noble the success-at-any-cost mentality of his times by likening his own devious plans to enrich himself to a nation's war fought in the interest of peace. Continuing the analogy of war, he will allow himself to be governed later by an oxymoronic law of "controlled savagery" in his dealings with banker Baker and Danny, his childhood friend.[25] Earlier, in his self-absorbed and solipsistic musings on what happens to him when he goes to his womb-like "Place" to escape the pressures of the world, he foreshadows this rationalization that blurs distinctions between black and white and wrong and right. It does not matter whether what happens there is good or bad, he muses, because it is "right for me."[26] Thus devoting himself to a delusion that he is the measure of right and wrong, good and evil—that there is no ethical standard outside of himself—his moral moorings fall away, and he has failed to arrive at either goodness or truth. From this point and this perspective, his entire world accordingly shrinks to the size of his own small-souled, conniving self.

Nor will he succeed in experiencing beauty—rather, he will find the horrors of nightmare in its place. For in his relationship with Danny, Ethan's encounters with the beauties of nature, friendship, and the remembered joy of childhood take a grotesque turn to reflect a deep psychic grief and guilt over his contemplated betrayal of this friend who has been like a brother to him since boyhood. Dreaming of a dizzyingly bright and beautiful day, he has a stark and horrifying vision of Danny's demise and realizes that it is a direct result of his own Cain-like betrayal of a brother. In this dream it is "early summer," he and Danny Taylor are no longer children but in late adolescence, and they have gone on an adventure to explore a dried-up lake and the ruins of a house. Ethan notices in detail the glorious beauty of the day with trees and grass in rich, full foliage, loaded down with the full growth of their own leaves and blades so that he himself feels "fat and crazy too" with the warm weight of the season.

Then the horror begins. From behind the column of a straight, slender juniper, he hears Danny's voice, but it is distorted as though he were "under water." Running to him, Ethan finds him "melting and running down over his frame." Frantically, he tries to push his features back into place—as though he were freshly poured cement—but he fails. Danny's "essence" continued to run downward between his fingers. And the more he tried, the more Danny contin-

ued to melt.[27] Shaken to his very core, still Ethan is undeterred from the course
he has determined. He will betray Danny, deceive Mr. Baker, and turn the aging
Marullo over to the immigration authorities for deportation. Such is the price he
is willing to pay for riches and success in the eyes of the world. He is now the
degenerate Every American.

Until the very end when he is spared by an epiphany, he similarly fails at
achieving love as well as beauty. Despite his constant, and often absurd, en-
dearments for Mary—"Miss Mousie," "darling chicken-flower," "ladybug"—his
love for her does not succeed in mooring him, stabilizing him, bringing him to
maturity.[28] He toys with the idea of an extramarital affair with Margie Young-
Hunt and contemplates and almost commits suicide without consideration of his
responsibility to Mary and their children. He likewise turns away from his
daughter, Ellen, and goes out into the night with suicide on his mind. Self-
absorbed, he determines to act on what he believes to be right for himself, un-
aware that he is losing his own best self in the process. Still, it is love that inspires the epiphany that will enable him to transcend his circumstances and will
call him back and restore him to their love and these familial responsibilities.

In order to find meaning and rise out of the vacuity he has created for himself, ultimately Ethan must rise to the challenge to change himself, transcend his
circumstances, and grow up—facing the world with a mature sense of responsibility. Frankl states that "logos," or meaning, "is deeper than logic." Human
beings cannot simply think themselves out of their dilemmas. Whereas Ethan
has tried to find success and meaning in his life by rationalizing, plotting, and
planning for self-aggrandizement, he has been left with emptiness and loss. He
must overcome what Frankl calls the modern malaise, "the existential vacuum."

Ethan does not fully recognize the emptiness of his life until his son, Allen,
plagiarizes his essay in an "I love America" contest and flippantly refuses to
acknowledge any wrongdoing—chiding his father and maintaining that everybody does it. Racked with guilt for contributing to Danny Taylor's death, for
betraying Marullo to the immigration officials, and for planning a bank robbery,
Ethan despairs and determines to commit suicide. With no sense of self or reality, in his "Place" on the shore, the tide rising around him, he reaches for the
razor blades in his pocket. One swift slash of the wrists will do it.

But he does not slash his wrists. Instead of the razor blades, he pulls from
his pocket a luminescent family talisman that his daughter, Ellen, evidently
placed there in a convulsive hug as he left home. Then he experiences an epiphany of light that moves him out of his solipsism into an awareness of his responsibility to life, to his daughter, and, by strong implication, to God. He has been
aware that there are some whose lights are still burning even though they have
gone on before: Marullo's, old Cap'n's, and Aunt Deborah's. Despairing,
though, he feels that his own "light is out" and that "there's nothing blacker than
a wick." His reality no longer linked to a house or a family, he prays: "I want to
go home—no not home, to the other side of home where the lights are given."
And his prayer is answered by the talisman and thoughts of his responsibility to

be a lightbearer for Ellen and to pass the light on to her. In a sense of responsibility to her and love for her, he has finally found himself. He has reached self-actualization. He has grown up. All that remains is to struggle out of that cave, against the pounding surf and "brisking waves" so that he can "return the talisman to its new owner." He determines not to let that light "go out."[29] Love triumphs over death and fills what had been an existential vacuum. Ethan finally has his moment of triumph.

This ending—so contrary to the cynicism of Hemingway and the darkness of Faulkner—carries Steinbeck's American epic to a prophetic conclusion. This story began *in medias res* with *The Grapes of Wrath* and its depiction of the Oklahoma Dustbowl and the contrasting greed and heroism of Americans; continued with *East of Eden* and its insistence that Americans can choose good over evil, hospitality and love over greed; and now concludes with *The Winter of Our Discontent* and its prophetic implications that the lights of this nation will continue.[30] Although some Ivy League critics have labeled and derided *Winter* as sentimental, after the events of September 11, 2001, when so many Americans became heroes, saints, and martyrs by triumphing over tragedy, Steinbeck's persistent optimism, his love for America, and his prophetic voice declaring the possibilities of transcendence over the national penchant for greed ring true. Like Ethan Allen Hawley, in Steinbeck's vision of America, the American people have been actualized and have entered into the realm of reality, revealing a nation capable of growing up and assuming moral responsibility for its own future. Steinbeck is not only "the poet of our dispossessed," as an early critic described him, he is also the poet who has seen most clearly this nation's potential for greatness of spirit and moral leadership to offset greed and power. This is the actuality in which Steinbeck, like Frankl, so passionately believed. Self-transcendence can overcome the malaise of the existential vacuum and restore meaning to those like Ethan, the Every American, who are caught in the limbo of their own self-absorption.

Notes

1. Viktor Frankl, *Man's Search for Meaning: An Introduction to Logotherapy* (New York: Simon and Schuster, 1959), 131.

2. John Steinbeck, *America and Americans* (New York: Viking Press, 1966), 105: emphasis added.

3. Frankl, 111.

4. Steinbeck, *America and Americans*, 105.

5. Ibid., 106: emphasis added.

6. Frankl, 111: emphasis added.

7. Ibid., 112: emphasis added.

8. Steinbeck, *America and Americans*, 106: emphasis added.

9. Frankl, 115-16.

10. John Steinbeck, *The Winter of Our Discontent* (New York: Penguin Books, 1961), 357.

11. Frankl, 112.

12. Steinbeck, *The Winter of Our Discontent*, 135-36.

13. Ibid., 136.

14. Ibid.

15. Ibid., 132.

16. Ibid., 98-99.

17. Frankl, 112.

18. Ibid., 111.

19. Steinbeck, *The Winter of Our Discontent*, 89.

20. Ibid., 46.

21. Ibid., 65.

22. Ibid.

23. Ibid., 116.

24. Ibid., 117.

25. Ibid., 137.

26. Ibid., 3.

27. Ibid., 131.

28. Ibid., 57.

29. Ibid., 357-58.

30. Like Ralph Waldo Emerson, it is likely Steinbeck believed that "a foolish consistency is the hobgoblin of small minds," and to claim that he adhered to a single metaphysic would be unwise indeed. However, in three of his novels—*The Grapes of Wrath*, *East of Eden*, and *The Winter of Our Discontent*—there is a remarkably consistent mythopoeic vision of human potentiality. As Laura F. Hodges has pointed out in "Arthur, Lancelot, and the Psychodrama of Steinbeck" (*Steinbeck Yearbook*, volume 2, 2002) Steinbeck "gives us characters who represent aspects of his own self-image in a psychodrama, dominated by Arthur and Lancelot who represent the immature and mature man coexistent in every man." In a poignant observation of the American people in *America and Americans*, he defines, by its absence, the quality that is for him a mark of nobility: "It as though the quality of *responsibility* had atrophied" [emphasis added]. In these three novels Steinbeck shows that without this sense of responsibility, Americans have lost their moorings, their anchor, their very soul. And like Frankl, he demonstrates that there is no meaning for the one, single, solitary individual who has no sense of the other—that only in community may human beings find true identity. This, I believe, is the essence of his moral philosophy of the human condition.

Part II: Ethical Explorations of Steinbeck's Fiction

Moral Experience in *Of Mice and Men*: Challenges and Reflection

RICHARD E. HART
Bloomfield College

Does John Steinbeck's *Of Mice and Men* contribute anything to morality and thinking about morality? Does the obvious social message and social conscious-ness of the work tweak the moral imagination and invite critical philosophic reflection? Some scholars and critics have appreciated what I call the "moral dimension" of the book, while others have expressed considerably less regard for that aspect. Skeptics seem to have gathered around the perennial charge of sentimentality and moral simplicity. Perhaps the most famous allegation of that kind came from Alfred Kazin in his definitive study, *On Native Grounds*. Kazin sharply attacked *Of Mice and Men* for its sterile "moral serenity" that led to the "calculated sentimentality" of the story.[1] Edwin Berry Burgum echoed Kazin when he wrote that Steinbeck "swung in his various novels from the extreme of a deep and legitimate admiration for working people to that in which all values are paralyzed in the apathy of the sentimental."[2] Similarly, John S. Kennedy stated that Steinbeck "can be acutely sensitive and true for a chapter, then em-barrassingly sentimental and cheaply trite."[3] Are such characterizations reflec-tive of what Charlotte Cook Hadella calls "critical elitism" or are they somehow on the mark?[4] If accurate, then *Of Mice and Men* would seem to be of little rele-vance to serious reflection on morality. Rather, it would be scarcely more than a popular little book/play for the masses who are absorbed by the sentimental. And as Jackson Benson has written, "'Sentimental' is the ultimate pejorative in modern literary criticism, tending to disqualify anything so labeled from further serious consideration."[5]

Hadella astutely points out that "For five decades *Of Mice and Men* sur-vived charges of animalism, sentimentalism, melodrama, and trite social pro-test."[6] In the 1980s assessments began to change. John Timmerman praised Steinbeck for "exploring the enduring questions of the nature of humanity, of good and evil, of tragedy and triumph."[7] Many readers and critics have surely been moved by the sense of social responsibility they find in *Of Mice and Men*. Louis Owens contended that Steinbeck's vision of America "is an ideal of commitment to humankind and to the environment, a holistic reverence for life. In this light, *Of Mice and Men* emerges as a skillfully rendered dramatization of the precepts to which Steinbeck dedicated his life's work."[8] *Steinbeck and the Environment: Interdisciplinary Approaches* would seem to enhance and extend Owens's regard for Steinbeck as an early ecologist with a humanistic moral sensibility. Finally, Hadella observes that Steinbeck's "stories themselves raise ethical questions,"[9] while Michael Meyer applauds him for being "the moral conscience of the American reading public."[10]

What is to be made of such contradictory views when applied to the subject of morality in *Of Mice and Men*? It cannot be simultaneously a simple-minded morality tale and a genuine provocation to the reader's thinking and feeling. I propose an approach to this novel that is both consistent with Steinbeck's philosophy (loosely speaking), and which allows the text to address a variety of moral issues and questions. I distinguish here between moral philosophy (as traditionally understood) and moral experience. By experience I mean simply undergoing the moral drama and tension and conflict that the characters in the story witness and reflecting sensitively on that experience (theirs and ours).

Though I am a philosopher for whom ethics is a specialty, I choose not to approach *Of Mice and Men* as a moral theorist, considering it generally fruitless to ponder whether Steinbeck represents and applies a certain type of ethical theory—is he a Kantian deontologist, a utilitarian in the manner of Bentham or Mill? Does he embrace "virtue ethics"? Is he Aristotelian or Platonist or Marxist in leaning, absolutist or relativist? There can be no reasonable or definitive answers to such questions because Steinbeck was not interested in philosophic theory divorced from lived experience. This is not to say, however, that he was not interested in morality and raising ethical questions in and through his work. When a reporter for the Associated Press asked what is the major function of an author in today's society, Steinbeck replied, "Criticism, I should think."[11] He was, indeed, a social critic, and such functioning can be highly conducive to meaningful thinking about morality. In a postscript to a questionnaire for a graduate student at Ohio University, he commented on his philosophy: "And as to the questions as to what I mean by—or what my philosophy is—I haven't the least idea. . . . I don't like people to be hurt or hungry or unnecessarily sad. It's just about as simple as that."[12] His approach to morality and philosophy may be simple, but that does not necessarily make it trite and sentimental. As Hadella points out, with *Of Mice and Men* and other works, Steinbeck "wished to challenge his audience's sense of values."[13] When a reporter asked what his last novel, *The Winter of Our Discontent*, was about, for example, Steinbeck replied in one word—"morals."[14] Steinbeck was interested in morality and shed important light on it in most of his fiction. The exact sort of light—and what we do with it—is what most interests me here.

This focus on experience and the thinking and feeling it engenders, rather than on philosophical theory, is motivated in part by what I take philosophy "in" literature to be. Literature (and other arts as well) is a uniquely powerful vehicle for philosophical exploration. It does not, however, provide logical arguments for this or that position or theory. The writer's function is not to construct or defend a particular philosophy or ideology. A story or a poem is not a series of propositions woven together by the force of reason. A work of literature shows, it exhibits, it offers multiple and unique perspectives not always available to reason and argument. It causes the reader to undergo the experience of how something looks and feels. If honest and well constructed, it has the capacity to present the "truth" of a situation (factually and emotionally), and such truthful experience has the power to make the reader think about life, society, and the world. Albert Camus once remarked that his *Myth of Sisyphus* essays gave a theoretical explanation of his philosophy of the absurd while his novel, *The Stranger*, enabled readers to witness and to feel such ideas as lived through human characters and situations. Both Jean-Paul Sartre and Albert Camus are excellent interdisciplinary examples of the interconnectedness of philosophy and literature. Both help to explain and justify the approach to fiction I am taking here.[15]

Of Mice and Men presents dramatic situations and characterizations that allow us to see and hear and feel ethical dilemmas and such social problems as racism, sexism, and economic exploitation in an immediate, first-hand way. Such issues are dramatically contextualized so as to provoke reader reflection. One cannot escape the moral burdens and provocations of the story. Steinbeck, of course, offers no resolutions or sweeping answers. Such is not his purpose or function. He means to agitate, to provoke, to anger, to cause doubt and raise a multitude of questions. In the manner of Socrates, this is the first honest step toward philosophizing.

What I have said here about literature is also consistent with what may loosely be called Steinbeck's philosophic method, non-teleological "is" thinking. As Hadella observes, with *Of Mice and Men* "Steinbeck was breaking new ground philosophically as well as formally in writing his play-novelette. By 1936 he had become very interested in non-teleological thinking, the scientific philosophy that concentrates on the conditions of existence rather than on causes and effects of these conditions."[16] Of prime importance here is the "conditions of existence," what human existence in a particular setting is really like from the inside. What do such conditions feel like when actively experienced? Hadella points further to Steinbeck's reluctance to explain causes and effects— how existence got to be a certain way and what it is leading to. This approach lent itself to a holistic, integrated vision of humanity and nature in which all things are literally united. This point of view carries important implications for morality because it "accepts things as they are without assigning blame to individuals or situations."[17]

In *Of Mice and Men* Steinbeck basically reports something that happened on a ranch (the original title was to be *Something That Happened*). He does not take sides and does not engage in normative ethical reasoning. He portrays rather than judges. Readers, or the audience for the play, are left to draw their own conclusions and to contemplate the good and the bad, the callous and the indifferent. Steinbeck knew that readers would raise their own questions and provide their own explanations, believing that honest writing has as its basic theme understanding humanity. This refers to the characters created by the author as well as the audience for the story. Humans feel and think. Thinking and feeling typically are rolled into one. When they encounter a moral problem either in life or in art, humans feel bad. They are often confused and want to know what caused it and how it could possibly be remedied. It is our natural disposition to ask why and search for answers. Though he doesn't theorize or explain, all this is perfectly compatible with Steinbeck's focus on responsibility and what people owe to each other. As an artist and a teller of stories, he does not assign blame or make an "argument" for right or wrong, leaving the reader to carry forward the moral burden of the things that happened. As Hadella observes, "Happily, the novel proved to be a successful marriage of form and philosophy. With a dramatic structure focusing on the character's dialogue and actions, Steinbeck achieved a narrative intensity that is largely untainted by authorial voice."[18]

Moral issues weave their way through *Of Mice and Men*. There are moral dimensions in the depiction of love and friendship as well as the profound moral dilemma George faces at the end of the story.[19] Critics have discussed as well the immorality of economic exploitation as represented in the class, ownership, and power structures of the ranch. Clearly, the great dream that George and Lennie share concerns human camaraderie and a realization of a sense of community. But the dream is largely about escape from an economic prison and the immorality of a dispossession and extreme poverty that restricts human freedom and opportunity. Two other moral issues, however, have perhaps not garnered quite as much attention—sexism and racism.

A discussion of sexism in the story must focus on Curley's wife, the only woman on the ranch. But her situation and the gender discrimination she is forced to endure has a moral impact on the male characters as well. She is a morally ambiguous character, with two distinct sides to her personality and behavior—both associated with male-dominated, sexist attitudes of the time and culture. Both sides of her personality grow directly from such pervasive gender attitudes and values, and each says something important about Steinbeck's portrayal of the situation of women at that time.

Curley's wife is not given a proper name. Apparently she does not merit it. Or could her anonymity be a deliberate suggestion that she is not just an individual, but represents all women? On the surface, she is cast as the classic seductress, the wily female who is the despoiler of paradise. She manipulates men into lust and sin through her aggressive sexuality. She exploits the sexual impulse in an effort to get things her way. She's the killer of male-centered dreams of fraternity and independence. Steinbeck seems to offer her as a crude, unsympathetic stereotype, as a nice-to-touch object—perhaps, in one interpretation, as simply a projection of misogynistic hostility toward women. With the possible exception of Slim, all the men on the ranch are suspicious of her. They don't like her, except to look at her, fearing that she is nothing more than "jail bait." But in all this is she her own person? Does she act freely—always knowingly—whereby the veil of moral responsibility would naturally descend upon her? Or has she been conditioned by society to utilize her assets as a mechanism for survival, likely the only one she knows? Is she largely on automatic pilot? In any case, what is to be said about the morality of her situation? Is there a larger story to realize about her?

Curley's wife views herself as a commodity, an object of sensuality. Clearly, she is regarded as property, as chattel of the ranch like the other powerless workers. But is her self-realization a willing thing, and is she comfortable about it? Are readers? Hadella argues that "free will . . . hardly seems to exist for people like Curley's wife and Lennie," that "she plays the only role she knows how to play."[20] Quickly disillusioned by the severely limited role of wife of a cruel and brutal ranch owner's son, she dreams of escaping to Hollywood, a totally unrealistic fantasy. Hadella's focus shifts from the earlier depiction of a manipulative bitch to that of a person "whose life is severely limited, a sympathetic character."[21] Mimi Gladstein points out that "There is a school of Steinbeck critics who respond to the castigations of Steinbeck's limited and repellent portrayals of women by explaining that Steinbeck's purpose in doing so is to critique woman-less or woman-oppressive culture."[22] Cutting women out of the male fraternity that the ranch symbolizes, then, creates a sterile condition that lacks diversity and wholeness.

Steinbeck's own account of Curley's wife supports such a sympathetic reading, for he described this character to Claire Luce, who played the part on Broadway and wanted to understand her role more fully. Curley's wife, Steinbeck wrote, is "a nice, kind girl and not a floozy. No man has ever considered her as anything except a girl to try to make. She has never talked to a man except in the sexual fencing conversation."[23] He also suggests that to really know Curley's wife would be to love her, that she is a trusting yet hardened girl accustomed to a male-dominated society, pretending to be something she is not, alone and unloved. Hadella observes that "*pretend* is the operative verb here, and it is on this question of pretended worldliness versus innate evil that an assessment of Curley's wife depends." It also rests, perhaps, on coming to grips with an "American society in which vulnerable, unfortunate young women must survive."[24]

At one point Curley's wife reveals for a moment her less sharp, more human side, speaking of her profound loneliness—similar to that of the ranch hands—and her unfulfilled need simply to have someone to talk to. Whereas the ranch workers apparently have one another, she has only a self-obsessed, hateful little husband who talks but does not listen. She's not some foolish kid, she tells Lennie, Candy, and Crooks in the scene in the barn. She could have had a bright future in Hollywood: "I tell ya I could of went with shows. Not jus' one, neither. An' a guy tol' me he could put me in pitchers."[25] Her naive beliefs about the "guy" and about what her life could have been reinforces the sad truth of her social as well as mental confinement. In this scene she reveals the hardness driven into her by life as she vents her resentment at being left behind with Lennie, Candy, and Crooks while the others go into town on a Saturday night. She admits that she has come because she is desperate for conversation. When Candy reveals the dream of the place he, George, and Lennie were going to share, she immediately douses it by cutting the men down at the knees. Guys like them, she says, are all alike. Give these men a little money, and they would spend it on whiskey. She seems to know them much better than they could ever know her.

When Curley's wife encounters Lennie alone in the barn, she again insists that she never gets to talk to anyone and is terribly lonely. For someone so spiteful, hard, and calculating, she surprisingly develops a momentary rapport with Lennie and his simple impulses. She consoles him over the dead puppy and speaks soothingly in convincing him that it is okay for him to talk to her. When Lennie protests that George forbade him to have anything to do with her, she cries, "Wha's the matter with me? . . . Ain't I got a right to talk to nobody? . . . I ain't doin' no harm to you."[26] She does not fully comprehend the fateful, awful reality of her situation: "Seems like they ain't none of them cares how I gotta live. I tell you I ain't used to livin' like this. I coulda made somethin' of myself. . . . Maybe I will yet."[27] Yet maybe not. She recalls once again that she had believed herself destined for stardom in the movies because some man thought she was a natural. She could have had beautiful clothes; she could have spoken on the radio. She does not seem to fully grasp the pathetic image of such a "future" in which, even in success, she would have become all the more a surface object, a nice thing to touch but not to know or to love. One of her would-be rescuers was to have written her from Hollywood, but she thought her mother must have stolen the letter. How could her own family stand in the way of her freedom, her being somebody? She marries Curley to escape from the narrow confines of her home, breaking away from what she perceived as family repression, only to find herself ironically confined to a ranch, wife of a relatively well-to-do little monster. The social and cultural context, it seems, will not permit her to better herself, regardless of where she is.

When Steinbeck prepared the play script for the Broadway production, one of the only two modifications to the novella involved an expanded role for Curley's wife. In Steinbeck's letter to actress Claire Luce he had tried to give a broader, sympathetic account of who the woman really was, what made her tick. In this letter he addressed social context and described the character more fully. In the play version he expanded her role in the barn scene with Lennie, "giving her an opportunity to tell Lennie about her childhood—dialogue that adds a sympathetic dimension to her character."[28] She tells Lennie of a violent, alcoholic father who once tried to run away with her only to be stopped by the authorities. It was an escape she longed for, perhaps setting the tone for the rest of her life. Indeed, in the barn scene in the play she carries a suitcase that she intends to hide, waiting for an opportune moment to sneak away to Hollywood. Hadella points out that "even in pursuit of her personal vision, she has no solid notion of herself as a worthwhile person. Her dream is to . . . become a cinematic image that occupies no space in the real world."[29] She is at base all about loneliness and the barriers that reinforce it. She unwittingly joins forces with all humans who also yearn for warmth and contact. As Hadella surmises, Steinbeck's little story "has something to tell its audience, not just of mice and men, but also of *women* who may find themselves in a world where they are unknown and therefore unloved."[30]

So what does Steinbeck tell his audience, and what does the audience say in reply? Hadella has it right, I believe, regarding the morality of sexism in this story. For a time the audience may see Curley's wife as a coy, one-dimensional manipulator. But once the broader parameters of her situation are revealed, she must be increasingly seen as a victim. Moral questions become an inevitable part of the audience's experience. We wonder what this woman has done to deserve such entrapment. Nothing, it seems, except to be born in a particular time and place. We are left to wonder whether freedom to be and to do must, as the Existentialists told us, be at the very essence of humanity. In the realm of morality, freedom and responsibility go hand in hand. Can one be held morally accountable for actions if the freedom of choice has been denied? And what of the immorality at the heart of vicious gender stereotypes which make mere caricatures out of real human beings? Any and all reductionistic images of others, whether predicated on gender, race, or class, are simply unacceptable and immoral. Steinbeck is not, however, preaching about morality, as perhaps I am. He does not have to. It is neither his inclination nor his purpose. If an author approaches a story with honesty and renders characters in their totality without bias, the moral issues emerge on their own—with a life and integrity of their own within the dramatic context. Curley's wife's drama, her loneliness and frustration, is nothing less, for the reader or theater audience, than rumination on the morality of how people are to be understood and treated. Freedom, individuality, the respect of others, and opportunity are at the very heart of morality. The opposite is repression, the spiritual death of a human being. Curley's wife stands as a glaringly bitter and ironic illustration of the immorality of narrow minds and the social conditions that produce them.

Besides sexism, racism is perhaps the most poignant moral issue in *Of Mice and Men*, which confronts the full effects of prejudice, principally on a lone black man, but also on the whites who live and work around him, to reveal a debilitating moral erosion. The obvious textual identification of racism involves the use of the derogatory "nigger," "god-damn nigger," or even supposedly complimentary references to how well the "nigger" plays horseshoes. But the

use of such hateful words is but a surface reflection of deeper, underlying hap-
penings and social structures rooted in racial misunderstanding and rejection.

Crooks, the black "stable buck," lives for all intents and purposes an existence of bondage, absent the chains. He is different, separated physically and
psychologically from those with whom he works daily. In part, this separation is
a result of the economic system of slavery resulting from ignorance and warped
attitudes. Louis Owens describes Crooks as

> an animated reminder of America's slave-holding economy, his twisted back
> evidence of the human cost of that economy. The fact that Crooks's family
> once possessed a farm identical to the dream-farm George and Lennie yearn for
> underscores his commonality with these men who are fodder for the machine,
> but the volume of the California Civil code for 1905 that sits on Crooks's shelf
> testifies to his awareness of difference.[31]

Any felt commonality with whites is, however, extremely short-lived. Difference that leads to isolation and unbearable loneliness is the prime moral force
embedded in the tragic existence of Crooks.

A highly detailed description of Crooks's separate living quarters, complete
with a manure pile right under the window, is one of the most vivid, powerful,
and succinct depictions of racism's effects in American literature. The very arrangement of his room and its contents reflect his situation as a proud, aloof
man. When Lennie appears in his doorway Crooks proclaims his "rights" to
have the room all to himself, to be left alone. In his mind he can justifiably reject just as much as he has been rejected. Sadly, he lives in a permanent syn-
drome of rejection: "I ain't wanted in the bunk house, and you ain't wanted in
my room."[32] Why is he not wanted? Solely because he is black, and the others
think he stinks like Candy's old, sickly dog. Crooks, then, can play horseshoes
"outdoors" with the men, but he is not permitted to go "inside" to their living
space.

Probably for the first time ever, Crooks shares with a white person, Lennie,
some details of his childhood when his family had a chicken ranch and he
played with white children, some of whom were nice. The boy could not understand his father's disapproval of his playmates. But his subsequent life experience, including the present ranch, made him understand his father's reasons. His
life situation is summed up in one sentence: "If I say something, why it's just a
nigger sayin' it."[33]

Crooks, like Curley's wife, simply needs someone to talk to, someone to be
with, some way to overcome his ostracized social condition. Although Lennie
appears to be a momentary talking companion, Crooks takes advantage of his
slow-wittedness, torturing him with talk of George's never returning and Lennie
being locked up in a booby hatch. That mild-mannered Crooks would feel im-
pelled to attack a similarly helpless person is witness to the moral depravity of
his circumstances. When Lennie becomes physically threatening, Crooks re-

treats into his story of isolation and misery: "A guy needs somebody—to be near him."[34] Such racism culminates in sickness and people on both sides being crazy with hurt and sadness.

Crooks is also stubbornly skeptical about the dream that George, Lennie, and old Candy share for a place of their own but gradually changes his mind as something magically comes over him, allowing him, probably for the first time in his life, to dream of happiness and liberation. He offers to work for nothing but his keep on this dream farm. But at that very moment Curley's wife arrives, momentarily bemoaning her own loneliness and desperation and then belittling them and crushing their dream into oblivion. If she cannot have a dream, neither can they. Then a terrible transformation comes over Crooks. After but a fleeting moment of contemplating a better future, like a frightened turtle Crooks retreats into his racial shell. Among the most insidious effects of racism is this unrelenting denial of freedoms—even the freedom of thought and dreams.

Here occurs an explosive merger of the ugly forces of sexism and racism. As Hadella writes, "Both Curley's wife and Crooks are obviously starved for companionship and acceptance as both are systematically ostracized from the ranch community—Crooks because of race and Curley's wife because of gender."[35] Nothing less than a volcanic moral collision is realized when Crooks becomes agitated to the point of trying to throw Curley's wife out of his room and threatens to tell the boss on her. She retaliates with a merciless scorn that opens the flood gates of her own pent-up frustrations and anger, asking whether he knows what she can do to him if he dares speak, threatening lynching. The moral outrage of the situation is revealed in the change in Crooks as he reduces himself to nothingness—all personality and ego gone. When she leaves, Crooks urges the others to leave also, telling him that her words are true and that he has no desire to work on their dream farm.

The scourge of racism has exacted its full toll, leaving behind a decent man of interests and background who is now reduced to nothingness. The mental beating he has absorbed made him a stranger even unto himself. The only stand he can make on his behalf is to proclaim his rights to have his own protected space, to be totally alone, rejected by everyone. What may appear as his autonomy is a defense against chronic loneliness and illness. A proud man is left with nothing to be proud of except his isolation. A few vengeful words from a desperately trapped white woman, whose husband has power, are sufficient to extinguish even a passing dream of improvement. Her words are emblematic of a lifetime of social injustice, centuries in truth, all based solely on race.

But the others are morally injured as well. Curley's wife, helpless victim of discrimination herself, becomes victimized in a second way. Her only recourse in life is to be hateful and inhuman. She can only assert herself by spewing racial venom on a helpless old black man, someone she perceives to be lower than she is. She neither hates Crooks nor desires to see him killed. But the unbalanced, depraved moral universe that both inhabit makes her into the spiteful bitch everyone expects. And Candy does not, probably cannot, understand the deeper meaning behind Crooks's statement that he does not want to work for them on the farm. He does not grasp the social and psychological realities of racism that lie behind and beneath the words. Like Curley's wife, Candy and the other men are likewise victims of the blinding powers of racism. All are caught in a moral drama beyond their control, one which they did not create. They are unwitting actors on a stage arranged by forces—historic, economic, political— beyond their own capacities to understand.

By portraying the lived realities of racism and sexism—in dramatically ugly but honest terms—Steinbeck wants us to go inside the skins of all those affected by the shaping conditions of social existence and to feel their bitter loneliness and desperation. He invites us to join the characters in their dreams of a better life, confront moral issues, and ponder moral questions as they grow out of the experience of his characters. Literature shows, it highlights, it lobbies in its own mysterious ways for a rethinking of the world we live in. Steinbeck believed that honest and true literature was all about trying to understand human be- ings—what makes them up and what keeps them going. Through the experience of sexism and racism as I read and feel them in *Of Mice and Men*, moral ques- tions become as compelling as they are inevitable. In this view I believe I am true to Steinbeck's purpose.

Notes

1. Alfred Kazin, *On Native Grounds* (New York: Doubleday Anchor Books, 1956), 309.

2. E. W. Tedlock, Jr. and C. V. Wicker, ed. *Steinbeck and His Critics* (Albuquerque: University of New Mexico Press, 1957), 104.

3. Ibid., 120.

4. Charlotte Cook Hadella, Of Mice and Men: *A Kinship of Powerlessness* (New York: Twayne, 1995), 20.

5. Jackson J. Benson, *The Short Novels of John Steinbeck* (Durham, N.C.: Duke University Press, 1990), 5.

6. Hadella, 23.

7. John H. Timmerman, *John Steinbeck's Fiction: The Aesthetics of the Road Taken* (Norman: University of Oklahoma Press, 1986), 8-9.

8. Hadella, 23.

9. Ibid., 35.

10. Michael Meyer, "Travels With John: My Journey as a Steinbeck Scholar" in *John Steinbeck: A Centennial Tribute*, ed. Stephen K. George (Westport, Conn.: Praeger, 2002), 147.

11. Thomas Fensch, ed. *Conversations With John Steinbeck* (Jackson: University Press of Mississippi, 1988), 79.

12. Ibid., 27.

13. Hadella, 9.

14. Fensch, 70.

15. For more on the relations between philosophy and literature, in particular morality as treated in literature, see Martha C. Nussbaum's *Love's Knowledge: Essays on Philosophy and Literature* (New York: Oxford University Press, 1990) and Richard Rorty's *Contingency, Irony and Solidarity* (Cambridge: Cambridge University Press, 1989), particularly his essays on Orwell and Nabokov. Also see Justus Buchler, *The Main of Light: On The Concept of Poetry* (New York: Oxford University Press, 1974).

16. Hadella, 12.

17. Ibid.

18. Ibid., 14.

19. See my essays "The Concept of Person in the Early Fiction of John Steinbeck" in the *Personalist Forum* 3.1 (Spring 1992); "Steinbeck on Man and Nature: A Philosophical Reflection" in *Steinbeck and the Environment: Interdisciplinary Approaches*, ed. Susan Beegel, Susan Shillinglaw, and Wes Tiffney, 1997; and "Steinbeck and Agrarian Pragmatism" in *The Agrarian Roots of Pragmatism*, ed. Paul B. Thompson and Thomas C. Hilde, 2000.

20. Hadella, 49-50.

21. Ibid., 43.

22. Mimi Gladstein, "Steinbeck and the Woman Question," *John Steinbeck: A Centennial Tribute*, ed. Stephen K. George (Westport, Conn.: Praeger, 2002), 110.

23. Elaine Steinbeck and Robert Wallsten, *Steinbeck: A Life in Letters* (New York: Viking, 1975), 154-55.

24. Hadella, 71.

25. John Steinbeck, *Of Mice and Men* (New York: Penguin Bantam, 1984), 86.

26. Ibid., 96.

27. Ibid.

28. Hadella, 68.

29. Ibid., 71.

30. Ibid., 73.

31. Louis Owens, "Deadly Kids, Stinking Dogs, and Heroes: The Best Laid Plans in Steinbeck's *Of Mice and Men,*" *Steinbeck Studies* (Fall 2002), 4.

32. Steinbeck, *Of Mice and Men*, 75.

33. Ibid., 77.

34. Ibid., 80.

35. Hadella, 58.

Of Death, Life, and Virtue in Steinbeck's
Of Mice and Men and *The Grapes of Wrath*

ALLENE M. PARKER
Embry-Riddle Aeronautical University

Today, over 100 years after his birth, John Steinbeck has the dubious honor of being, as Jackson Benson suggests, "probably . . . the most banned author in America."[1] Even with the meteoric rise of J. K. Rowling's Harry Potter series since 1998, it is safe to say that Steinbeck continues to be the most consistently challenged *American* author—having held that position for 67 years. While five of his works of fiction[2] and his 1941 film *The Forgotten Village* have all been threatened with censorship at some time, two of Steinbeck's novels—*Of Mice and Men* (1937) and *The Grapes of Wrath* (1939)—have been consistently challenged every year since their publication, with 2002 statistics citing *Of Mice and Men* as the second-most-challenged book of 2001.[3] Although Steinbeck is not among the most-challenged authors for 2002,[4] objections to his works remain prevalent. In this essay I propose to consider the ethical dilemmas Steinbeck poses at the conclusions of his two most contested novels, together with some of the moral implications of these scenes, as informed by ideas from virtue ethics. Such a reading provides the possibility for considering the life and death consequences of these endings as morally defensible and even virtuous outcomes within the context of the novels as a whole, despite their frequent selection as targets for criticism and censorship.

The conclusions in *Of Mice and Men* and *The Grapes of Wrath*—often euphemized as disturbing situations due to violence or sexuality—have been identified as being particularly offensive to readers and, thus, justifiable grounds for banning or challenging these novels. Political agendas, regardless of specific reasons stated for censorship, are obvious when the censorship histories of both novels are examined carefully. For example, Lee Burress's study of the censorship of *The Grapes of Wrath* from 1950-1985 finds that the novel is "a typical illustration of a book being charged with obscenity, when the real reason . . . seems likely to lie elsewhere."[5] "Elsewhere" is found, I believe, in the superficial judgments about certain characters' use of non-standard English or profanities and about what characters are doing within particular social contexts, both of which create discomfort for particular readers. Given the Joads' socioeconomic background, for example, it seems ridiculous to expect that they would speak standard American textbook English. Yet, this fact was the stated grounds for censorship of *The Grapes of Wrath* on more than one occasion soon after its publication.

Nicholas Karolides, Margaret Bald, and Dawn B. Sova's *100 Banned Books: Censorship Histories of World Literature* documents a number of late-twentieth-century challenges to Steinbeck as well. They note that when censorship surfaces in the United States, it is often grounded in someone's fear that children will be adversely affected by "political values and images" or that it is "deemed unpatriotic" to examine "flaws in American society."[6] One obvious flaw is California's treatment of the Dust Bowl migrants in the 1930s—a historical reality central to *The Grapes of Wrath*. The plight of other homegrown migrant laborers—bindle stiffs like George and Lennie—is another such flaw. California's inhumane treatment of migrant labor both before and after the 1930s has been well documented.[7] However, well-developed characters in novels may move and disturb us even more deeply than historical accounts dealing with the same issues; thus, depictions of human behavior will unavoidably involve potentially sensitive "political values and images."[8]

While Aristotle makes the point that his inquiry into ethics, which forms the basis of our understanding of virtue ethics, is, in fact, "a sort of political inquiry,"[9] a full consideration of American politics as applied to Steinbeck's literary work and critical reception is beyond the scope of this essay. However, once the notion of "values" appears, we find ourselves within the purview of ethics. What ethical issues provoke such distress and fear at the conclusions of *Of Mice and Men* and *The Grapes of Wrath*? I believe one possible set of answers appears in Steinbeck's portrayal of ethically complex situations that challenge our notions of good or virtuous behavior. Steinbeck's characters must act in difficult circumstances, but their actions demonstrate the power of ordinary people to act virtuously in the face of great adversity. Throughout both novels, Steinbeck also shines as a writer who takes seriously "the sufferings of ordinary people."[10]

By showing us these sufferings, Steinbeck pushes us to contemplate the meaning of such events, however difficult such contemplation may be, as well as our feelings about these events. How do we feel at the end of each novel? Who do we feel most strongly for? Such questions are especially relevant when we recognize that both novels have repeatedly led people to praise Steinbeck's work highly or to condemn it strongly: same work, but very different reactions! Carol Bly introduces her anthology, *Changing The Bully Who Rules The World: Reading And Thinking About Ethics*, by emphasizing literature's power to help us think about a wide range of ethical dilemmas. She observes that "in ethics, wise people have always taken note of *passing feelings* as scrupulously as they have taken note of new ideas."[11]

Although feelings themselves are not to be equated with virtue or vice from Aristotle's perspective, human emotions clearly are comprised within certain virtues and vices and are also clearly connected to human actions, often in complex ways. Compassion—a virtue associated with both George's and Rose of Sharon's behavior—is at least partially comprised of a deep emotion that may motivate human action even if such feelings themselves are not action. For Aristotle, "Feelings neither the virtues nor vices are; because in light of the Feelings we are not denominated either good or bad, but in light of the virtues and vices we are."[12] Thus, human actions are judged according to differing criteria (based in part on specific historical and social contexts) as manifesting virtue or vice. Since actions themselves are ambiguous, multiple and conflicting interpretations of these actions are to be expected; that is where questions of virtuous character arise.

As Alasdair MacIntyre observes, "From an Aristotelian standpoint to identify certain actions as manifesting or failing to manifest a virtue or virtues is never only to evaluate; it is also to take the first step towards explaining why those actions rather than some others were performed."[13] If we apply this idea about human behavior to understanding virtue or vice as presented in a work of literary fiction, it is critical to consider the actions of a character or characters in light of the whole work and not just a part. This is not to say that a reader should not be disturbed by a particular incident; however, that incident must be thoughtfully examined as one part of a larger work. When considering matters of censorship, generally one part of a work is condemned as representative of the whole, and matters of context are considered insignificant, if considered at all.

As Aristotle reminds us, "by acting in the various relations in which we are thrown with our fellow men, we come to be, some just, some unjust. . . . [Further,] we are inquiring not merely that we may know what virtue is but that we may become virtuous."[14] Since action requires a context for more than a superficial understanding, I will explore the virtuous behavior in the controversial conclusions of Steinbeck's most censored novels by first discussing the two characters who manifest this virtue: George in *Of Mice and Men* and Rose of Sharon in *The Grapes of Wrath*. After considering the characters themselves, I will then discuss related aspects of each novel before offering some concluding ideas about the ongoing relevance of Steinbeck's ability to make us consider ethically challenging issues in human life.

George and Rose of Sharon

At the conclusion of *Of Mice and Men*, George makes the decision to shoot his companion, Lennie, in the back of the head. George makes this choice when it appears certain that Lennie will not escape from a mob bent on violent revenge.

Slim, one of the ranch hands who knows that Lennie has killed Curley's wife, both counsels George that none of the apparent options for Lennie's future offer a good outcome and implies that something must be done by George regarding him. After George kills Lennie, Slim says, "A guy got to sometimes"; just a few lines later, in the penultimate paragraph of the novel, Slim continues, "You hadda, George. I swear you hadda."[15]

A different scene of human suffering appears at the conclusion of *The Grapes of Wrath*. Even though she is physically exhausted—as well as caught up in grief at the loss of her baby and her family's continuing misfortunes—Rose of Sharon offers her breast milk to a starving man when the Joads seek shelter in a barn and find it occupied by a boy and his father. Ma Joad and Rose of Sharon communicate nonverbally: they "looked deep into each other." Then Ma Joad "herded" everyone from the barn so Rose of Sharon has privacy to feed the starving man. Finally, Rose of Sharon overcomes the man's feeble protests with the simple words "You got to"[16]—a response that echoes Slim's words to George in *Of Mice and Men*.

The implied questions in both scenes are simple to ask but less simple to answer. Why did George *have to* shoot Lennie? Why does Rose of Sharon *have to* feed the starving man? Steinbeck does not answer these questions for us; "You hadda" or "You got to" seem insufficient for purposes of philosophical inquiry and analysis. Still, in both scenes Steinbeck appears to insist on a moral grounding for human behavior that requires compassionate treatment of our fellow human beings—even under the most extreme circumstances when human character is most truly revealed. Further, Steinbeck demonstrates in both novels that no matter who a character happens to be and what situation the character finds himself or herself in—whether a homeless bindle stiff, part of a family of Dust Bowl migrants, or a privileged rancher or landowner—the artificial distinctions between "us" and "them" can be overcome by the power of the human spirit to cope, adapt, and survive against great odds. This remains the case even when some characters fall by the wayside. Both novels also demonstrate that virtuous behavior is not determined by socioeconomic status, or the lack thereof. In fact, the behavior of many of Steinbeck's characters, including George and Rose of Sharon, supports Aristotle's perception that virtues are "habits or trained faculties" which humans have the power to develop over time.[17] If we grant Aristotle's idea that virtues may be developed over time, then within the context of both novels George and Rose of Sharon have had the opportunity to develop their virtuous qualities, even though these qualities might not be manifested in every situation. George and Rose of Sharon are complex and contradictory characters, yet they are able to rise to the challenge of virtuous action when confronted by extreme life and death circumstances. Steinbeck's development of these two characters is consistent with a vision of human nature he will articulate even more explicitly at the beginning of a later novel, *Cannery Row*, whose "inhabitants are, as the man once said, 'whores, pimps, gamblers, and sons of bitches,' by which he meant Everybody. Had the man looked through another peephole he might have said, 'saints and angels and martyrs and holy men,' and he would have meant the same thing."[18]

One answer to the question of *why* George and Rose of Sharon make the decisions they do and proceed to act on them might suggest a notion of simply doing one's duty as prescribed by a set of human laws. Following Kant's deontology and his well-known idea that "the presence of a good will is what makes an action morally good, regardless of its consequences,"[19] it would be possible to construct an argument in favor of both George's and Rose of Sharon's good intent, given their development as characters throughout both novels. However, ideas from virtue ethics can lead us beyond the idea of merely doing one's duty with good intent—however difficult or unpleasant the duty may be—because the concluding scenes in both novels appear to stand outside human law or unwritten social codes, and, as such, challenge our understanding.

Virtue ethics as formulated by Aristotle asks us to consider issues of *being* apart from *doing*—i.e., whether or not an individual (or, by extension, a character in literature) is of good character and has a virtuous nature. This is not to discount the importance of human action; however, it does allow us to consider a single action in light of both an immediate context and the larger context of a character's virtuous or non-virtuous nature over time or as revealed in the context of a novel. As Nina Rosenstand observes, "Aristotle. . . is not so much interested in our response to singular situations as he is in our response in general."[20] Aristotle is also interested in the practical implications of his ideas; thus, he provides flexibility of application, recognizing that "in practical matters and questions of expediency there are no invariable laws."[21]

Both George's and Rose of Sharon's singular actions in the context of situations demanding immediate resolution do, in fact, contradict established legal or social conventions. Yet, paradoxically, their actions reinforce an overall understanding that both George and Rose of Sharon are virtuous characters who believe they are doing the right thing at the right time. Even though challenges to their virtue during a moment of crisis result in conventionally unacceptable behavior, their behavior may still be understood as virtuous. Thus, both characters offer examples that disturb comfortable, convenient ideas about right and wrong. Rose of Sharon's behavior when she rescues the starving man appears to offer a close parallel to the Biblical parable of the Good Samaritan, but this parallel seems inapplicable when considering George's shooting of Lennie. However, the sequence of George's actions when he shoots Lennie does reveal something of George's character that might bring him back within the scope of the parable. Frans de Wahl writes of the Good Samaritan story that "the biblical message is to be wary of ethics by the book rather than by the heart."[22] In the world of mob justice posed at the end of *Of Mice and Men*, where Curley is motivated to seek revenge above all else, we are already far beyond ethics by the book in the form of law. In addition, given the way the narrative progresses, we are far from any compromise between characters that would allow an ending without further violence and bloodshed. George is acting from his heart when he pulls the trigger, given the nature of his association with Lennie and the harsh reality of the context at the end of the novel.

Throughout *Of Mice and Men* we are shown that George has spent years looking out for Lennie, with little reward except that he has Lennie's companionship. We also know that George assumed the responsibilities of a caregiver at some point, taking upon himself the role probably once filled by Lennie's Aunt Clara. Although George knows that without Lennie he could live as he chooses and perhaps even find peace in life, when Lennie offers to leave, George backs down: "George said, 'I want you to stay with me, Lennie. Jesus Christ, somebody'd shoot you for a coyote if you was by yourself. No, you stay with me. Your Aunt Clara wouldn't like you running off by yourself, even if she is dead.'"[23] Thus, when George shoots Lennie, however reluctantly, he reveals his compassion through virtuous action under extreme circumstances, as does Rose of Sharon when she feeds the starving man. The moral implications of these human actions from the heart, fictional though they are, will no doubt continue to disturb, challenge, and motivate readers to further reflection for years to come.

Of Mice and Men

What if something bad happens and there is no clear evidence of cause and effect or action and consequences? For example, John Steinbeck told people that the character of Lennie was based on a real worker he knew in the fields of Salinas—a worker who killed another worker with a pitchfork because it just happened that way.[24] When something is "just that way" and humans are faced with impossible decisions, then virtue ethics suggests that the most humane decision under the circumstances may have to suffice where there is no clear-cut mean of moderation or where none of the possible choices appear to be acceptable.

In his article, "Deadly Kids, Stinking Dogs, and Heroes: The Best Laid Plans in Steinbeck's *Of Mice and Men*," Louis Owens argues for a nonsentimental reading of this novel that begins with an understanding that "no one is to blame for the fact that Lennie kills things, and no one is to blame for Lennie's inability to survive within society. . . . If they'd gotten the dream farm, Lennie would have killed the rabbits. He would have killed the neighbors." Further, Owens argues that Slim "is playing God" when he encourages George to help "get 'im."[25] Slim may indeed be playing God, but it is still George who must decide in the end whether or not to pull the trigger, not Slim. Louis Owens's reading of *Of Mice and Men* views the novel as "a cautionary tale deeply engaged with the profound human crisis of [Steinbeck's] times," including the cases of euthanasia ("mercy killings") associated with "the rise of Fascism in Germany."[26] I agree with Owens's assessment that Lennie's death—

parallel to that of the drowning of the unwanted ranch puppies and the shooting of Candy's "worthless" old dog—is not one to be preferred; however, the novel also precludes other options.

George's angry litany of complaints in the novel's first chapter demonstrates his dilemma with respect to Lennie:

> "An' whatta I got," George went on furiously. "I got you! You can't keep a job and you lose me ever' job I get. Jus' keep me shovin' all over the country all the time. An' that ain't the worst. You get in trouble. You do bad things and I got to get you out." His voice rose nearly to a shout. "You crazy son-of-a-bitch. You keep me in hot water all the time."[27]

Despite the fact that no one is to blame for Lennie being the way he is, the novel makes it clear that George feels responsible for Lennie, getting him out of trouble when Lennie cannot even remember what happened and being an ever-present accessory to any number of relatively minor incidents. So what is to be done about Lennie when he finally goes too far and it becomes obvious that their shared dream of a farm with rabbits is unattainable?

Although George—in anger, and to his shame—also expresses in the first chapter the idea that "I wisht I could put you in a cage with about a million mice an' let you have fun,"[28] he recognizes that this is not a reasonable solution. For Lennie, life in a "cage," whether a prison or some other institution, is not a valid option. Slim reinforces this idea at the end of the novel when he says, "An' s'pose they lock him up an' strap him down and put him in a cage. That ain't no good, George." Even if the novel allowed for the option of a defense by establishing Lennie's mental limitations (which it does not), life in an institution has already been ruled out as "no good."[29] Lennie is unprepared to cope with a life without George. Given the evidence presented in the novel, Lennie would not be able to understand what he did wrong or why he has been separated from his friend, even if he were otherwise being cared for appropriately.

The other option offered is Curley's pronouncement that "I'm gonna shoot the guts outa that big bastard myself, even if I only got one hand. I'm gonna get 'im."[30] If Curley kills Lennie, the resolution can be considered revenge for the killing of Curley's wife. If Slim or another one of the ranch hands kills Lennie, the resolution can be considered frontier justice at the hands of one or more parties who are playing their expected roles as members of a search party.

However, if George kills Lennie, he has a far more personal stake in the consequences, especially when his longtime role as Lennie's caretaker is taken into consideration. Lennie is doomed no matter what. And George is also doomed; he must ultimately sacrifice his friend and their shared dreams in a choice among multiple evils. But George can choose to make Lennie's end as quick and painless as possible—which he does. In this context, George's choice is still virtuous, as it exemplifies Aristotle's teaching related to the question of extremes: "For of the extremes one is more dangerous, the other less. Since then it is hard to hit the mean precisely, we must 'row when we cannot sail,' as the proverb has it, and choose the least of two evils."[31] If Lennie must die as the consequence of his actions, however ignorant, it is less extreme and more humane for George to kill Lennie out of compassion than for Lennie to be killed by Curley and his posse out of vengeance.

Research in the field of primate study suggests an additional avenue of exploration with respect to George and Lennie's situation. In his book, *Good Natured: The Origins Of Right And Wrong In Humans And Other Animals*, Frans de Waal notes that although humans and other primates tend to display special treatment toward the handicapped that is predominantly benevolent in character, such benevolence can lead to potentially negative consequences in the form of "sympathy entrapment." Primates, including humans, tend to "take care of distressed individuals."[32] This caretaking behavior can also render individuals vulnerable to exploitation by others who exploit sympathy toward the handicapped for harmful purposes. From this perspective, George does appear to suffer from sympathy entrapment in his relationship with Lennie—an entrapment that, while mutually beneficial to the degree that it provides a support system for both men, finally works against both of them as well.

Slim can influence George's actions toward Lennie and prevail upon him to pull the trigger because there are no good options available that will allow George to rescue Lennie one more time. The question of purpose is also relevant here, as, up to this point, George has been very successful in his attempts to take care of Lennie. While I do not mean to suggest that George's ultimate purpose as a human being is to care for Lennie, caring for Lennie has indeed become one of George's apparent purposes in life, and he has been very good at it—which, by Aristotle's standards, is also a measure of George's virtue. However, we must then consider what happens when circumstances beyond George's control interfere with this purpose.

George does shoot Lennie, but he does so only after he becomes convinced that it is the right thing to do; Slim offers George a rationale for taking decisive action, and George accepts Slim's argument. Even at the end, however, George displays virtue in his attempt to comfort and calm Lennie; George again tells Lennie the story of their dream home with the rabbits, and Lennie never suspects that he is about to be shot. After Lennie has been killed, George takes responsibility for the killing; moreover, after the deed is done, he does not appear to be consoled by Slim's earlier assessment of the situation. Carlson, another ranch hand, gets the last word. As he watches Slim and George walk away up the trail, Carlson asks a companion, "Now what the hell ya suppose is eatin' them two guys?"[33] The novel leaves us with this final question as well.

I teach *Of Mice and Men* occasionally and continue to appreciate the power of the novel's ending when students encounter it for the first time. Often, they express feelings of shock and outrage, coupled with observations that they can also understand why circumstances compel George to shoot Lennie or that George is also killing his own dream for the future when he kills Lennie. This recognition—that, besides Lennie, George appears to have the most to lose as a result of his action—is not meant to be a reassuring idea. But it is a plausible outcome given George's history with Lennie, a person who cannot recognize basic distinctions between right and wrong. Even so, I do not believe that the moral of the story is that we should shoot our friends when the odds are stacked against them and us. Rather, the novel presents us with a horrible choice and the action that follows from that choice. I believe the novel's conclusion is intended to "eat" on our consciences and make us think about our own sense of who we are as human beings, as well as what we decide to do based on who we are. It may also help us be more aware of and sensitive about difficult decisions other people must make.

The Grapes of Wrath

Steinbeck's presentation of the Dust Bowl migrants confronted early readers with social problems that remain unsolved in California and elsewhere today, more than sixty years later. This enduring legacy of challenge is a major—if seldom directly acknowledged—factor in the continued banning or challenging of *The Grapes of Wrath*. From 1939 to the present, Steinbeck's novelistic presentation of the migrants' experiences has been a disturbing revelation to many readers. Rose of Sharon's feeding of the starving man is the culmination of an entire series of actions in the novel that reveal the power of the individual as a vehicle for compassion as well as social change, not to mention the power of individuals linked to a community, no matter how low that community appears to be on the social hierarchy.

One outcome of the participation of individuals in a community involves the acquisition of sufficient power to begin to change unfavorable conditions, even on a small scale, ultimately tipping the balance in favor of the people who are being oppressed. This theme of power attained through community is developed in a variety of ways: it shows up in the descriptions of the model migrant camp; it is evident in Jim Casy's attempts to unite the migrants around common goals and shared needs; and, finally, it culminates in Rose of Sharon's feeding of the starving man.

In contrast to George's decision, which makes him a virtuous agent of death, Rose of Sharon is a virtuous agent of life. Her gesture of compassion is, in one respect, an act of claiming personal power to do the right or good thing and make a positive difference in a bad situation. At the same time, it is also a compelling, practical solution to the problem of how to feed one starving man— Rose of Sharon literally has the power to bring life in the face of death. Her action may even be considered defiant, as it reveals the power of human beings to survive against great odds in the face of extreme oppression, through an exercise not of cruelty but of virtue. However, this theme can be conveniently ignored if Rose of Sharon's gesture is interpreted (and subsequently, discredited) as nothing more than a demonstration of sexual perversity on the part of the character, not to mention in the mind of the author.

At the novel's conclusion, Rose of Sharon chooses to take virtuous action under extreme circumstances. Her physical nakedness beneath the "comfort" as she feeds the man is not a demonstration of licentiousness. Within the context of the novel, Ma Joad directs Rose of Sharon to remove her clothing because she (along with everyone else) has been soaked by the storm; Ma Joad also screens Rose of Sharon with the "comfort" offered by the boy. By next wrapping Rose of Sharon in the dirty "comfort," Ma Joad both attempts to observe social conventions and also takes practical action to ward off a health risk for her daughter. Rose of Sharon is at risk because she has just had and lost a child; however, these difficult circumstances also give her the ability to serve as a wet nurse—a capacity that is not normally viewed as being offensive. Consequently, Rose of Sharon has the individual power to redeem this particular life-threatening situation.

Of course, what has shocked some readers over the years is the simple fact that Rose of Sharon is nursing a grown man, not a child. However, that is hardly the most shocking implication of this concluding scene. I believe readers should be far more shocked by the entire chain of circumstances—many of them caused by vices such as greed and prejudice—that lead the remaining members of the Joad family to be in the execrable circumstances in which they find themselves long before disastrous weather conditions force them to seek shelter in a barn.

Still, despite appalling conditions, Rose of Sharon offers hope at the end of the novel as she suckles the starving man: "She looked up and across the barn, and her lips came together and smiled mysteriously."[34] Despite the fact that both Rose of Sharon and the starving man have been brought together in a predicament they did not cause, Rose of Sharon has not been rendered powerless by greater powers in society (all the factors contributing to the Dust Bowl Migration in general and the individual and collective human misery of the migrants) or the seemingly unpredictable forces of nature that result in flooding. Rose of Sharon can triumph over calamity by manifesting compassion through virtuous action.

Circumstances, including natural processes, have made her a mother without a child. Rose of Sharon could choose to remain isolated in her own grief and indifferent to the starving man's plight; she could certainly claim that the man's plight is not her problem. She is moved beyond self-pity with the assistance of her mother, but Ma Joad does not force her to act or verbally tell Rose of Sharon that she has to suckle the man. Although Ma helps engineer the opportunity for her daughter to act in a virtuous manner, it is still Rose of Sharon who must decide what to do. When Rose of Sharon tells the man, "You got to,"[35] she is perhaps speaking to herself as well. She must use the only power she has at her disposal to offer the possibility of life in the face of otherwise certain death. Rose of Sharon's act appears to be motivated by feelings of compassion, but it becomes an act of virtue in Aristotelian terms not only because it is advantageous to another person but also because it involves some personal difficulty or risk. Perhaps her act even meets the criteria for justice, which Aristotle describes as the "perfect Virtue."[36]

Conclusion

T. Walter Herbert has observed that "powerful literary art keeps warring voices alive and at odds . . . [and] such conflicting voices will persist within readers of literature so long as there are unresolved moral dilemmas in the cultural axioms by which our social selves are constituted."[37] The moral dilemmas in *Of Mice and Men* and *The Grapes of Wrath* remain with us today not only in fiction, but also in contemporary headlines dealing with such issues as starvation, poverty, and euthanasia. Steinbeck's work can lead us to think about difficult ethical issues that we might prefer not to think about; this characteristic of his work is both a mark of Steinbeck's success and of his ability to irritate critics. In his Nobel acceptance speech, Steinbeck proclaims, "The ancient commission of the writer has not changed. He is charged with exposing our many grievous faults and failures, with dredging up to the light our dark and dangerous dreams for the purpose of improvement."[38] By participating in the possibility of human improvement, the writer is potentially advancing the development of human virtue by offering readers an opportunity to learn from the successes and failures of the characters created in a particular work.

The 21st century brings new opportunities to celebrate and enjoy the works of a major American writer whose words continue to inspire, challenge, and potentially offend his readers. However, thoughtful readers should not be afraid to encounter the deeper ethical issues in *Of Mice and Men* and *The Grapes of Wrath* and to consider their wide-ranging implications. If change can be a consequence of taking literature seriously, then perhaps literature *is* as dangerous as many critics have claimed. On the other hand, to refuse to read these novels or actively prevent others from experiencing them based on superficial readings and judgments deprives individuals and communities of the opportunity to respond to an ethical imperative insisting on virtuous treatment of our fellow human beings. While the conclusions presented in *Of Mice and Men* and *The Grapes of Wrath* may disturb us, these scenes also point us in the direction of an understanding of human virtue that underscores the idea that no one is expendable and that illuminates the power of courage, compassion, and goodness even under the bleakest of circumstances. I am convinced that as we move into a second century with John Steinbeck's literary influence, future generations of thoughtful readers will continue to benefit from their explorations of death, life, and virtue in *Of Mice and Men* and *The Grapes of Wrath*.

Notes

1. Jackson Benson, "The Favorite Author We Love to Hate," in *The Steinbeck Question: New Essays in Criticism*, ed. Donald R. Noble (Troy, N.Y.: Whitston, 1993), 21.

2. *The Red Pony, In Dubious Battle, Of Mice and Men, The Grapes of Wrath*, and *East of Eden* are the five challenged works.

3. "Harried Potter," *The Arizona Republic*, September 28, 2002, p. 2.

4. *American Library Association* [Web site]; available from http://www.ala.org/; accessed January 4, 2004.

5. Lee Burress, *Battle of the Books: Literary Censorship in the Public Schools, 1950-1985* (Metuchen, N.J.: Scarecrow, 1989), 46.

6. Nicholas Karolides, Margaret Bald, and Dawn B. Sova, *100 Banned Books: Censorship Histories of World Literature* (New York: Checkmark Books, 1999), 1.

7. Two excellent sources documenting the past and present treatment of migrant workers in California are Carey McWilliams's *Factories in the Field: The Story of Migratory Farm Labor in California* (Boston: Little, Brown, 1939) and Eric Schlosser's "In the Strawberry Fields" (*The Atlantic Monthly*, November, 1995).

8. Karolides, Bald, and Sova, 1.

9. Oliver A. Johnson, ed., *Ethics: Selections from Classical and Contemporary Writers*, 4th ed. (New York: Holt, Rinehart, and Winston, 1978), 64.

10. Jane Tompkins, *Sensational Designs: The Cultural Work of American Fiction, 1760-1860* (New York: Oxford University Press, 1985), 195.

11. Carol Bly, *Changing The Bully Who Rules The World: Reading And Thinking About Ethics* (Minneapolis, Minn.: Milkweed Editions, 1996), xxv.

12. Johnson, 25. For more connections between the emotions and virtues/vices, see Justin Oakley's *Morality and the Emotions* (Routledge, 1992) and George's "The Emotional Content of Cruelty" in the present volume.

13. Alasdair MacIntyre, *After Virtue*, 2nd ed. (Notre Dame, Ind.: University of Notre Dame Press, 1984), 199.

14. Johnson, 21.

15. John Steinbeck, *Of Mice and Men* (New York: Viking, 1937), 117-18.

16. John Steinbeck, *The Grapes of Wrath* (New York: Penguin, 1976), 580-81.

17. Johnson, 79.

18. John Steinbeck, *Cannery Row* (New York: Viking, 1945), 1.

19. Nina Rosenstand, *The Moral of the Story: An Introduction to Ethics*, 4th ed. (Boston: McGraw Hill, 2003), 221.

20. Ibid., 375.

21. Johnson, 76.

22. Frans de Wahl, *Good Natured: The Origins Of Right And Wrong In Humans And Other Animals* (Cambridge: Harvard University Press, 1996), 87.

23. Steinbeck, *Of Mice and Men*, 14.

24. *John Steinbeck: An American Writer*, Arts & Entertainment Television Networks, 1998. videocassette.

25. Louis Owens, "Deadly Kids, Stinking Dogs, and Heroes: The Best Laid Plans in Steinbeck's *Of Mice and Men*," *Steinbeck Studies* (Fall 2002): 3-5.

26. Ibid., 8.

27. Steinbeck, *Of Mice and Men*, 12.

28. Ibid., 12

29. Ibid., 106.

30. Ibid., 107.

31. Johnson, 85.

32. de Waal, 44.

33. Steinbeck, *Of Mice and Men*, 118.

34. Steinbeck, *The Grapes of Wrath*, 581.

35. Ibid., 581.

36. Aristotle, *The Nichomachean Ethics*, trans. D. P. Chase (New York: Dover, 1998), 78.

37. T. Walter Herbert, "Mozart, Hawthorne, and Mario Savio: Aesthetic Power and Political Complicity," *College English* 57 (1995): 404-5.

38. Jay Parini, *John Steinbeck: A Biography* (New York: Holt, 1995), xx.

Judging Elisa Allen: Reader Entrapment in "The Chrysanthemums"

TERRY GORTON
Brigham Young University-Idaho

> "It ain't the right kind of life for a woman."
> "How do you know? How can you tell?" she said.
>
> —"The Chrysanthemums"

> For the study of literature may not only result in ethical consequences, but through these very consequences, should reveal something of the specific makeup of ourselves and our faculties, which are activated and acted upon by literature.
>
> —Wolfgang Iser in *Prospecting*

> Re-vision—the act of looking back, of seeing with fresh eyes, of entering an old text from a new critical direction—is for women more than a chapter in culture history; it is an act of survival. Until we can understand the assumptions in which we are drenched we cannot know ourselves.
>
> —Adrienne Rich in *On Lies, Secrets, and Silence*

One important aspect of ethics that I think literature is particularly well suited to teaching is the relationship between our ethical judgments and our cultural imprintings or conventions. The classical Greek formulations of ethics established this crucial link between ethics and culturally-derived habits of thought and action. The word *ethical* (as well as the Latin word "moral") is derived from the Greek *êthos*, meaning "character" or "disposition," and carries with it an earlier sense of "custom," "usage," or "habit." For Aristotle, as for his teacher, Plato, the most important struggle for each of us involves making choices based on our passions and false impressions or else making these choices based on "reason" and critical self-awareness. Achieving the greatest potential or happiness for ourselves requires that we allow both reasoned analysis and the conscientious development of "good habits" to guide us in making judgments and acting on those judgments. Such a course would ultimately determine our moral character.

But Aristotle is aware of how our judgments, actions, character, and happiness are affected by unexamined—and potentially harmful—"dispositions," "customs," or "habits." Indeed, an ability to free ourselves from acting from "mere custom" is so crucial in his philosophy that Aristotle suggests that even if we happen to make good or virtuous decisions while simply following an ingrained—and unexamined—disposition, our ultimate character, and therefore happiness, will not be enhanced. Our greatest happiness only results from making the most virtuous choices based on the most critically conscientious judgments. Eventually, those "dispositions" and "customs" that were before based simply on passions or unexamined habits will be replaced by the more refined and virtuous "dispositions" that we have deliberately struggled throughout our lives to nurture.

Certainly, in this respect, most critics today who plead for more ethical judgments (which I would argue is the primary goal of contemporary literary criticism) remain Aristotelians: the Marxists who want us to escape purely economic motivations by helping us to see more clearly how other ideologies can be traced to greed and materialism; the Freudians who would uncover the hidden mechanisms of the subconscious; the feminists and multiculturalists who show how deeply ingrained sexist and racist biases remain; new historicists, who radically question the traditional historical perspectives; even deconstructionists (often accused of eschewing ethical agendas), who would free us from an unexamined and sometimes insidious reliance upon age-old metaphysical or logocentric foundations and presumptions. Indeed, a primary reason for the ascendancy of these critical voices was the apparent apathy of their new-critical predecessors to examine those (often dominant and sometimes harmful) dispositions and biases affecting authors, readers, and characters apart from the aesthetic quality of the text. In a real sense, it was a concern for an ethical dimension of the literary experience that united these groups in their near unanimous rebellion against New Criticism. And as Wayne Booth has convincingly argued, despite their protestation all of these groups—aesthetic, political, ideological—in reality practice ethical criticism.[1]

Literary Analysis as an Ethical Exercise

Good literature is disturbing in a way that history and social science writing frequently are not. Because it summons powerful emotions, it disconcerts and puzzles. It inspires distrust of conventional pieties and exacts a frequently painful confrontation with one's own thoughts and intentions.

—Martha Nussbaum in *Poetic Justice*

As one of the consequences of this rebellion, the phrase "close reading" acquired a peculiarly odious connotation, summoning the various sins associated with New Criticism. However, ironically, though decrying New Criticism, each of these theories strenuously maintained, and even improved upon, this primary methodology. Does anyone think that Jane Tompkins, Jacques Derrida, Stephen Greenblatt, Stanley Fish, or Henry Gates is a less thorough practitioner of close textual analysis than New Critics?

Once we expand upon the narrow purpose of New Criticism—to the ethical perspectives most critical approaches insist upon—the New Critical methodology of close scrutiny of texts remains essential, and we achieve these other purposes best when we continue to read carefully and closely. As well for critics today as for Aristotle, improving our ethical judgments (of texts as well as of people) demands careful reexamination of initial impressions in light of further evidence.

It would be hard to imagine a better forum for achieving critical self-awareness of how predispositions influence our points of view than the literary experience—especially since literature by its nature invites the reader to make various judgments of actions and decisions by characters whose own ethical choices are the core of any narrative. So the readers judge the characters' judgments, and in doing so the readers are able to critically examine the process of making both good and bad judgments—their *own* as well as the characters'. Essentially, the latest published interpretations may be seen simply as yet another reader who says: "As I experienced this text lately, I think I may have seen some other important things; gotten past some of my initial presumptions, biases, or faulty judgments; and uncovered additional evidence that may help give a fuller picture, or additional perspectives." Is there any more ethical pursuit?

Ethical Entrapment

We become aware of our potential to remake knowledge only after we remember that something is always missing, that *learning starts with the sensation of being trapped.* . . . Being trapped is indeed a socially and discursively induced pain, and we are only beginning to learn how it feels to start learning in such placcs.

—Kurt Spellmeyer in *Common Ground*

One of the more specific and powerful ways the literary experience provides such opportunities is through the process of entrapment: our entrapment in the literary experience often helps us become aware of some ways we are entrapped extra-textually by dispositions and habituations that are simply very difficult to shake.[2] Because of its symbolic and multileveled nature, its narrative point of view often far-removed from the author, its emphasis on conflict and character instead of exposition, as well as its predilection for irony, ambiguity, suspense, participation, and discovery, the literary experience is particularly well-suited to evoking ethical dilemmas and involvement in its readers through the process of entrapment.

I would like to consider how Steinbeck's story, "The Chrysanthemums," plays upon readers' tendencies to make judgments based on unexamined first impressions and culturally-derived dispositions in order to draw and entrap readers, and how this entrapment helps reveal significant ethical struggles taking place not only within, but also beyond the story. The main ethical question at stake in the reading experience of "The Chrysanthemums" has been well expressed by many critics. These readers suggest that the story dramatizes how women (in this case Elisa Allen) and "femininity" itself tends to be limited and undervalued by our society. I think Marilyn L. Mitchell puts the struggle best when she says the conflict in "The Chrysanthemums" is "between society's view of what constitutes masculinity and its view of what constitutes femininity." In this conflict, Elisa is "trapped between society's definition of the masculine and the feminine" and is "struggling against the limitations of the feminine." "Steinbeck reveals fundamental differences," says Mitchell, "between the way women see themselves and the way they are viewed by men."[3]

If we can agree that one of the most important ethical struggles of the story concerns how a woman's role and value tends to be limited in society, I think we should take the opportunity to look at that struggle from two separate but interrelated perspectives—one as we look at the struggles of characters inside the story, and one as we look at the struggles of readers outside the story. *Inside the story* we can examine Elisa Allen as she seeks to understand her role and value as a woman—especially her struggles to appreciate her personal strengths and contributions and to escape from any traps (especially societal presumptions about the capabilities and roles of women) that may cause her to limit or undervalue these strengths. *From outside the story*, we can examine the challenges that readers encounter as they evaluate Elisa, especially the readers' struggles to escape from various traps: both literary traps which seduce us into hasty judgments based on initial—and often false—impressions, but also extra-literary traps, such as ingrained attitudes, habits, or customs in society that may cause us to limit or undervalue a woman's role and strengths.

It might be surprising to some to think that Steinbeck of all people would call into question and challenge simplistic notions of gender roles or speculate on the "limitations of femininity."[4] But as dozens of published essays on the story attest, readers continue to find the story a powerful provocation for these issues. Steinbeck himself previews the interpretive challenges[5] he wove into the story: "['The Chrysanthemums'] is entirely different, and is meant to strike without the reader's knowledge. I mean he reads it casually and after it is finished feels that something profound has happened to him although he does not know what nor how."[6] We will find that the ethical challenges he provokes—as well as the kinds of ethical responses he elicits from readers—are as rich and relevant today as they were when he wrote the story almost seventy years ago.

The Will-o'-the-Wisp versus the Reader

"That's a bright direction; there's a glowing there."

—"The Chrysanthemums"

One commentator gives the following thumbnail sketch of John Steinbeck's "The Chrysanthemums":

> On a foothill ranch live the Allens, a middle-aged, childless couple, seemingly successful with their ranch and their marriage. As the story opens, Elisa Allen works in the flower garden as her husband Henry completes a sale of thirty steers to buyers for a meat company. To celebrate the sale, the couple decide to spend the evening in Salinas. As Elisa expertly prepares new chrysanthemum sprouts from old roots, an itinerant repairman of kitchenware arrives unexpectedly. Although no work is available, Elisa finds pans for repair after the man plays on her pride. She responds strongly also to accounts of his way of life. The tinker soon leaves with a half dollar for his work and a flower pot of sprouts for someone down the road. Later, Elisa becomes upset after discovering the discarded sprouts and dirt lying on the road.[7]

Just a thumbnail sketch, of course, but the published commentators tell us about this same Elisa Allen: she fails "as a woman" when she tries to go beyond "her feminine self, her capacity for fructification and childbearing," and turns to "the spectacle of the violent prize fights, to pleasure in the thought of vindictive assault on men";[8] "Elisa's sexual feelings are [thus] expressed through her physical actions and statements, by the flower symbolism, and through her envy and even hatred of males."[9] The main "ingredient of Elisa's emotion is . . . her basic feminine sexuality," which causes her to "become her own victim." And since Elisa, like other women, is "fundamentally emotional, as evidenced by tears or sexual arousal," she soon "operates at less than a rational level and is victimized both by her basic nature and by others."[10] She is also "unable or unwilling to satisfy her partner sexually," finds the "act of love wholly distasteful and to be avoided whenever possible," and over the years has "deprived, emasculated, her husband."[11] In her encounter with the pot mender, Elisa reveals "her erotic potential"—as when she finds herself "below him in the traditional female position for intercourse, . . . subconsciously contrasting him with her husband as a potential sexual partner."[12] At this point in the story, Elisa "becomes a parody of a bitch in heat."[13] Elisa, we are told, is a "courtesan" who is "repelled by sexual reality," renders her husband "effectively sterile by [her] subversion of the natural sexual process," and ultimately remains "a pitiable victim of male domination and female disadvantage."[14] "She has transformed her workaday self into a sex object but could as easily be the manipulative temptress as the docile toy."[15]

I read these comments from the most often cited interpretations of the story to my "Introduction to Literature" students after they hand in their critical analysis papers on the story (for which they are prohibited from accessing any published resources). "What story did they read?" the students ask, looking somewhat shell-shocked. Certainly, in a Steinbeck story we should not be surprised to find an emphasis upon sexuality, but what is particularly interesting about critical reactions to this story is 1) how little explicit sexual detail is to be found in the story; 2) how anxious readers seem to be to ferret out and magnify the least suggestion of any sexual aspect of Elisa as the key to all else that she does or says, 3) what significant details about Elisa and the other characters these critics are ready to disregard in order to maintain the erotic focus, and 4) how this "erotic imperative"[16] in critical commentary upon Elisa is often accompanied by other limiting attitudes about women and femininity—attitudes that seem to confirm how tenaciously viable some debunked cultural and historical attitudes about women remain today.[17]

Much physical, social, emotional, and spiritual entrapment exists in the story. We sense above all Elisa's entrapment and wonder how she feels and how aware she is of these traps. It will be the interpretive opportunity of each reader, of course, to decide what those traps are and what she seems to have discovered about herself as she becomes aware of these traps. Like Elisa, perhaps we, too, will find ourselves unexpectedly entrapped, and then also like Elisa, perhaps this experience will help us discover other traps we may be caught in—traps that extend beyond the story we have been reading.

One interesting traditional metaphor for this kind of entrapment—based on initial impressions which we later have to adjust or even abandon—is the idea of the "will-o'-the-wisp," which is based upon a natural phenomenon that is sometimes observed at night near bogs and river bottoms where gases formed by rotting organic matter spontaneously combust. From a distance, a bright band of yellow light can be seen flickering above the swampland. The light might appear, recede, and appear again. When one approaches the light it disappears or seems to change its position. Also referred to as *ignis fatuus* (foolish fire), or jack-o'-lantern, the will-o'-the-wisp has come to mean any deceptive attraction or delusion.

In the opening paragraph of the story, we are introduced to both the will-o'-the-wisp and its accompanying theme song, variations on the word "seemed," which serve throughout the story as a red flag to the reader, warning us not to be fooled by appearances, as in: Elisa's figure "*looked* blocked and heavy." The tinker's life "*sounds* like a nice kind of way to live." Along the river there "*seemed* a thin band of sunshine." Elisa was crying "weakly—*like* an old woman." We are clearly told "there was no sunshine in the valley," yet we find that "the yellow stubble fields *seemed* to be bathed in pale cold sunshine." "The thick willow scrub along the river," we read, "flamed with sharp and positive yellow leaves."[18]

The sudden, unexpected visit from the itinerant pot mender can be seen as a will-o'-the-wisp which causes Elisa Allen to briefly question her worth as a woman and to yearn, for a moment, after some superficially attractive qualities of the pot mender's life—representative, we shall see, of a man's life in general ("That's a bright direction. There's a glowing there,"[19] she whispers as he departs). The visit of the pot mender can be a will-o'-the-wisp for readers also as we become every bit as mesmerized as Elisa, every bit as hasty to draw conclusions based on first impressions only. If we are not careful, our society's ingrained customs and dispositions may cause us to likewise misjudge Elisa, and in a similar "trance-like state" ("her eyes half-closed, so that the scene came vaguely into them")[20] undervalue her role as a woman.

It is well to note why Elisa—and the reader—might be particularly prone at this point to be trapped into finding the tinker's life comparatively attractive. He has no ties to coop him up on a ranch, no land, no obligations. He has the sky for a canopy and moves with good weather. The tinker's life may *seem* especially inviting when it is contrasted with several apparently unattractive elements of Elisa's life at the moment. The ranch house is so "hard swept" and "hard polished" that it seems dull. The boredom of ranch life is pronounced because the month is December, and at this time of the year "there was little work to be done." The readers have missed the intense activity of harvesting and plowing: "The hay was cut and stored and the orchards were plowed up." The ranch life seems even further restricting at this point because the fog has closed off the valley "from the sky and from all the rest of the world." For the Allens, for ranchers in general, December is a "time of quiet and waiting."[21]

It is important to keep in mind that this pall in the Allen's life is only temporary. If we look carefully—beneath the soil's surface, up into the foothills, and inside the silos—we may find what was not obvious at first glance: clear evidence for the fertility and activity that normally characterize their life, indicated by the "deep" and "black" soil, the "shaggy and rough-coated" cattle,[22] the orchards and hay fields. But during this momentary quietus, as the drifter comes on the scene, we may be tempted, with Elisa, to unfairly balance her own strengths against the tinker's and decide "that sounds like a nice kind of way to live." Both Elisa and the unwary reader are about to come under the spell of the will-o'-the-wisp and thus distracted from the very real virtues of her own life as a woman.

Demonstrations of the Superior Quality of Elisa's Lifestyle

"You might be surprised. . . . I could show you what a woman might do."

—"The Chrysanthemums"

First of all, the physical descriptions of Elisa and the pot mender, I think, point to the greater richness and attractiveness of her lifestyle, though (as usual) not at first glance. It is interesting to see how deliberate and congruent the list of contrasting features is between Elisa and the pot mender: their hair, eyes, clothes, hands, hats, horses, dogs, etc., all clearly inviting us to contrast them, as suggestive of the quality of their respective lifestyles.

When we first meet Elisa she does not seem to be a very feminine or attractive woman. She is dressed in mannish work clothes with a hat pulled over her eyes and clodhopper shoes. However, if we look under the hat we see that her eyes "were as clear as water" and that her hair is dark and pretty. Underneath a corduroy apron, she is wearing "a figured print dress"; heavy work gloves cover and protect what we learn is the very symbol of her womanhood—her planter's hands.[23]

Likewise our first impression when we are introduced to the pot mender is of a jovial man with a hearty laugh. But the laughter in his face and eyes disappears "the moment his laughing voice" ceases. It is an empty laugh. "Although his hair and beard were graying" the pot mender "did not look old." A reader sympathetic to the pot mender might figure that he has retained his youthful vigor in his maturity, but this could as easily indicate that his lifestyle has aged him prematurely. The pot mender's clothes are greasy, his hat battered, and his eyes "dark." That "every crack" in his hands was "a black line"[24] is not a good sign of his past or future.

The conversation between Elisa and the pot mender shows her to be the more witty, the one who has had deeper, more complex experiences, though we would suspect none of this at first. It is ironic that the itinerant, carefree tinker, "a very big man,"[25] is outshone so completely by someone we may easily fool ourselves into believing is a dull ranch wife. In particular, her superior wit and conversational skills are demonstrated in their exchanges over the animals. After his dog retreats from her shepherds ("the dog lowered his tail, and retired under the wagon"), the pot mender quips "that's a bad dog in a fight when he gets started." Elisa laughs and good-naturedly tops this with a quick and witty reply: "I see he is. How soon does he generally get started?" A moment later, in offering directions, Elisa expresses some helpful concern about the ability of the pot mender's team to cross a particular ford in the river. The man takes this friendly suggestion as an insult, reacting with "some asperity" as he responds: "It might surprise you what them beasts can pull through." Instead of reacting in kind to the tinker, Elisa uses humor again to relieve the potential tension and recover a more neighborly atmosphere, echoing his previous words in a very funny retort: "When they get started?" Her tactful response succeeds, eliciting a brief smile from the man. And then, instead of just letting him find out for himself the hard way, she again goes out of her way—without being confrontational—to encourage him to take another route: "Well," said Elisa, "I think you'll save time if you go back to the Salinas road and pick up the highway there."[26]

Elisa's richer life is also evidenced by her futile attempt to tell the pot mender about "planting hands"—her ability to nurture and give tender care to plants. Her efforts fail, as he seems incapable of appreciating such an experience. But when he begins to talk about his nights in the wagon, Elisa quickly interrupts and shows that she has shared some of the feelings and experiences that might seem the unique realm of someone like the pot mender. And she uses words that reach and touch the stars: "I've never lived as you do, but I know what you mean. When the night is dark—why, the stars are sharp-pointed, and there's quiet. Why, you rise up and up! Every pointed star gets driven into your body. It's like that. Hot and sharp and—lovely."[27] These words have become another will-o'-the-wisp for many critics who, with McMahon, insist that the "sexual implications" here are "unmistakable"[28] and then pursue them throughout the story. Certainly, we seem to be invited to recognize an erotic passion in these words. What becomes problematic, however, is how concentrated, obsessive, and exclusive the emphasis on Elisa's sexuality then becomes—as if that is all that makes her tick and all we should focus on if we really want to understand and appreciate Elisa.[29]

A comparison between the animals of the ranch and those of the pot mender also suggests the richness of Elisa's life, while foreshadowing a productive future for her and a sterile one for the pot mender. (Of course Steinbeck, the ardent naturalist and author of *The Grapes of Wrath*, with its symbolic intercalary chapters linking the actions of various creatures—such as a turtle struggling to cross a road—with the actions of his characters, would expect us to notice these correspondences.) A "crawling team" consisting of an old horse and a burro, which "drooped like unwatered flowers," draws the pot mender's wagon.[30] Crossbreeding of a horse and a burro produces a mule, which is sterile, suggesting the ultimate sterility of the pot mender's life. His dog is a mongrel, nondescript, of undefined ancestry. This is also suggestive of the pot mender, who is never given a name. Elisa's dogs, however, are a particular breed—shepherds; they are a team and their offspring will not be mongrels. And they are stronger than the mongrel, causing him to retreat, all of which symbolically point to Elisa's richer, stronger life.

A peculiar tendency I have found scattered throughout the secondary literature on this story is the critical attempt to symbolically attach the feeble actions and condition of the pot mender's dog with Elisa Allen while completely ignoring her own dogs and the richer connotations such associations would imply about her life. Such contorted juxtapositioning allows critics to assign to Elisa their preferred labels of submissive, retreating, and unproductive while simultaneously sidestepping any associations of superior strength, dignity, and productivity that Elisa's shepherds would symbolically give her. Astoundingly, when a commentator finally does notice Elisa's shepherds, there is an attempt to transfer their richer associations to the tinker instead of to Elisa. For example, Ernest Sullivan writes:

> Anyone reading John Steinbeck's "The Chrysanthemums" cannot help being struck by the repeated association of unpleasant canine characteristics with the otherwise attractive Elisa Allen. These *associations identify her with the visiting tinker's mongrel dog, further suggesting a parallel between the Allen's two ranch shepherds and the tinker.* . . . The correspondences between people and the dogs elucidate the social and spiritual relationships of the three humans, as

well as foreshadow and explain Elisa's failure at the end of the story to escape from her unproductive lifestyle.[31]

For some reason, we are told, this interaction supplies clear evidence foreshadowing "Elisa's eventual failure to escape her confined lifestyle. When the mongrel darts from its accustomed position beneath the tinker's wagon, the two ranch dogs shepherd it back. The mongrel considers fighting, but, aware that it could not overcome the two dogs secure on their home ground, retreats angrily back under the wagon and protection of its owner." In other words, when we see the *tinker's dog* "retreat . . . angrily back under [*the tinker's*] wagon, . . . aware that it could not overcome [*Elisa's*] two dogs secure on their home ground,"[32] we are supposed to construe a symbolic victory for the tinker and failure for Elisa. Such manipulation of symbolic evidence to support a preconceived interpretation suggests, rather, how a reader's entrapment in presumptions may in turn direct the way he reads, as well as to what lengths he may go to preserve these presumptions. Of course, the downside of symbolically associating Elisa's animals with Elisa's life and the pot mender's animals with his life is that Elisa comes out ahead.

Elisa's Hands

"I don't how to tell you." She looked deep into his eyes, searchingly.
Her mouth opened a little, and she seemed to be listening.
"I'll try to tell you," she said.

—"The Chrysanthemums"

Keeping in mind the interpretive challenge which Steinbeck presents the reader of "The Chrysanthemums," we have yet to consider that aspect of Elisa's life which is at once the most persistently developed image in the story, the most sharply defined characteristic of her femininity, the greatest source of her fulfillment and most earnest attempts at communication with the other characters in the story (and the reader). This aspect is particularly crucial because it is also the part of her life most conspicuously ignored or undervalued by the critics—Elisa's planter's hands. The key to understanding what is fulfilling in Elisa's life, the key to overcoming the delusions of the will-o'-the-wisp which would cause us as readers to miss her potential triumph and fulfillment, lies in Elisa's hands. Although her planter's hands are invariably associated with the chrysanthemums, it would be wrong to limit their significance and reach to these flowers alone. The hands may be seen as a symbol and testimony of the crowning quality of her womanhood—a reverence for life.[33] It is significant that her mother had this "gift," and that the men of the story conspicuously lack it.

The images associated with men in the story demonstrate either a pragmatic, irreverent, or antagonistic attitude toward life. When we meet Henry Allen he is closing a business deal with two other men from the Western Meat company, to whom he has just sold "thirty head of three-year-old steers." That is "good" for Henry, Elisa says. While Elisa is busy with the chrysanthemums, the men all "studied" Henry's automobile, suggesting their fascination for inanimate objects. The tinker's mismatched team "drooped like unwatered flowers" and his lonely mongrel was "lean."[34] The tinker's main concern is with profit, so the chrysanthemums are as expendable for him as another person's respect and trust, but the lifeless pot is valued for its pragmatic worth.[35]

The most pointed contrast between Elisa and the men—as symbolized by what each do with their hands—is finally made at the climactic moment of the story when Elisa and Henry head off to town. Just as the delusion of the will-o'-the-wisp is overcome by approaching the swamp or riverbed from which it emanates, Elisa awakens completely from her delusion that the tinker's life (a man's life) is more appealing than her own when their car approaches the tinker's wagon alongside the river and she notices the roughly discarded chrysanthemum sprouts tossed on the road. She then seems to awaken from her deluded trance as she draws some conclusions about the kind of life a moment ago she had coveted.

At first she wonders why he couldn't just have tossed the pot and plants off into the brush: "He might have thrown them off the road. That wouldn't have been much trouble, not very much." Then the answer dawns on her—the man had his priorities and what he found valuable and worth preserving was the lifeless pot. The chrysanthemums she had so tenderly placed in his care were disposable. "But he kept the pot," she explains to herself. "He had to keep the pot. That's why he couldn't get them off the road." A lot of other things now seem to add up in Elisa's mind. "The thing was done," we read. "She did not look back." Henry notices that she has broken free from her trance—from her delusions about the appeal of a life like the pot mender's—and says, "Now you're changed again."[36]

There is some silence as they drive, as Elisa registers all that has happened, and then perhaps the most important conversation in the entire story takes place. Elisa asks about the fights, about what men do with their hands in the name of recreation: "Henry, at those prize fights, do the men hurt each other very much?"[37] All readers perceive her inquiry about the fights as a crucial question in our understanding of Elisa. What do we learn about how she is struggling with "the differences between society's definition of femininity," and about "the limitations of the feminine" from her inquiry? And what do we learn from her question about the "ways women are viewed by men (and other women, and society) compared to the ways they view themselves?"[38]

When Elisa shows interest in the fights, she seems simply to be expressing amazement that men could "enjoy" such cruelty. And we as readers are thereby better able to learn the distinction in a man's and woman's perspectives on such things. Henry's response to Elisa's question about violence—"Sometimes, a little, not often"—suggests he is much more oblivious to the bloody pummeling going on at "prize fights." Moreover, the usual explanation as to why she sud-

denly asks Henry about the boxing matches is that she wants to vent her anger at
men by vicariously punishing them as she talks about, or even attends, a boxing
match. And so when she expands her inquiry, she vents even more venom and
enjoys more vicarious vengeance: "Well, I've heard how they break noses, and
blood runs down their chests. I've read how the fighting gloves get heavy and
soggy with blood."[39]

I don't know of any comments about the story that mystify or astound me
more than these kinds of explanations about Elisa's closing questions. I think I
know why people draw such conclusions. Primarily, they need to find an explanation, any explanation, for all this talk about boxing. They know the questions
are critical as they come at the end of the story. And they know how hurt, how
crushed, Elisa feels after seeing the discarded chrysanthemums. And so they
find an easy answer. But is there anything in the story that even remotely suggests that Elisa possesses such vindictiveness, such petty animosity and sadistic
projections? One almost has to turn to Freud to conjure up such rancor in the
woman we have been observing so far.

Are there any other possible explanations for her questions we may want to
consider? Haven't we agreed that the story has been portraying how men and
women value things differently, how a woman's view is often unappreciated and
misunderstood, how a woman is often limited? Keeping in mind that the encounter with the pot mender has focused upon the contrasts between the respective strengths and values of men and women, and keeping in mind that Elisa has
been wondering if she is missing out on something in life because she is a
woman, shouldn't we consider if Elisa's questions have something to do with
the ongoing exploration of these respective strengths and values rather than her
getting in a quick right uppercut as the bout ends?

And then, in case we still haven't caught that all this talk of boxing has been
motivated not by vindictiveness but by Elisa's struggle to understand some fundamental differences between men's and women's values, she asks perhaps the
key question of the entire long afternoon on the ranch, the Rosetta stone to guide
all other interpretations of her character and actions: "*Do any women ever go to
the fights*?"[40] Aren't we supposed to connect her specific question with the rest
of the contrasts between men and women in the story, and also with the fact that
it was a man who just dumped the flowers on the side of the road so that he
could keep the pot? Then, when Henry again invites her to go the fights, aren't
we supposed to understand by her forceful negative response that she now understands the difference between her values and a man's and that she simply
prefers her feminine values? "Oh, no. No," she insists, "I don't want to go. I'm
sure I don't."[41]

Many readers refuse to accept Elisa's sincerity behind these four clear and
negative responses to whether or not she wants to go to the fights. Most resolve
this "problem" simply by insisting—against her contrary statements—that Elisa
actually wants to go the fight and would enjoy seeing those scenes of brutality
she has so graphically described.

The Gift Is in the Hands, Not the Womb

"It's the budding that takes the most care."

—"The Chrysanthemums"

The most serious mistake the reader can make when viewing Elisa's most cherished gift—her planter's hands—is to suppose that it is limited to what one critic called her "capacity for fructification and childbearing"[42]—or as most other critics would have it, to sexuality. Yet the gift is not in the womb but in the hands. When Henry wishes that Elisa would "raise some apples" as big as the chrysanthemums, we ought not be too quick to assume that raising apples or children is beyond Elisa or a part of life which she has rejected. She says "maybe I could."[43] And maybe she will.

Still, a valid question remains: Why, then, is the Allen's home childless? Certainly, Elisa's gift of planter's hands has as its most obvious culmination the raising of children. The only answer to this question from within the story is that we simply don't know that they are childless. But if we would *suppose* they are childless, we still can do so without consigning Elisa a failure for not using her gift. A few possible reasons why Elisa might be childless are that perhaps she (like one out of eight other women) is sterile; perhaps her husband is sterile; perhaps their children were stillborn; perhaps they are considering adoption. Perhaps they have children but the kids are singularly unobtrusive or are away visiting their grandparents.

A more relevant question is to ask why Steinbeck would choose to make the Allens *appear childless*. One possible reason is that he wanted to emphasize that Elisa's gift of planter's hands—her reverence for life—is a trait of her womanhood and not just her motherhood. Or perhaps he was concerned that some readers might too readily dismiss his portrayal of such a gift as a stereotype and gain no deeper appreciation for the gift or for Elisa. In any case, the essence of Elisa's gift is not with the biological ability to give birth to children but with the love and protection and nurturing of children—more especially of life in general. Women physically or socially or psychically precluded from bearing children can still exercise completely this gift of womanhood.

Steinbeck makes this idea clear by linking Elisa's work with the chrysanthemums to what can be called postnatal care.[44] When she turns the soil over and over, smoothes it and pats it firm, then prepares "ten parallel trenches to receive the sets," she acts like a nurse in an obstetrics unit. Her next action includes all the images of a doctor delivering a child: "She pulled out the little crisp shoots, trimmed off the leaves of each one with her scissors and laid it on a small orderly pile." When Elisa prepares chrysanthemums to be transplanted (i.e., adopted) by a lady the tinker says he knows, Elisa says, "You *can* raise them from seed, but it's much easier to root the little sprouts you see there" (original emphasis), which Elisa describes as "Beautiful, oh, beautiful." She then shakes out "her dark pretty hair"[45] as further testimony that her reverence for life is the essence of her femininity.

That Elisa's gift is most important *after birth* is again suggested by the timetable she gives to the pot mender to pass on to the lady. Steinbeck goes out of his way to delineate a nine-month period until the most important of Elisa's tasks begins—the budding. Note that Elisa gave the pot mender the sprouts in December; they would then take root "in about a month" and the buds would start "[a]bout the last of September." From January to September is nine months, the period of gestation. And it is *after gestation* that the most crucial work takes place; as Elisa tried to teach the pot mender, "It's the *budding* that takes the most care." As Elisa says these words she is not only talking to the pot mender but just as surely to the reader. "I don't know how to tell you," she says as she looks deeply into our eyes, searchingly, listening. "I can only tell you what it feels like. . . . Everything goes right down into your fingertips. You watch your fingers work. They do it themselves. You can feel how it is. They pick and pick the buds. . . . Do you see? . . . Do you see that? Can you understand that?"[46]

Do we see? Can we understand that? Elisa is now reaching her hand toward us, almost touching us. Are we interested in what she is saying or only in a meal and a pot? Does she discover that we aren't listening, and do we also cause her to feel ashamed—ashamed because she supposed we actually cared, and found we didn't, after all? Are we, like the pot mender, so intent on finding something of Elisa's to fix, some weakness to exploit, that we don't see what is whole and good and strong about her? Because, ultimately, Elisa is presenting the gift of the chrysanthemums to us, the readers, placing them gently into *our hands*, asking us to watch them carefully, and then waiting to see what we will do with them. We, as readers, find ourselves, despite protestations of neutrality, inextricably bound with Elisa, Henry, the tinker, and the will-o'-the-wisp into the pages of the same story.

Parting Views of Elisa

"Mind," she called, "if you're long in getting there, keep the sand damp."
"Sand, ma'am? . . . Sand?"

—"The Chrysanthemums"

Sadly, as we have seen from a review of the critical history of "The Chrysanthemums," many readers and almost all critics follow most readily the promptings of the will-o'-the-wisp, judging Elisa as a failure and denying her character those qualities which bring her fulfillment. The critics are almost unanimous in attributing to her qualities which demean her. The favorite ploy of such extratextual wills-o'-the-wisp is to drum up some conflict between Elisa and Henry, using Henry as a stooge to abet their own insistence on the emptiness of Elisa's life. But Henry seems a decent man and a good husband to Elisa; if he isn't able to fully appreciate Elisa's gift, he does at least recognize it, encourage it, and give Elisa all the room she needs to exercise it. As Warren Beach puts it, "Nothing is said about the relationship of this married pair, but everything shows that it is one of confidence and mutual respect."[47]

The last sentence of the story is in some ways an ethical barometer, a final test for the reader in this evolving relationship to Elisa, to see if the reader has looked beyond shallow impressions to dispel the fog of seductive prejudices and to shake free from the trance of ingrained patterns of thought: "She was crying weakly—like an old woman."[48] How are we going to read these words? On a very simple level, the sentence simply could appropriately evoke a kind of frustration that is tinged with experience—fittingly suggesting that Elisa, even as she escapes the delusive attractions of a lifestyle such as the pot mender's, nevertheless is deeply hurt by the actions and manipulations of this man. But the critics have some other suggestions for us: Elisa is a hopeless, frustrated, and (perhaps most importantly for some critics) sexless failure. As many conclude: "At the end we see her as a woman, but only that ghost of a woman which nature and society have permitted her to be. She cries like an old woman because she has given in to passivity and potential desiccation."[49] ". . . [S]he was crying weakly—like an old woman'—like an old woman for whom all hope of romance is a thing of the past."[50] "The youthful energy and vitality she had felt is dissolved as she turns her head aside and breaks into tears."[51] "Part of the vision she must be seeing is herself as an old woman. Her dream of something in life beyond mere existence is crushed at this moment."[52] "Her dreams of feminine equality are . . . shattered . . . now she is only 'an old woman.'"[53] "Her tears at the end of the story are the tears of a bitter, defeated woman."[54] "She retreats to the safety of her accustomed unproductive and sexless role, 'crying like an old woman.'"[55]

If we would agree with such readings then we must be willing to make the following assumptions. First, we must conceive that it is a sign of failure to be an old woman; second, that crying is a sign of weakness; and third, that *weakly* has as its meaning impotent and feeble instead of, say, subdued, hushed, or delicate. What would it take for the readers to see "an old woman" as a sign of strength, dignity, beauty, and femininity? Would they be foolish, irrational, naïve, oblivious to evidence and reality, to allow for such a reading? What would it take to see "crying" as an indication not of weakness, but of tenderness, dignity, depth of feeling, compassion? What would it take to see Elisa Allen not as a failure, frustrated and unfulfilled, but as a woman who is complete, strong, and self-aware?

It would take a struggle. And through our reading of "The Chrysanthemums," we become fellow participants in this struggle, which leads us to reexamine not only our interpretation of Elisa, and women, but also the process of interpretation itself. The resonating echoes of this interpretation—which amplify at each rebound, making an apparently isolated dissection of Elisa a wave which envelops the reader in its motions—now includes as the subject of interpretation the reader, the latest protagonist in the ever-newly-created version of "The Chrysanthemums," a version catalyzed by Steinbeck's story but with a life of its own, committed to further propagation.

Notes

1. Wayne C. Booth, *The Company We Keep: An Ethics of Fiction* (Berkeley: University of California Press, 1988), 11-12.

2. I am aware that one of the more crucial questions in philosophical ethics involves the degree to which our values and behaviors are simply a matter of cultural imprinting, and that for many philosophers, as well as literary and critical theorists (e.g., much of what goes under the name of "poststructuralism") virtually all of our so-called ethical behavior is culturally determined or "constructed" and therefore beyond our capacities to critically examine, intervene, or adjust. Leaving aside the fatal inconsistency of any theory which attempts to reveal to others what it insists cannot ever be known by anyone, I am writing this essay under the simple assumption that, despite the reality of some imprinting, and construction, we ultimately retain the capacity to critically examine and adjust these dispositions. I also agree with Aristotle that all questions and definitions of "ethical behavior" hinge upon our capacities to make at least some non-determined choices and actions. I think the literary experience often both confirms such suppositions and expands such capacities.

3. Marilyn L. Mitchell, "Steinbeck's Strong Women: Feminine Identity in the Short Stories," *Modern Fiction Studies* 20 (Summer 1972): 304, 306.

4. Without suggesting that "biography is destiny" in an interpretive sense, I think some details of Steinbeck's life may help explain some possible motivations for his dramatizing the struggles of Elisa Allen, who shares much in common with Carol Steinbeck, his first wife. Perhaps Steinbeck wanted to show the many unappreciated and unexercised talents that were overshadowed by her role as a writer's wife. Perhaps he wanted to highlight certain qualities (such as Carol's work with the poor and constant concern for the downtrodden) that may have been dismissed as "stereotypical feminine attributes." Perhaps he wanted to recognize that her abilities and interests were not limited to the "feminine sphere" and at the same time suggest that even those women who do forego entrance into the market or into work outside of the home (as Carol did) should not necessarily feel that they are losing out. Carol, like Elisa, didn't have any children (though she expressed an intense maternal longing and—at Steinbeck's insistence—underwent a traumatic abortion that left her incapable of having children). Carol was an avid gardener and a great nurturer who took care of Steinbeck's parents in their old age. She was also, according to Steinbeck, his best editor and the motivation for much of his early success. Steinbeck, in his letters, expressed guilt about Carol's sacrifice of her own talents (she even had a manuscript of poems) and for his lack of appreciation for her efforts.

5. Two critics in particular explain how Steinbeck's narrative point of view presents formidable challenges to readers' interpretive efforts, demanding that readers base judgments of Elisa's motivations and feelings solely on concrete evidence from the story, without recourse to authorial revelation of her inner thoughts. Such a point of view, of course, may make the reader even more vulnerable to the kinds of presumptions Aristotle considered barriers to ethical judgments. However, R. S. Hughes applauds Steinbeck's

skill and says "his point-of-view in this tale merits special attention" because "[m]uch of the ambiguity—and the appeal—of Elisa Allen come from the *reader's never knowing precisely what she is thinking*. . . . The objective style insures the ambiguity of Elisa's character and helps to make 'The Chrysanthemums' one of Steinbeck's finest short stories" (26, emphasis added). Kenneth Payson Kempton, on the other hand, criticizes Steinbeck's oblique narration (*"instead of catching, we are caught and misled"*) but does encourage readers to pay close attention to the dynamics and details of the text as the key to understanding Elisa Allen: "So we must watch Elisa closely, stay alert, wait for small signs and portents, and be sure to catch each as it comes along" (322, emphasis added).

6. Elaine Steinbeck and Robert Wallsten, eds., *Steinbeck: A Life in Letters* (New York: Viking, 1975), 91.

7. Paul McCarthy, *John Steinbeck* (New York: Unger, 1980), 26.

8. Mordecai Marcus, "The Lost Dream of Sex and Childbirth in 'The Chrysanthemums,'" *Modern Fiction Studies* 11 (Spring 1965): 55, 57.

9. William V. Miller, "Sexual and Spiritual Ambiguity in 'The Chrysanthemums,'" *Modern Fiction Studies* 20 (Summer 1972): 5.

10. Charles Sweet, "Ms. Elisa Allen and Steinbeck's 'The Chrysanthemums,'" *Modern Fiction Studies* 21 (Fall 1974): 213.

11. R. Simmonds, "The Original Manuscript of Steinbeck's 'The Chrysanthemums,'" *Steinbeck Quarterly* 7, no. 3-4 (Summer-Fall 1974): 107-8.

12. Mitchell, 312-13.

13. Louis Owens, *John Steinbeck's Re-Vision of America* (Athens: University of Georgia Press, 1985), 111.

14. Stanley Renner, "The Real Woman Behind the Fence in 'The Chrysanthemums,'" *Modern Fiction Studies* 31 (Summer 1985): 306, 312, 314.

15. David Leon Higdon, "Dionysian Madness in Steinbeck's 'The Chrysanthemums,'" *Classical and Modern Quarterly* 11, no. 1 (September 1990): 65.

16. I have borrowed the phrase "erotic imperative" from Rene Girard who, in writing about some aspects of *Hamlet* criticism, notes that "we are often dominated nowadays in our literary criticism by what might be called an 'erotic imperative' no less dogmatic in its demands, and no less naive ultimately, than the sexual taboos that came before. In time, this rebellious child of Puritanism will grow old, let us hope, and it may then become possible to recognize that his effects . . . were no less detestable and destructive than those of his father." The sociologist Michelle Rosaldo, in *Women, Culture, and Society*, makes a similar claim about the ubiquity of such an imperative: "Cultural notions of the female often gravitate around natural or biological characteristics: fertility, maternity, sex, and menstrual blood. And women, as wives, witches, midwives, nuns, or whores are defined almost exclusively in terms of their sexual functions." Linda Alcoff explains how such tenacious cultural influences continue to serve as formidable obstacles even to feminists: "In attempting to speak for women, feminism often seems to presuppose that it knows what women truly are, but such an assumption is foolhardy given that every source of knowledge about women has been contaminated with misogyny and sexism. . . . For feminists, who must transcend this discourse, it appears we have nowhere to turn." (295-96).

17. For example, here are three quotations from published commentary on "The Chrysanthemums": 1) "Both Elisa Allen of 'The Chrysanthemums' and Mary Teller in 'The White Quail' display *a strength of will usually identified with the male* but which, in these cases, the husbands are not shown to have." 2) "Steinbeck continually refers to

Mary as 'pretty,' but he describes Elisa's face as 'eager, mature, and handsome,' interesting masculine adjectives." 3) "In each case the woman chooses a traditional feminine activity, gardening, as a creative outlet, yet the *dedication* with which each undertakes her project *is of the sort traditionally considered masculine.*" These critical statements should provoke such questions as: Why should anyone identify "dedication" and "strength of will" as exclusively masculine traits? What sort of a tradition allows men such a monopoly? Why would the critic expect the reader to make such a distinction? And even if we concede that "handsome" seems to fit men better than women, why would a critic expect us to agree that "eager" or "mature" apply better to men? Interestingly, these three quotes all come from the single most often lauded, reprinted, and quoted essay on "The Chrysanthemums": Marilyn Mitchell's "Steinbeck's Strong Women: Feminine Identity in the Short Stories," (*Southwest Review*, Summer 1976), reprinted in Harold Bloom's *John Steinbeck: Modern Critical Interpretations*, Tetsumaro Hayashi's *Steinbeck's Women: Essays in Criticism*, and R. S. Hughes's *John Steinbeck: A Study of the Short Fiction.*

18. John Steinbeck, *The Long Valley* (New York: Viking, 1956), 9-10, 14, 23: emphasis added.

19. Ibid., 20.

20. Ibid.

21. Ibid., 9-10.

22. Ibid., 9.

23. Ibid., 10.

24. Ibid., 13-14.

25. Ibid., 13.

26. Ibid., 13-14

27. Ibid., 18; here is another point of view about what these same events reveal about Elisa's personality: "When the man first arrives, she deprecates (in semi-humorous fashion) the prowess of his dog and then of his mismatched team. Later she insists that she would be equal to living his rough open-air life with all that it entails and finally she challenges his own prowess, claiming that she could sharpen scissors and mend pots just as efficiently, if not better, than he" (Simmonds 109).

28. McMahon, 457.

29. I think Leon Lewis, in an essay for the *Master Plots* series, provides a helpful, nonsexual explanation of what is taking place between Elisa and the pot mender. "Elisa is fascinated by his way of life," writes Lewis, "overlooking the harshness and uncertainty of his existence in her eagerness to romanticize his style." When the tinker shows interest in her flowers, Lewis notes that he has tapped into "her passionate involvement with the process of planting. . . . The consequence of their conversation is very dramatic. Elisa feels energized and appreciated, delighted by her opportunity to share her special skill and excited by the chance to share, at least in her imagination, a totally different kind of life."

30. Steinbeck, 12-13.

31. Ernest Sullivan, "The Cur in 'The Chrysanthemums,'" *Studies in Short Fiction*, 16 (1975): 215: emphasis added. Later Sullivan insists that this forced retreat of the tinker's dog by Elisa's shepherds somehow reflects Elisa's passivity, sexual rebuff, and defeat.

32. Ibid., 216.

33. I am not suggesting here that "a reverence for life" *is* the "crowning nature of womanhood," but only that Steinbeck seems to be suggesting such in this story, and that his character, Elisa Allen, seems to exemplify this. Further, Steinbeck symbolically associates Elisa's print dress, her long hair, "curves," lingerie, as "feminine" qualities in contrast with the more symbolically masculine qualities of her earlier "costume" (man's hat, clodhopper shoes, work clothes).

34. Steinbeck, 10-11, 13.

35. Kenneth Pellow explains the contrast between the men and Elisa as follows: "For [Henry], living things, organic beings, are to be sold, killed, broken, enslaved; to her, they are to be nurtured. And the tinker is just as much a disappointment to her. . . . It should not surprise us that the tinker keeps the manufactured, inanimate portion of Elisa's 'gift' to him, while throwing away the part—the main part, indeed—that is natural and organic. Elisa seems to understand the separateness of his actions, when she sees the flowers lying on the road" (13).

36. Steinbeck, 22-23.

37. Ibid., 23.

38. Mitchell, 304, 306.

39. Steinbeck, 23.

40. Ibid.: emphasis added.

41. Ibid.

42. Marcus, 57.

43. Steinbeck, 11.

44. The notion of an "erotic imperative" may again help explain some critical attempts to determine the interpretive significance of the central symbol in the story—the chrysanthemums themselves. Different critics tell us that the chrysanthemums represent either the female or male sexual anatomy: they are "shaped like a woman's breasts" and "suggest the voluptuous softness of a sexually mature woman" (McMahon 455); "The flower stems can be regarded in the story's context as phallic ('too small and easy for her energy')" (Miller 3); the flowers are "phallic symbols" over which "she exercises complete mastery" (Simmonds 107); "Early in the story the chrysanthemum stalks resemble phalluses, and Elisa's 'over eager' snipping of them suggests castration. Then in the 'rooting' bed Elisa's inserting the 'little crisp shoots' into open, receptive furrows of earth suggests sexual coition" (Hughes 25).

45. Steinbeck, 12, 16.

46. Ibid., 17-18.

47. Joseph Warren Beach, *American Fiction, 1920-1940* (New York: Russell & Russell, 1960), 311.

48. Steinbeck, 23.

49. Marcus, 58.

50. McMahon, 458.

51. Ray B. West, Jr., *The Short Story in America: 1910-1950* (Chicago: Henry Regnery, 1952), 49.

52. Mitchell, 314.

53. Sweet, 213.

54. Simmonds, 110.

55. Sullivan, 216.

The Power of Strange Faces: Revisiting *The Grapes of Wrath* with the Postmodern Ethics of Emmanuel Levinas

MICHAEL D. HANSEN
Independent Scholar

John Steinbeck did not like moralists. This is too bad because he was such a committed moralist himself. He once said of Ed Ricketts that, as a "true biologist," he understood that "morals are too often diagnostic of prostatitis and stomach ulcers," and Steinbeck praised his friend for not confusing "a low hormone productivity with moral ethics."[1] His main complaint with moralists may simply have been the facile but widespread contemporary denunciations of his characters' openly sexual lifestyles, colorful language, or supposedly "communist" rhetoric. However, Steinbeck's distrust of morality went much deeper than a few superficial actions taken by outraged school boards. His preoccupation with the profound limitations of moral thought is obvious in several aspects of his work, from his and Ricketts's exposition of "non-teleological thinking," to his explorations of the moral shortcomings of both sides of the political spectrum in *In Dubious Battle*, to the central conflicts and images in *The Grapes of Wrath*.

The aesthetic power of the final image of *The Grapes of Wrath* would be hard to explain if there were not a fundamental moral tension between a woman offering her breast to an adult stranger and Rose of Sharon's almost mystical selflessness to another. It would also be difficult, without resorting to moral language, to account for the power of the extra-Christian martyrdom of a lusty, fallen preacher or to explain the ethical indignation produced by truckloads of food being destroyed simply to keep prices artificially high. Yet despite this obvious preoccupation with morality and ethics in his novels, Steinbeck's body of work as whole, particularly his essays and letters, still seem to caution against any easy readings based on any particular moral schema.

Many years ago Frederick Carpenter detailed the way that the novel is infused by several strands of American philosophy, including moral philosophy.[2] However, many of the more universal issues that Steinbeck addresses through this most American—and somehow most universal—novel are notably crippled when examined through a purely American lens. These unavoidably moral topics range from the justice of economic relationships to the underlying nature of familial relationships and, most profoundly, the complex relationship of the self to the other— particularly as that relationship plays itself out in groups. I would suggest that we may find a properly subtle yet still productive moral lens in the philosophy of one of the most influential European post-modern ethicists, Emmanuel Levinas.

In the late 1930s and early 40s, Steinbeck and Ricketts were formulating their own philosophical "modus operandi" which they called non-teleological thinking. This naturalist-inspired credo sought to move beyond the puritanical American impulse to uncover and root out the moral causes of a problem in favor of a "conscious acceptance" of things as they are. They believed that through non-teleological thinking they would be capable of "great tenderness" and an "all embracing-ness" that would come from greater acceptance.[3] Across the Atlantic, a relatively obscure philosophy student, Emmanuel Levinas, was studying under and writing about some of the most important continental philosophers of the day, Edmund Husserl and Martin Heidegger. Although radically different from Steinbeck and Ricketts in their methods and goals, Husserl and Heidegger, the fathers of phenomenology, also questioned the way that Western philosophy had forever tried to categorize and understand the way things are by referencing some sterile signifying uber-concept. For Heidegger, the question of Being was best summed up in the German phrase "*Es gibt.*" As commonly used, *es gibt*—"there is"—signified mere existence, as in *Es gibt viele Autos in den USA*—"There are a lot of cars in the USA." Literally translated, *Es gibt* also signified "It gives." As Heidegger saw it, existence itself was a kind of gift or giving-ness, a concept not radically different from Steinbeck and Ricketts's "all embracing-ness."

As a Jew born to Lithuanian parents, Emmanuel Levinas was profoundly affected by World War II. The application of Nietzsche's ontology of "will to will" or "will to power" left Europe in shambles. Heidegger's "giving-ness" seemed like a hollow and naïve refuge from the horrors of Nazism. While Levinas labored away in a prison camp, his wife and child hidden in a monastery to escape the concentration camps, Heidegger accepted a Nazi appointment to a prestigious academic post. Levinas would focus the remainder of his life's work on formulating an ethics that could somehow get past the ontological tendency to reduce being, to explain it away in some philosophical system, however sophisticated. For Levinas, ethics, not ontology, had to be first philosophy.

Levinas therefore counters Heidegger's German concept of *Es gibt* with its French equivalent *Il y a*. The equivalent French signifier does not carry with it the illusion of giving. It means nothing. Levinas speaks of the *Il y a* in paradoxes: a "rumbling silence" or "nothingness, even though there is nothing." The nothingness of this existence is terrible and the self tries to free itself but cannot. There is no salvation from the *Il y a* through this set-up identity, by moving from impersonal being to something, says Levinas.[4] As he sees it, the self or ego can only fully escape the solitude of Being by relinquishing its sovereignty, by "being for the other." The Other, Levinas's most important and influential concept, is another being that opens up the possibility that I do not encompass the entire knowable universe, that there is more than me.

In English, we might speak of "knowing" this other person in a similar sense as we might speak of "knowing" that the capital of California is Sacramento. For Levinas this would be a mistake. Knowledge, in this sense, implies a relationship in which the object can be thematized, ingested, and reduced to the Same. While we may know facts about the other, the existence of the Other cannot be reduced to knowledge, nor is there any escape from the solitude of being in simply knowing about the other. The essential experience I require to break the solitude of my own existence, my own being, is the face-to-face relationship with the Other.

Levinas speaks of the face-to-face relationship with the Other in terms that seem almost kabbalistic but which always return to our responsibilities for the Other. He writes that the Face of the Other, in its destitute nakedness and vulnerability, comes to me from below, pleading for my help and service. From this level arise the virtues of good will and charity but also the possibility of human family and community. On another level the Face comes to me from above, demanding obedience to the commandment "Thou shalt not kill." This responsibility is better thought of as the ability-to-respond rather than the "blame" Steinbeck and Ricketts try to avoid in their non-teleological thinking. It is also non-reciprocal. Levinas states that "I am responsible for the Other without waiting for his reciprocity, were I to die for it. Reciprocity is his affair."[5] Justice then arises not from any claim that I may personally have against an "other," but from the fact that I am simultaneously responsible for and face-to-face with many others. These "other others" can claim justice for me or I for them, but it is never mine to claim for myself.

The experience of otherness, of alterity, does not happen at once of course, but continues throughout our everyday lives. Indeed, Levinas argues that this relationship precedes and gives rise to consciousness. Even before words, the very face of the Other is expression, and the expression of the Other reveals my egoism and calls me to responsibility. This relationship, which we call discourse, allows both parties to remain absolute and separate. Discourse with the Other also opens the possibility of self-discourse, or thought, and then conditions the nature of that thought. Because it conditions all thought, the face-to-face relationship with the Other prefigures all meaning. Behind all symbolic expression, such as reading or hearing, there is an other that produced those symbols. Levinas asserts that the Other is the linguistic signifier which comes to the aid of his signs and gives them meaning.[6] The signifier, or the Other, seems elusive because he is elusive; we cannot, by definition, ever completely grasp him. Thus, we never arrive at "the" correct meaning of a sign or series of signs because we never fully possess the signifier, who remains other by definition.

For reasons we will now explore more fully, this is precisely the kind of ethical system that can help uncover the moral-aesthetic power of *The Grapes of Wrath*. Like many good critical approaches, Levinasian criticism applies a particular focus—in this case, not the text's treatment of women or economic sympathies, but the type and nature of ethical relationships present in the text. Our reading will then arrive at an evaluative ethical judgment—not that Ma was a strong woman character or that Steinbeck was a non-committal Communist, but that the text handles a series of morally significant conflicts that it works out to varying degrees of satisfaction. Levinasian ethics are radical ethics. In attempting to expose some of the face-to-face relationships in the text in as much complexity as the critical medium will allow, we will take a different direction than many previous approaches. We begin with an examination of the historical context of *The Grapes of Wrath*, looking at the face-to-face relationships with the farm workers and farm owners that engendered the novel. We will then look at Casy's "gospel" in light of Levinasian ethics. Finally, we will examine the way the Levinas explanation of eros expands our understanding of the Joads as a mythic or archetypal family.

A Historical Discourse: The Many Faces of *The Grapes of Wrath*

Many different historical relationships are involved in the text: Steinbeck's relationship with the migrant workers and owners' associations, the owners' relationship to the migrant workers, and the publisher's relationship to Steinbeck and his readers, to name just a few. Behind each of these relationships are countless face-to-face ethical encounters. In a similar way, *The Grapes of Wrath* is itself in relationship to countless readers—past, present, and future. Each of these many relationships implies ethical obligations and experiences, involving and indicated by the Face, which we can analyze using Levinasian ethics. In this discussion, I will explore the face-to-face encounters that led Steinbeck to produce this novel, which faces left traces in this text, and how these faces affect the text's contemporary readers. I will also look at which faces were significantly left out of the text. All of these reveal important details about the historical and rhetorical context of *The Grapes of Wrath* as well as the power of the face-to-face experience.

In August of 1936, Steinbeck's friend George West asked him to do a series of articles on migrant farm labor in California for the *San Francisco News*. Steinbeck agreed and set off in an old bakery truck to do research. He spent the next few years working closely with the migrants and the federal government trying to improve the migrants' living and working conditions. During the time Steinbeck was documenting the suffering of many of the farm workers, he met Tom Collins, the government camp manager to whom the book is dedicated (along with Steinbeck's first wife Carol). Collins not only provided the model for the white-suited camp manager who welcomes the Joads to the Weedpatch camp, he also gave Steinbeck literally volumes of information on the migrants' habits, experiences, and dialect. Steinbeck considered these details very important. He notes in his working journal several times that "we have to know these people," the characters he is creating, or as he puts it, "the family I am to live with for four months." He correspondingly worked hard to include enough detail to make his characters realistic, to make them "intensely alive the whole time." Especially as he was working on the beginning of the book, Steinbeck notes that he "must take time in the description, detail, detail, looks, clothes, gestures."[7]

Though some critics have praised *The Grapes of Wrath* for its realistic detail, the novel differs from traditional "realist" or "naturalistic" works. The text does not describe "what happens" as though characters were powerless, and it does not ask readers to suspend their sympathy. Though Steinbeck produced more traditionally "realistic" texts like *Of Mice and Men* and *In Dubious Battle*, the world of *The Grapes of Wrath* asks readers to care intensely about what happens to the Joads at every step of the journey. Unlike a Jack London or Stephen Crane, Steinbeck sets up the novel on the premise that humans deserve better and are essentially different from animals. "Them's horses," the men remind us, "we're men."[8] Furthermore, the Joads' experience at the government camp shows us that they can be helped, that they are not doomed by nature to suffer and die, but that a better life is available to them.

The novel's realism thus functions not as an end in itself but as a means to the end of social awareness. In a letter to Elizabeth Otis, Steinbeck relates a similar opportunity to raise awareness by taking a photographer from *Life* magazine to the migrant camps during the floods. Steinbeck laments the workers' suffering, "where the water is a foot deep in the tents and the children are up on the beds and there is no food and no fire, and the county has taken off all the nurses because 'The problem is so great that we can't do anything about it.'" He is excited about doing the story for *Life* though because "If *Life* does use this stuff there will be lots of pictures and swell ones. It will give you an idea of the kind of people they are and *the kind of faces*. I break myself every time I go out because the argument that one person's effort can't really do anything doesn't seem to apply when you come on a bunch of starving children and you have a little money."[9] The faces of the Okies became Steinbeck's goal for the *Life* story; I think they were also one of the more important reasons why he incorporated so much detail into *The Grapes of Wrath*.

The novel re-presents the faces of the Okies so that I, the reader, will have an ethical experience with Okies analogous to the one that so profoundly moved Steinbeck. In the introduction to the book version of *The Forgotten Village*, a documentary film Steinbeck helped produce just after *The Grapes of Wrath*, he explains the ethical phenomenon he attempts to create in this way:

> A great many documentary films have used the generalized method, that is, the showing of a condition or an event as it affects a group of people. The audience

can then have a personalized reaction from imagining one member of that group. I have felt that this is the more difficult point of observation from the audience's viewpoint. It means very little to know that a million Chinese are starving unless you know one Chinese who is starving. In *The Forgotten Village* we reversed the usual process. Our story centered on one family in a small village. We wished our audience to know the family well, and incidentally to like it, as we did. Then, from association with this little personalized group, the larger conclusion concerning the racial group could be drawn with something like participation.[10]

If Steinbeck believes that it means little to know that thousands of Mexican families are going without proper medical care (as in the film) without knowing one Mexican family intimately, it also stands to reason that it means little to know hundreds of migrant farm workers are starving without knowing one migrant farm family that is starving. This family is the Joads. By knowing the Joads and "hopefully liking them," we are brought by "something like participation" into the situation confronting the whole group. This experience is parallel to that of the ethical experience of the face of the Other.[11]

The Grapes of Wrath recreates the ethical experience with the face on varying levels. First, as we have just noted, the plight of the Joads represents on a broad level the hundreds of migrant workers who had or are having similar experiences. The novel also recreates the ethical experience of the face in specific textual instances of representation, such as Ma and Uncle John's experience with a group of starving kids. Note the emphasis Steinbeck gives to the faces of the children:[12]

> The children stood stiffly and looked at her. Their faces were blank, rigid, and their eyes went mechanically from the pot to the tin plate she held. Their eyes followed the spoon from pot to plate, and when she passed the steaming plate to Uncle John, their eyes followed it up. Uncle John sunk his spoon into the stew and the banked eyes rose up with the spoon. A piece of potato went into John's mouth and the banked eyes were on his face, watching to see how he would react. Would it be good? Would he like it?[13]

Steinbeck can be accused of sentimentality for scenes like this one. Such objections, the same kind used a half century earlier with Harriet Beecher Stowe's *Uncle Tom's Cabin*, rest on the premise that "art" should be distant from the emotions of the reader, appealing instead to the reader's intellect and more refined aesthetic sensibilities. This attitude toward art reveals in the critics who make such charges a certain arrogance. Levinas reminds us that ethics is prior to knowledge: hence, sympathy for the naked face of an other is also prior to the intellectual or aesthetic stimulation of a good turn of words. By prior I mean not only in time but in ethical importance and value. "Sentiment" of the sort found in *The Grapes of Wrath* is not an artistic flaw so much as it is an ethical virtue, especially knowing what we do about Steinbeck's own life experiences with suffering others.

To say that Steinbeck illustrates or represents the ethical experience with the Okies is not to say that his representation is historically perfect. Floyd C. Watkins and other critics have pointed out that while *The Grapes of Wrath* incorporates many factual details about California agriculture, there are also many details the novel gets wrong. Watkins finds scores of factual errors in the text and, more significantly, shows it to be unrepresentative of many of the cultural and religious traditions of the so-called Okies. If we judge the novel as essentially historical fiction, these problems do prove significant, from the trivial errors—there are no irrigation ditches for baptizing in Sallisaw, Oklahoma—to the more substantial—Granma and Grampa's characters are stripped of the gentility and religious sensibility that the older generation of Bible Belt farmers would likely have possessed.[14]

However, it is worth noting that while Steinbeck was very concerned about making the characters in *The Grapes of Wrath* live, he did not seem to be concerned about making them historically accurate. In fact, he calls his characters an "over-essence of people."[15] Steinbeck's choice of words here—"over essence"—bears out Levinas's definition of art. Levinas says that "an artwork prolongs, and goes beyond, common perception. What common perception trivializes and misses, an artwork apprehends in its irreducible essence. . . . Where common language abdicates, a poem or painting speaks. Thus an artwork is more real than reality. . . . "[16] I will leave to other critics the matter of whether or not Steinbeck used the most effective stylistic techniques or historical detail to apprehend that "irreducible essence." What concerns me is the fact that "surrendering to the text"[17] of *The Grapes of Wrath* produces for me, and has produced for other readers, an essential experience of otherness "more real than reality." Critical reevaluation of the experience with the novel does reveal some flaws, but they are not fatal ones and they do not significantly diminish the power of my acquaintance with the Joads.

The Grapes of Wrath is a biased text, and the pro-worker bias it assumes limits its ability to fully present the faces of all others in California agriculture. The situation of the migrants in the interior valleys was a subject that Steinbeck had strong feelings about, including strong feelings about who was right and wrong in the conflict. However, he attempts, as we have noted, to take a nonteleological approach to the problem and avoid blaming individuals for their part in the conflict. Toward the end, the novel presents the faces of characters who were "other" to the Joads—the tractor drivers, the large landholders, and the business people (whom Steinbeck affectionately calls "shitheels"). In one instance, an evicted tenant says to the tractor driver who just plowed up his land, "Why, you're Joe Davis's boy!" The identification puts a face and a name to the driver who had previously only been described as "the man sitting in the iron seat" who does "not look like a man." Then we learn a little about why Joe Davis's boy does what he does: "Three dollars a day [his wage]. I get damn sick of crawling for my dinner—and not getting it. I got a wife and kids. We got to eat. Three dollars a day, and it comes every day." In a similar cameo, Mr. Thomas, the landowner who gives a temporary job to Tom Joad, regrets not being able to pay the men a higher wage because the Farmer's Association and the bank have threatened to close him up if he doesn't cut the wages he is paying.[18] All theses scenes portray the "grower men" as similar to the Joads—human beings who would care, would do more, except that they are caught up in something larger than themselves.[19]

These two examples should not blind us to the fact, however, that for the most part *The Grapes of Wrath* does not represent the faces of the growers and business people. This is true both figuratively—we get very little of the owners' side of the dilemma—and literally—we seldom see (or read a description of) the faces of the growers. Many times the text refers to the owners as simply "The Farmer's Association." At other times they are identified by how they are dressed or what they carry, but never with any description of how they or their faces look. Pa has nearly half a page dedicated to his face, but the "owner men" who come to contract workers, the men who burn down the Hooverville, the boys hired to break up the dance, and the men who converge on Tom and Casy are all faceless "voices [that] came out of the darkness." Tom never even sees the face of the man he kills. The novel describes how Tom sees the pick handle in the flashlight beam, grabs it, hits the man on the shoulder the first time and on "the second time his crushing blow found the head, and as the heavy man sunk down, three more blows found the head."[20] The impersonal description of the blows (almost as if the pick were swinging itself) and the anonymity of the encounter contrast sharply with the first murder Tom commits in which Tom personally knew the victim and the victim's family.

The scene in which Tom kills Casy's murderer is morally the most problematic in the novel. As I noted in the introduction to Levinas, one of two essential features of the face is that it commands me not to kill. Tom kills "the heavy man" without any idea of who he is, having never even seen the man's face. Later Tom apologizes for what happened, saying that "I didn' know what I was a-doin', no more'n when you take a breath. I didn' even know I was gonna do it."[21] In fact, Tom has no idea what is going to happen when he sets out for a walk that night, but he gets caught up in something larger than himself—the strike and Casy's leadership role. Killing someone, whether it be a strike leader like Casy or a strike breaker like "the heavy man," is not something that just happens, though, and it is difficult to allow Tom to merely "I didn' know" his way out of it. The pick handle wrested away from the man and the multiple blows all point to a purposeful act. Ma justifies Tom with a "you done what you had to do,"[22] but the facelessness of the encounter and the absence of information on the heavy man remain troubling and morally significant absences, particularly since the simplistic response could just as easily be used by the growers to justify their own unethical actions.

A second limitation that *The Grapes of Wrath* assumes in representing 1930s agriculture in California is the significant absence of Mexican or Mexican-American workers. The Joads, like other Okies, lay claim to American land because they were "born on it," because they worked it, and because they died on it. Their forbears even "had to kill the Indians and drive them away."[23] The Joads mention a relative that fought the American Revolution and never mention any family traditions or experiences that predate the family's arrival in America. All of these factors serve to emphasize the Joads' American-ness. Steinbeck insisted in a letter to his publisher that the full text and music of "The Battle Hymn of the Republic" appear in the first edition because "The Battle Hymn is American and intensely so, . . . So if both words and music are there the book is keyed into the American scene from the beginning."[24]

In emphasizing the Joads' American-ness, *The Grapes of Wrath* achieves a significant rhetorical effect: the primarily American audience note that sixth- and seventh-generation Americans are being driven from their land, that Americans are being paid lousy wages, and that Americans are starving to death in California. However, in appealing to a primarily nationalistic sense of injustice, Steinbeck also says what he probably would not want to have to say: if we care more that a sixth-generation American is starving, we care less that a Mexican or first- or second-generation Mexican-American is starving. Some time before *The Grapes of Wrath* was written and for a good time since, Mexican and Mexican-American labor has been the group primarily responsible for harvesting California's crops. But society and the novel has typically paid less attention to the ignominies that they have had to endure. For every family Joad in California history there are probably twenty families Hernandez. Their plight is perhaps the subject for another great American novel.

A Philosophical Discourse: Casy's Gospel and Levinasian Ethics

At first glance, the character of Jim Casy doesn't seem to know what he believes and therefore doesn't seem to make a very good preacher, possessing merely a certain folksy, common-sense kind of wisdom that he passes along to others as occasion permits. Upon further reflection and plot development, however, it becomes apparent that Casy's character possesses a complex and significant "gospel" complete with a disciple in the form of Tom Joad. Casy's "gospel" contains at least three separate veins: Christianity, American Transcendentalism, and phalanx theory. The combination is tenuous but gives Casy a fascinating philosophical perspective of the Joads' situation. Though it would be productive to merely identify the different strains of Casy's thought and how they work together, in an ethical evaluation we want to take that analysis one step further and examine whether or not Casy's thought is actually tenable and ethical. Levinas warns us that the history of Western philosophy has been one of universal synthesis in search of Totality. Philosophers have sought a system that was a "reduction of all experience, a reduction of all that was reasonable, to a totality wherein consciousness embraces the world, leaves nothing other outside itself, and thus becomes absolute thought. The consciousness of the self is at the same time the consciousness of the whole."[25] Does a system like Casy's gospel, which attempts to synthesize three widely divergent philosophical systems, move toward a totalizing unity? Or does it merely point to the way in which we all tend to call on widely different systems of thought to explain our widely different experiences?

The first vein of Casy's thought stems from Christianity. When we first see Jim Casy, he is singing "Yes, sir, that's my Savior" to the tune of "Yes, Sir, That's My Baby," setting the tone for the unusual version of Christianity he then advances. Casy explains to Tom that he used to be a preacher until he had an Augustinian conversion while sleeping under a tree. His experience leads him to the conclusion that sin may be "just the way folks is" and that "maybe we been whippin' the hell out of ourselves for nothin'." He also comes to the conclusion that the Holy Spirit is just love and that "all men got one big soul ever'body's a part of."[26] Though shedding the doctrines of sin, the Spirit, and the individual soul, Casy's gospel remains partly Christian. He speaks of his own conversion and Tom is later converted. Casy preaches the importance of love between all men. He emphasizes the need to be a part of the people, especially the poor, and his disciple Tom prepares to "go forth among all nations," teaching people to help one another and avoid hypocrisy.[27]

Casy's Christ-like teachings are supported by his Christ-like role in the novel. Not only do Jim Casy and Jesus Christ share the same initials, they share many of the same attributes and functions. Like Christ, Casy undergoes a wilderness experience and comes back to serve among the poor. Casy atones or takes upon himself the blame for Tom Joad's assault on the policeman and "saves" the family by preventing Tom from getting sent back for broken parole. When Tom toasts Casy, Casy does not allow Tom to call him "the preacher," leading to the statement "here's for the man," a parallel to the scriptural Ecce Homo. The most powerful parallels between Christ and Casy occur in the final scene of Casy's life. The attacking men come at night to get Casy, just as Christ's enemies came at night to get Him. One of the lynchers identifies Casy as "that shiny bastard," a reference to both Christ's holiness and the virgin birth. Casy's last words, "You fella's don't know what you're doin'," parallel Christ's words on the cross, a connection that Ma picks up on and which leads her to remark that "I wish Granma could a heard." Finally, the attackers solidify the connection with a pun: "Jesus, George. I think you killed him."[28]

Nevertheless, Casy is a Christ-like figure who preaches a gutted Christianity. The novel substitutes elements of Steinbeck's phalanx theory to fill in the gaps left by what Casy has abandoned in Christianity. For instance, where there was once sin and the fall, Casy inserts the doctrine of wholeness and disunity. Casy teaches this doctrine to the family during the "prayer" for their trip to California. There was a time, he teaches, that "mankin' was holy, [because] it was one thing." But then, "it only got unholy when one mis'able little fella' got the bit in his teeth an' run off his own way, kickin' and draggin' and fightin'. Fella like that bust the holiness."[29] In Casy's gospel, actions that lead men to work together are righteous and holy. Actions that break the unity precipitate a fall and are considered sin.

In the intercalary chapters, we get a similar construction of sin, this time from a more sociological perspective. The text relates how several families would come together and form a camp. Once formed, the camps soon developed an unspoken code of rights. These included "the right of privacy in the tent; the right to keep the past black hidden in the heart; the right to talk and listen; the right to refuse help or to accept, to offer help or decline it," and "the right of the hungry to be fed," with "the rights of the pregnant and the sick . . . transcend[ing] all other rights."[30] As in Casy's sermon, the actions which lead to the group's survival are respected, even accepted as virtues, while those which lead to the group's disintegration are shunned as sins.

Based on the doctrine contained in Casy's gospel that social unity is a virtuous, paradisiacal state and that being apart is a fallen or negative state, we can trace the development of the novel through the unity and disunity of the Joad family. Prior to the beginning of the novel, the family has fallen; it is apart. Tom has been in prison, Uncle John has been living a lonely life in his own house, and the rest of the Joad family lives an insular life, concerned mainly with their own well-being. The novel begins with Tom coming home, and the family moving toward greater unity. Eventually the entire family, including Tom and Casy, get together at Uncle John's house and begin their trek across the United States to California. They meet up with another family and bring them into the social circle. At this point the "fambly" has reached its largest size and greatest unity.

Phalanx theory in *The Grapes of Wrath* is made explicit in chapter 14, an intercalary chapter inserted into the text while the Joads and Wilsons are together that details a collectivist trend among the migrant workers. The movement begins with the "I," as when one man says "I have lost my land," to "we," as when a group of men say, "We have lost our land." The men together are stronger, "not as lonely and perplexed as one man," and represent a greater threat to the old order. As Steinbeck puts it, "This is the thing to bomb. This is the beginning—from 'I' to 'we.'"[31] This chapter, central to the philosophical and ideological direction of the novel, neatly summarizes the role of Steinbeck's phalanx theory in Casy's gospel.

A third line of thought in Casy's gospel is American Transcendentalism. Frederick Carpenter was one of the first critics to document the presence of American philosophical thought in *The Grapes of Wrath*. Carpenter notes that the "one big soul that ever'body's a part of" that Casy preaches constitutes a thinly veiled version of the Emersonian oversoul. Though Casy does not stress self-reliance or individualism, as Emerson does, he does advance a belief in the unification of peoples, something that Carpenter identifies with Whitman's idealized mass democracy. The ideals of the mass soul and mass democracy take the place of the Christian emphasis on the individual soul. Unlike Christianity, in which individuals respect each other based on their sense of God's commands or fear of individual damnation, individuals in Casy's gospel respect each other out of a kind of enlightened self-interest. Since all members are part of an organism—"manself," or the "big soul"—individual cells should not take actions against each other because their action is ultimately self-defeating—by wounding the organism they are compromising their own chances for survival. Casy tells Tom Joad to tell the workers that if they continue to pick peaches and break the strike, "they're starvin' us and stabbin' themselves in the back" because the wages will drop back down to their original level when the owners break the strike.[32] According to Casy, acting against the group, like acting against the organism, is equal to acting against yourself.

From the point the Joads help the Wilsons to the end of the novel, the Joads learn what it means to act for others in order to help themselves. Though the family gradually gets scattered again, the members of the Joad clan learn to act for the greater good of those around them. With the exception of Connie and Noah who strike out on their own, the Joads shift from "I" to "we." In the Weedpatch camp, Ma becomes part of a Ladies Committee, Ruthie is taught through ostracism how to play civilly with other children, and Tom joins a crew of men. Some of those men teach Tom the importance of "a-workin' together." As they put it, "Depity can't pick on one fella in this camp. He's pickin' on the whole darn camp. An he don't dare. . . . Fella organizin' for the union was a-talkin' out on the road. He says we could do that any place. Jus' stick together." In the floods, Pa must call on the help of other men to try and stop the floodwater with a dike. Ma has to rely on another woman, Mrs. Wainwright, to help take care of Rose of Sharon. This is a trying experience for Ma, who has always been able to take care of her own. She remarks, "Use ta' be fambly was fust. It ain't so now. It's anybody. Worse off we get the more we got to do."[33] Ma's comment indicates that the family really has learned the lesson Casy teaches: they have sacrificed everything, even family to some extent, for the greater good of "manself."

Initially, then, Casy's gospel appears to be capable of great ethical good. According to Warren French, the Joads receive "an education of the heart" during the course of the novel which brings them to greater proximity with and responsibility for others.[34] Their Christian background has predisposed them to help others. By trying to rid them of the notion of individual sin, Casy attempts to take the family one step further and "save" them from the paralyzing self-blame that has nearly ruined Uncle John. Furthermore, Casy directs the family's attention away from themselves and toward the humanity, the others, who need their help. In their service to others, the Joads also become a model for the reader of how it is possible to help, that no situation is "so great we can't do anything about it." Finally, Casy's gospel reminds us of our dependence on others and that by serving others we ultimately serve ourselves.

However, from the standpoint of Levinasian ethics, Casy's gospel also advances unethical, or at least less ethical, philosophies and behavior. There are at least three ethical flaws in Casy's thought—the "we" fallacy, the "absolution" fallacy, and the "introspective" fallacy. We first consider the "we" fallacy. As previously noted, Levinas sees true union not as synthesis, or bringing together two entities to form one new entity, but as the union of the face-to-face in which both parties maintain their "secrecy" or individual existences. Levinas specifically attacks what he calls the third term, "we," in which I and the other are brought together under the auspices of a new term. For Levinas, ethical reality is always a matter of the "I/you" relationship, not the fusion of "I/we."[35] Levinas's thinking on the matter thus directly counters that advanced by Casy. For Casy, the primordial state was one of human "togetherness" which was broken by the individualistic action of a group member. For Levinas, the primordial relationship is one of separation and secrecy, the essential "sin" lying in ignoring the absolute separation of the Other. The problems inherent in Casy's "we" construct are numerous, some of which come out in the novel.

Chapter 14 of the novel offers the move from "I" to "We" in biological terms. It describes how one man saying "I lost my land" gets together with another man who lost his land and they start to talk together. Steinbeck then warns:

> Here is the node, you who hate change and fear revolution. Keep these two squatting men apart; make them hate, fear, suspect each other. Here is the anlage of the thing you fear. This is the zygote. From here "I lost my land" is changed; a cell is split and from its splitting grows the thing you hate, "We lost our land." The danger is here, for two men are not as lonely and perplexed as one.[36]

This biological terminology reveals Steinbeck's organismic conception of group man, an entity almost beyond the control of any "I." The problems with this construct lie in the fact that the "we" principle works whether or not the group fulfills an ethical purpose. The same description that worked for two Okies getting together also works for two Tutsi or Hutu tribesmen (or Serb/Bosnian or Israeli/Iraqi villagers). When the two Tutsis become "we," the other, the Hutu, matters very little. The unethical behavior that then flows from the "we construct" can be devastating. Historically, humanity has conceived of itself politically, as groups of "we's" that sometimes work together and sometimes work against each other. Levinas warns us that the political must always be "checked and criticized starting from the ethical [the I/you]."[37] If not so checked, the result will always be a dangerous totality whether it takes the form of a powerful government or a small mob of angry strikers. Contrary to Casy's gospel, behavior must be judged not against a primordial background of togetherness but one of absolute separation.

The separation between Self and Other results in my responsibility to and for the Other. This responsibility defines me: as Levinas states, "I am I in the sole measure that I am responsible."[38] Inasmuch as my very identity depends on it, this responsibility cannot be abdicated or put off. Traditionally, Christianity has taught this concept with the doctrine of sin. Casy, noticing the misapplication of sin in his own culture, rejects the doctrine in his gospel. However, he never clearly presents an alternative construct by which I, the self, can remind myself of my responsibility to the Other or remind other Others of their responsibilities. This leads to the second fallacy, the fallacy of absolution, in which the self believes that it can put off responsibility because of its role in the politics of the group. This is especially true of the "owner men," who are said to be "caught in something larger than themselves," and, though "some of them hated the mathematics that drove them," they "would take no responsibility for the banks or the companies because they were men and slaves, while the banks were machines and masters all at the same time." As Casy sees it, the owner man, like others, is "just doin' what he's gotta do."[39] In order to have justice, then, Casy must break the world down into "Us" and "Them."

Ethics dictates that the owner men are responsible to the Okie farmers. They should do what they can even if their efforts do not "make a difference" in the larger system of dispossession and poverty. Again, ethics is not ontology. Simply because the owner men should take responsibility does not mean they will. However, since ethical responsibility is non-reciprocal, the fact that the owners are not taking care of their responsibility does not entitle the Okies to neglect their responsibility to attend to the "poverty" of the owners (poverty, in the Levinasian sense of the term, is not limited to physical possessions but seems to apply to any personal lack, be it material, moral, or spiritual). Sometimes my obligation to other Others will supersede my obligation to an owner, for instance, and I will have to strike or speak out in condemnation. The needs of other Others never replace the needs of any other, however. The ethical requires that I always recognize the existence and needs of the Other; it offers no absolution. Once again, Tom's revenge killing is so troublesome precisely because we never really encounter Tom's responsibility to that other; it is swallowed up in the "you done what you had to do."

Finally, we consider the problematic ethics of the transcendental epistemology advanced by Casy's gospel. Casy's disciple Tom aligns himself with previous transcendental thought when he explains to Ma Casy's doctrine of the "great big soul": "Says one time he [Casy] went out in the wilderness to find his own soul, an' he foun' he didn' have no soul that was his'n. Says he just got a little piece of a great big soul."[40] Tom goes on to tell Ma that she needn't worry about him since, if Casy was right,

> "Then it don' matter. Then I'll be all aroun' in the dark. I'll be ever'where—wherever you look. Wherever they's a fight, so that hungry people can eat, I'll be there. Wherever they's a cop beatin' up a guy, I'll be there. If Casy knowed, why, I'll be in the way guy's yell when they're mad an'—I'll be there in the way kids laugh when they're hungry an' they know supper's ready."[41]

Tom's speech resembles the thought of many earlier American transcendentalists, who, as Carpenter has pointed out, proposed the existence of an "oversoul," or Nature's self, to which men had access by way of meditative epiphanies. In *Nature*, Emerson describes these epiphanies as moments when "all mean egotism vanishes" and the self becomes a "transparent eye ball." During this time "currents of the Universal Being" circulate through the individual and he becomes "part and parcel of God."[42] To participate in these epiphanies, the individual must "go into the woods" where he can find solitude. Casy tells of a similar experience where "There was the hills an' there was me, an' we wasn't separate no more. We was one thing. An' that one thing was holy."[43]

In these Emersonian experiences the lone self becomes the channel for the universal and introspection becomes the essential epistemology. In light of Levinas, we will call this the introspective fallacy. Introspection is not an unethical act in Levinasian ethics, but it is also not the essential experience or epistemology. To turn into the self, to introspect, usually means turning away from sociality or the company of others—to "retire from society," as Emerson put it. For Levinas, sociality or the company of others is the fount of experience and wisdom, the essential epistemology. The individual cannot experience what is other—absolutely and infinitely other than himself—except in what the face of the Other opens up to him; "transcendence" occurs only in the face-to-face.

When Casy decides that he "didn' have no soul that was his'n," he decides to go out into the world to seek his soul. Levinas might also recommend this approach with the important admonition that the self not enter into the sociality of the world expecting to achieve a mystical communion with his fellows. Tom will not be "wherever you look"; he will always be face-to-face with someone, someone other than himself. These encounters with the Other will call into question the knowledge Tom has acquired from Casy and his experience. Knowledge and thought, in a Levinasian system, does not occur as a singular moment of "enlightenment" but in "discourse"—a relationship and series of experiences with the Other. As such, knowledge is always in flux. Perhaps this is why Tom must admit to Ma's "I don't really know" that he doesn't really know either.

A Mythic Discourse: The Metaphysics of Family

The Grapes of Wrath treats two levels of family experience: the first, a pragmatic and political level, based largely in the extended family and centered on the character of Ma Joad; the second, a mystical and erotic level, based principally on the immediate family and centered on the character of Rose of Sharon. I wish to consider both levels in light of Levinasian ethics, group theory, and a new critical lens, that of mythic/archetypal experience. While *The Grapes of Wrath* is undoubtedly a realistic novel, based on sociological and scientific thought derived from Steinbeck's acquaintance with friends like Ed Ricketts, it is also a mythical and allegorical novel, based on universal symbols and types of human experience derived from Steinbeck's acquaintance with literature and friends like Joseph Campbell. In this section I will give some consideration to the mythical characterization of the novel.

The extended Joad family, composed of eleven individuals, is first introduced through its individual members, but in the middle of chapter 10, a mystical experience unites the family into one whole. The text introduces this union
as "the congress, the family government" that goes into session "without any
signal" and then describes the action of the participants as seeming "to be a part
of an organization of the unconscious. They obeyed impulses which registered
only faintly in their thinking minds." In this Jungian congress, Pa, Uncle John,
and Grampa make up the "nucleus" around which a line is formed composed of
Tom, Al, and Connie. The women are further to the outside taking their places
"behind the squatting men."[44] The children are placeless but stand beside the
women. In the seating arrangement, the text introduces the traditional political
makeup of the Western extended family. From this clan organization is derived
the ideal organization of the family which, like all ideals, is shown to be impossible (and perhaps undesirable) to realize.

From the beginning it is obvious that Ma holds a power beyond that which
her place in the seating arrangement assigns her. When the family considers the
possibility of bringing Casy along, they must defer to Ma who holds a kind of
veto power over anything the family does. When asked if the family "kin feed
an extra mouth" Ma replies:

> "It ain't kin we? It's will we? . . . As far as 'kin,' we can't do nothin', not go to
> California or nothin'; but as far as 'will,' why we'll do what we will. An' as far
> as 'will'—it's a long time our folks been here . . . an' I never heerd tell of no
> Joads or no Hazletts, neither, ever refusin' food an' shelter or a lift on the road
> to anybody that asked."

Ma's reply defies the impossible and shames Pa to the point that "his spirit was
raw from the whipping."[45] He abdicates to her authority.

Ma's authority comes from an inner strength greater than that of any other
character or force in the novel. We catch a glimpse of this inner force when her
face is described for the first time near the beginning of the novel:

> Her full face was not soft; it was controlled, kindly. Her hazel eyes seemed to
> have experienced all possible tragedy and to have mounted pain and suffering
> like steps into a high calm and a superhuman understanding. She seemed to
> know, to accept, to welcome her position, the citadel of the family, the strong
> place that could not be taken.

Ma, as spiritual citadel of the Joad family, realizes that if she ever swayed or
doubted, the family would "fall, the family will to function would be gone."[46]
Mimi Gladstein has shown how Ma's character surpasses any of Hemingway's
or Faulkner's female characters, both in her willingness to subvert male authority and in her multidimensionality. Gladstein argues that Ma is seen as an "indestructible woman" because women are better able to cope with change and adapt

to disaster, citing Ma's reference to women as rivers that continually flow where men live their lives in "jerks."[47]

As the family meets with more and greater disasters, then, one would expect Ma's role in family government to increase. It does. When Pa wants to separate the family for a few days, for instance, Ma revolts, grabs a jack handle, and takes control. When Tom objects to Ma's plan, "The eyes of the whole family shifted back to Ma. She was the power. She had taken control." Tom, too, then abdicates to Ma's authority in matters of the family. In the final scenes of the novel, the "ideal" organization of the family outlined in chapter 10 has so far broken down that Pa says, "Funny! Woman takin' over the fambly. Woman sayin' we'll do this here, and we'll go there. An' I don' even care."[48] Through the family's long ordeal and the character of Ma, Steinbeck reverses traditional opposition pertaining to the politics of the family: man as the strong leader and woman as the weak follower.

Steinbeck's reversal, or "deconstruction,"[49] of the traditional family political system accomplishes important ethical aims which hinge on understanding the ethics of the family, a matter of some importance to Levinas. Familial relationships hold a special place in the Levinasian philosophical system because they represent special cases of the I/you relationship. Levinas speaks especially to the erotic relationship, in which families are commenced, and holds the erotic relationship to be unique among all other human relationships because the Self seeks and values what is radically other in another. I, the Self, do not value the erotic relationship because there is a fusion, because I and the Other become one; Levinas denounces the "idea of love that would be a confusion between two beings" as a "false romantic idea." Instead, Levinas posits, "the pathos of the erotic relationship is the fact of being two, and the other is absolutely other." Levinas emphasizes that in the erotic relationship, "the other as other here is not an object which becomes ours or becomes us; to the contrary, it withdraws into its mystery."[50]

In the marital relationship, the legal and social extension of the erotic, humans have, as in philosophy, displayed dangerous tendencies toward totality. In the close contact of marriage, men (especially but not exclusively) forget that what they should most value in a spouse is her alterity, her complete otherness. In such totalizing relationships where the wife's independent behavior is not in line with the Same or husband's will, the man may employ various means at his social and physiological disposal to "bring her in line" or into a mastery of his will. This tendency, even a tendency to use violence, is apparent in *The Grapes of Wrath*. Pa says to his wife, "Seems like times is changed. Time was when a man said what we'd do. Seem like women is tellin' now. Seems like it's purty near time to get a stick." Steinbeck's reversal of the traditional family political system thus gives him the chance to intervene in the system. Ma reminds Pa that the traditional roles don't apply any more since Pa is no longer the provider. She then tells Pa that "you ain't lickin' no woman; you're a fighting 'cause I got a stick all laid out too."[51] Pa loses the argument and, more importantly, loses the illusion of total control. In much the same way, the Joads move beyond their narrow duties to their family to a consideration of their responsibilities to the outside world. As Ma says, "They was a time when we was on the lan'. There was a boundary to us then. Ol' folks die off, an' little fella's come, an' we was always one thing—we was the fambly—kinda whole and clear. An' now we ain't clear no more. . . . There ain't no fambly now."[52] Having already reversed the political structure within the family, the text then blurs the line between family and stranger, with the Joads learning to see themselves as part of the larger human condition.

By far the most important mythical character within the family is Rose of Sharon, who supplies the thread that ties together divergent elements in the text. Combining in one character the mysterious holiness of both the erotic and the maternal, she brings together most of the novel's important themes: displacement from the land, the movement from "I" to "We," and the ethical appeal of the migrant workers' plight. Any discussion of myth or family in *The Grapes of Wrath* would be incomplete without a careful consideration of her character.

The name, Rose of Sharon, originates in the Song of Solomon, chapter two, verse one: "I am the rose of Sharon, and the lily of the valleys. As the lily among thorns, so is my love among the daughters" (King James Version). Sharon, in this verse, refers to land along the Mediterranean Sea to the northwest of Jerusalem which was swampy, sandy, and generally unsuitable for human habitation or agriculture. The poetic figure "Rose of Sharon" thus rests on contrast, the beauty and fertility of the Rose being contrasted with the desolation and infertility of Sharon. The character of Rose of Sharon, like her name, is a symbol of fertility in the otherwise desolate existence of the Joads. Rose of Sharon's fertility arises not only out of her maternity but her sexuality. The Song of Solomon, like the poetic figures it contains, combines images of sexuality and fertility (in the sense of progeny). Traditional Christianity has also introduced a third element—sanctity—into the Song of Solomon and hence to Rose of Sharon's name. Chastity-minded Christians have always been uncomfortable with the erotic imagery of Song of Solomon, yet their belief in the Bible as the literal word of God creates a need to do something with the book. A traditional reading of The Song of Solomon has therefore taken the imagery to be allegorical, symbolizing Christ, the bridegroom, and his relationship with his bride, his Church. *The Grapes of Wrath* incorporates the religious symbolism into her character as well in a rich mixture of holy, erotic, and maternal symbolism, with Rose of Sharon's first appearance in the novel confirming her threefold nature. She is first introduced as "pregnant and careful." The novel then relates how "Her hair, braided and wrapped around her head, made an ash-blond crown," and how her face wore a look of "knowing perfection." Both phrases emphasize her elevated, holy role in the family as tied to her maternity. The continued description of "her plump body" and "full soft breasts," however, suggests erotic underpinnings, especially with its description of "hard hips and buttocks" that swing so "as to invite slapping and stroking." Rose of Sharon's mindset also confirms her role: "the whole world was pregnant to her; she thought only in terms of reproduction and motherhood."[53]

The maternal Rose of Sharon begins the novel as a symbol of fertility in an otherwise infertile world. Not only is the family farm barren from seasons of erosion and drought, the family is itself infertile—Granma and Ma are beyond child-bearing age; Noah, Tom, and Al leave the family; Ruthie and Winfield are too young. Rose of Sharon is the family's only current hope for continuance. Her sexual fertility is symbolically contrasted with the infertility of the old land in an incident that takes place as the family crosses into California. While everyone is sleeping, Connie and Rose of Sharon "struggle together," or have sex, under a blanket.[54] To Rose of Sharon's shock, they later learn that at the precise time they were together, Granma had died. The effect is to contrast the vital fertility and possibility of the new land and generation with the sterility of the old.

Once in California, Rose of Sharon's fertile fortunes take a turn for the worse. As the family moves from job to job, Rose of Sharon loses one by one the qualities that made her unique in the family. When Connie leaves to chase his pipe dreams, Rose of Sharon loses much of her sexuality. Her holiness, sexuality, and maternity are all attacked by the fundamentalist Elizabeth Sandry, who warns her that if she "hug dances" she will be "sinnin'" and will probably "drop her baby." Though Ma pierces Rose of Sharon's ears, and Tom compliments her on her looks, Rose of Sharon will only go to the dance if Ma promises that she won't "let nobody touch" her. What "hug-dancin'" and "play actin'" couldn't take from her, poor nutrition, overwork, and exposure do. By the time Rose of Sharon delivers, she is no longer the confident, innocent, and holy creature we met in the beginning but a frazzled, scared girl with her "faced flushed and her eyes shining with fever."[55] When the baby is stillborn she seems to have lost everything.

However, in the end Rose of Sharon brings together the elements of Casy's gospel—Christianity, Phalanx Theory, and American Transcendentalism—in an act that symbolically encompasses the entire human family. Rose of Sharon gives (of) her "life" in the penultimate Christian sacrifice, with critics observing that the sight of the "mysteriously smiling" Rose of Sharon breastfeeding a full grown man parallels paintings of the Madonna with the Christ child. Rose of Sharon's offer also signals the ultimate transition from "I" to "We." It is the most intimate of gifts offered to a complete stranger, someone not even connected to the family. Finally, Rose of Sharon's action lends her character a measure of the sublime. The man's age compared with an infant hints at the temporal transcendence of the act and the flow of life from one person to another suggests the act's spiritual and physical transcendence. We are reminded of Tom's promise that he would be there "whenever there's a fight so hungry people can eat" and Casy's scripture that "Two are better than one . . . for if they fall, the one will lif' up his fellow."[56] Rose of Sharon's character thus comes full circle: from a hopeful, self-absorbed, expectant mother to a stricken, desperate woman, and then back again to a type of universal mother. The family truly has received an "education of the heart."

Finally, the last scene has great ethical value. Many critics, including Steinbeck's own publisher, criticized the ending as being "all too abrupt." Steinbeck's curt response was that he could not change the ending, for "If there is a symbol, it is a survival symbol. . . . [I]t must be an accident, it must be a stranger, and it must be quick. The fact that the Joads don't know him, don't care about him, have no ties to him—that is the emphasis."[57] The fact that the man is a stranger, that we get almost no information about him, gives the incident its great ethical value. Except for the fact that he is a human being, we know nothing about the man. He is absolutely Other. Steinbeck lived in a time when it was becoming easier and easier to kill or order someone killed without even looking them in the face. This may absolve our perception of guilt, but the responsibility to the Other lies beyond perception. Levinas writes in *Ethics and Infinity* that

> You turn yourself toward the Other as toward an object when you see a nose, eyes, a forehead, chin, and you can describe them. The best way of encountering the Other is not even to notice the color of his eyes! The relation with the face can be dominated by perception, but what is specifically the face cannot be reduced to that.[58]

The scant attention given to the man fed by Rose of Sharon, attacked by some formalist critics as a hasty, undeveloped ending, actually serves to put the man beyond perception. It doesn't matter what he looks like or his age; the essential matter is that he is destitute and Rose of Sharon can help him.

In *The Grapes of Wrath* we have a powerful counter-symbol to the twentieth century experience with Totality. In a world and time where groups of men and women killed whole other groups of men and women because they were different, and often without even seeing their faces, Rose of Sharon's sacrifice to a man she does not know stands as a powerful reminder of the power of the individual, supported by the group, to intervene in situations that too often seem beyond our control.

Conclusion

Early criticism of *The Grapes of Wrath* focused on the "immorality" of the novel due to its language, adult situations, and the final scene, which was thought to be indecent for sensitive readers. In my attempts to apply a more rigorous moral methodology to the text, I have come to a different conclusion. The offensive language becomes part of Steinbeck's effort to recreate the experience of otherness he had with the Okies; the adult situations become mythic archetypes; and the final scene becomes a poignant symbol of our responsibility to attend to the needs of the Other—the stranger, the widow, the orphan. Indeed, the novel seems more moral and Christian than many of the "moral" and "Christian" criticisms used against it.

The Grapes of Wrath is also more than an aesthetic "work" hanging on the bare wall of a sterile literary museum, as much of later criticism has treated it. A reading that would strip the novel of its political and social context and dismiss the ethical concerns within the text in order to focus on Steinbeck's sentence structure as opposed to that of Hemingway seems itself guilty of a totalization of both the novel and the reader's experience. Our treatment of the text has shown that much of the novel's power—from a Levinasian perspective—arises from the perceptive way it treats our complex ethical relations to others. *The Grapes of Wrath* is a valuable, moral text not because it is aesthetically perfect or historically accurate (notwithstanding its strengths in these areas) but because it wrestles in profound ways with important ethical issues—right and wrong, responsibility and blame, family and community, self and other.

Notes

1. John Steinbeck, *The Log from the Sea of Cortez* (New York: Penguin, 1986), 33-34.

2. Frederick I. Carpenter, "The Philosophical Joads," in *Modern Critical Interpretations:* The Grapes of Wrath, ed. Harold Bloom (New York: Chelsea House, 1988), 7-15.

3. Steinbeck, *The Log from the Sea of Cortez*, 174.

4. Emmanuel Levinas, *Ethics and Infinity: Conversations with Philippe Nemo*, trans. Richard A. Cohen (Pittsburgh: Duquesne University Press, 1985), 49, 51.

5. Ibid., 98.

6. Emmanuel Levinas, *Totality and Infinity*, trans. Alphonso Lingis (Boston: Martinus Nijhoff, 1979), 181-82.

7. John Steinbeck, *Working Days: The Journals of* The Grapes of Wrath, ed. Robert DeMott (New York: Penguin, 1989), 29, 37, 40.

8. John Steinbeck, *The Grapes of Wrath* (New York: Penguin, 1976), 556.

9. Elaine Steinbeck and Robert Wallsten, eds., *Steinbeck: A Life in Letters* (New York: Viking, 1975), 161-62: emphasis added.

10. John Steinbeck, *The Forgotten Village* (New York: Photogravure and Color, Co., 1941), 1.

11. I say parallel because I cannot say identical. Levinas says that "you turn yourself toward the Other as toward an object when you see a nose, eyes, a forehead, a chin, and you can describe them. The best way of encountering the Other is not even to notice the color of his eyes! The relation with the face can surely be dominated by perception, but what is specifically the face is what cannot be reduced to that" (*Ethics & Infinity*, 85-86). A work of literature or art uses words or color or lines to represent the face; the face, however, is itself presentation. While the experience of the face cannot be broken down into language, language can recreate the face or, better yet, the subjective and personal experience of relationship to the face.

12. Steinbeck gives attention to the children's faces, but, more specifically, he focuses on their eyes. Levinas refers to the eyes as "unguarded, absolutely unprotected"

(see "Signature," 293, in *Difficult Freedom: Essays on Judaism*, ed. Seán Hand). For Levinas the eyes are the focus of the face, the most essential component.

13. Steinbeck, *The Grapes of Wrath*, 331.

14. Floyd C. Watkins, "Flat Wine from *The Grapes of Wrath*," in *Modern Critical Interpretations:* The Grapes of Wrath, ed. Harold Bloom (New York: Chelsea House, 1988), 60-64.

15. Steinbeck, *Working Days*, 39.

16. Travis Anderson, "Drawing Upon Levinas to Sketch Out a Heterotopic Poetics of Art and Tragedy," *Research in Phenomenology* 24 (1994): 72-73.

17. Wayne Booth, in *The Company We Keep* (University of California Press, 1988), argues that "surrendering to the text" is an essential step in the critical reading of literature. After we have surrendered to the text, we must then return to the experience with a more critical eye.

18. Steinbeck, *The Grapes of Wrath*, 45, 47, 378.

19. In recreating the conditions "larger than themselves" that led the California citizens to acts of hostility and violence, Steinbeck turns again to the power of the face. In chapter 21, an intercalary chapter describing the local citizens' reaction to the migrants, Steinbeck notes that "Men who had never been hungry saw the eyes of the hungry. Men who had never wanted anything very much saw the flare of want in the eyes of the migrants. And the men . . . gathered to defend themselves; and they reassured themselves that they were good and the invaders bad, as a man must do before he fights" (363).

20. Steinbeck, *The Grapes of Wrath*, 495.

21. Ibid., 503.

22. Ibid.

23. Ibid., 43.

24. Steinbeck and Wallsten, 174.

25. Levinas, *Ethics and Infinity*, 75.

26. Steinbeck, *The Grapes of Wrath*, 30-31.

27. Ibid., 537.

28. Ibid., 67, 495, 503.

29. Ibid., 105.

30. Ibid., 250.

31. Ibid., 194.

32. Ibid., 491.

33. Ibid., 460, 569.

34. Warren French, *John Steinbeck*, rev. ed. (Boston: Twayne, 1975), 98.

35. Emmanuel Levinas, *Time and the Other and Additional Essays*, trans. Richard A. Cohen (Pittsburgh: Duquesne University Press, 1987), 93.

36. Steinbeck, *The Grapes of Wrath*, 194.

37. Levinas, *Ethics and Infinity*, 80.

38. Ibid., 101.

39. Steinbeck, *The Grapes of Wrath*, 40-41, 494.

40. Ibid., 535.

41. Ibid., 537.

42. Ralph Waldo Emerson, "Nature," in *The Norton Anthology of Literature*, ed. Nina Baym, et al., 3rd shorter ed. (New York: W.W. Norton, 1989), 386.

43. Steinbeck, *The Grapes of Wrath*, 105.

44. Ibid., 128.

45. Ibid., 132.

46. Ibid., 95-96.

47. Mimi R. Gladstein, "The Indestructable Women: Ma Joad and Rose of Sharon," in *Modern Critical Interpretations:* The Grapes of Wrath, ed. Harold Bloom (New York: Chelsea House, 1988), 115-27.

48. Steinbeck, *The Grapes of Wrath*, 218, 541.

49. Some modern critics tend to look at deconstruction as an end in itself and might cringe at the suggestion that deconstruction could be used toward an ethical or moral end. Derrida himself explained the purpose of deconstruction as being to "put into practice a reversal of the classical opposition and a general displacement of the system. It is on that condition alone that deconstruction will provide the means of intervening in the field of opposition it criticizes and which is also a field of non-discursive forces" (in Culler's *On Deconstruction: Theory and Criticism After Structuralism*, 86). If the traditional family politics is a non-discursive field, and Steinbeck deconstructs it, then he does so to "intervene." As we shall see later this intervention is for an ethical purpose.

50. Levinas, *Ethics and Infinity*, 66-67.

51. Steinbeck, *The Grapes of Wrath*, 452-53.

52. Ibid., 503.

53. Ibid., 123.

54. Ibid., 289.

55. Ibid., 398-400, 434, 558.

56. Ibid., 535-37.

57. Steinbeck and Wallsten, 177-78.

58. Levinas, *Ethics and Infinity*, 85-86.

The Emotional Content of Cruelty: An Analysis of Kate in *East of Eden*

STEPHEN K. GEORGE
Brigham Young University-Idaho

It is sometimes the very irrationality of compassion, the residual capacity to respond with tenderness and love when all one's reason counsels otherwise, that
confers upon a compassionate act its sweetness, beauty, and nobility. In exactly
the same way does the irrationality of malice [or cruelty], the *pointless* but deliberate infliction of suffering, produce its acute and revolting ugliness.

—Richard Taylor in "Compassion"

"Mother—dear Mother—I'm going to show you how to run a whorehouse.
We'll fix the gray slugs that come in here and dump their nasty little loads—for
a dollar. We'll give them pleasure, Mother dear."

—Kate, *East of Eden*

Of all the depraved character traits, cruelty seems the most difficult to comprehend. In some fundamental way the cruel person defies rationality in her deliberate attempt to maim the lives of others "so that the victim can eventually trust
neither himself nor anyone else."[1] As a vice, cruelty goes beyond an "unjust or
callous use of force or power" that hurts or violates "another's rights or sensibilities," one of the common definitions for "violence."[2] Rather, cruelty is a deliberate and focused attempt to cause pain so that the torturer may receive pleasure in another's suffering. It is tearing off a butterfly's wings and then smiling as
the insect squirms on the ground. It is offering cutting remarks and then savoring
the attempt to salvage some dignity. It is the most ugly of all vices.

Such satisfaction in human suffering suffuses Cathy Ames' sarcastic words
above; as the pitiless whore of John Steinbeck's *East of Eden* reveals, the
"pleasure" will largely be hers as she fixes the "gray slugs" who frequent the

silk sheets of Faye's brothel.[3] Of all of Steinbeck's creations, Cathy (or Kate as she is later known) is his most evil and perhaps the most cruel character ever depicted in literature, a sexual sadist who could make even an Iago blush. At first the author posits Kate as a "psychic monster" incapable of kindness or con-science, and thus beyond the realm of ethical inquiry—she merely is what she is. But later Steinbeck revises this assessment, saying that her cruelty means little "unless we know why."[4] Much of this epic novel, which follows Kate from childhood to her final suicide, seeks to trace the emotional origins of this vice.[5] Literature, I believe, has never produced a more complete picture of the emo-tional underpinnings of evil.

This essay's focus will be on the most common form of cruelty, the "delib-erate infliction of suffering without justification,"[6] through an analysis of Kate's actions, attitudes, and emotions concerning others, especially men. If, as Martha Nussbaum contends, it is literature that provides the rich levels of observation, explication, and psychology needed to capture the full ethical dimensions of human nature and conflict,[7] then in the character of Kate (as well as in Kate's character) we may find the essence of cruelty: its desire to cause another "an-guish and fear,"[8] its preoccupation with "power over a creature's whole life,"[9] its giving of pleasure when the ordinary moral perception finds only "revulsion" and disgust.[10] I would contend that the real experience or "feel" of this vice can best be found in literary portrayals that mirror and highlight the true nature of cruelty. In Cathy, "Steinbeck's most demonic creation,"[11] we have a depiction of evil that exceeds any sum of features commonly used to describe the cruel per-son and that offers insights into the origination of cruelty itself, particularly in understanding its frequent basis in fear and hatred.

To my knowledge, such an in-depth analysis of the emotional content of cruelty has not been offered before. Philip Hallie, in "From Cruelty to Good-ness," reveals his own desire to find such essentials when he criticizes the over-emphasis of the pain element of cruelty; he observes (and rightly so) that "the word 'pain' . . . [seems] to be a simplistic and superficial way of describing the many different sorts of cruelty." Rather, as Hallie argues, the real "depths of an understanding of cruelty lie in . . . an understanding of human dignity" and in the power relationships that enable "the maiming of" that "dignity" or "crushing of a person's self-respect," for "a disparity in power . . . [lies] at the center of the dynamism of cruelty."[12] In examining cruelty from the vantage point of hierar-chies and human degradation, Hallie clearly opens a new avenue to our under-standing of the mechanisms of this vice.

However, this focus on power relationships does little to explain *why* a per-son is cruel and *how*, on a psychological and ethical level, that person can do what they do.[13] Yes, the cruel person has a degree of control over another person or group of people, as Kate does over her whorehouse clientele. An imbalance of power, in the most operative sense, is what makes the cruelty of the dominant party possible. But power itself does not equate to cruelty: "It [cruelty] may be connected with power, but is not identical with it. Many persons in high rank had power but were free from any signs of cruelty."[14] Rather, for reasons intimately connected with the cruel person's emotional and mental state, the cruel nature and cruel behavior seem to arise out of more primary and personal considerations. As will be argued here, fear and hatred are frequently the emotional pillars undergirding the vice of cruelty, and it is only by understanding the connections of these powerfully destructive emotions to this character trait that we can explain the cruel person's motivation for power, his desire to inflict pain, and his enjoyment of others' suffering. Fear and hatred, while not inevitably producing cruelty, are nevertheless often (and perhaps always) at the motivational and enabling core of this vice.

But how so? Certainly there is not a general tendency to associate the first of these emotions, fear, with cruelty. Such would seem a contradiction with our experience with this vice, for the merciless person—be it a ruthless terrorist or a brutal spouse—seems, at least outwardly, far from being afraid. Rather, cruel people inspire fear; Kate, as Steinbeck shows, brandishes fear as a weapon, for she "had always been able to shovel into the mind of any man and dig up his impulses and his desires" to use against him.[15] It is just this ability to inspire fear in others by playing on their vulnerabilities that keeps her whorehouse customers and workers in line, and thus maintains the "disparity in power" that Hallie describes as being "at the center of . . . cruelty."[16] Even her henchman, Joe Valery, who aspires to ruin Kate and take over her business, admits a grudging "admiration for . . . [his mistress] based on *fear*," for "Kate made a slave of him just as he had always made slaves of women. She fed him, clothed him, gave him orders, punished him."[17]

However, it is precisely this obsession with "power over a creature's whole life," this desire to render "the resistance of the victim ineffectual, making him [utterly] passive,"[18] that suggests the depth of the cruel person's inner fears—her own horror at being out of control or vulnerable or worthless in her own eyes. Such fear thus explains, at least in some instances, the cruel person's intense need for power, which can both prevent personal attacks while simultaneously bolstering a shaky sense of self-worth. Kate seems to have just such an inferiority complex that can be appeased only by an exertion of power, specifically when she entices men to perform degrading sexual acts in order to prove their innate depravity. The irrational but competitive model of hatred that Jean Hampton proposes is at work here, in which the cruel person, by "controlling or harming or mastering her enemy," endeavors "to diminish him" and thus indirectly elevate herself.[19] Kate's delight in her picture collection—in the "state senator" with "bubs like a woman" who savors whips, the "professor of philosophy" with a taste for "toilet" water, the "minister of the Gospel" who mixes masochism and matches—largely results from these photographs proving her higher value. They are the evidence that she presents to her former husband when Adam questions her humanity; her response—"Do you think I want to be human? Look at those pictures! I'd rather be a dog than a human"[20]—reveals her intense need for superiority, a need that may have its foundation in a panic over her own personal worth.

However, while Kate's fears of inferiority are suggested, her terrors at being controlled, manipulated, and "looked into" by others, particularly men, are undeniable. Irrational fear[21] is the primary emotion motivating Kate's horrible actions throughout the novel: burning her parents alive, maiming Samuel Hamilton, shooting Adam Trask, torturing her whorehouse customers. Of course Kate denies this, declaring to Adam that she is "not afraid of . . . [him] or anyone else"; but Kate, as the narrator observes, is also a pathological liar. Her extreme fear of vulnerability arises, often with an attendant rage and hatred, every time she loses control. For example, when her pimp and sexually-tormented lover, Mr. Edwards, tries to kill her, Cathy feels "real fear," for it "had been the only time in her life [that] she had lost [complete] control of a situation" and "she determined never to let it happen again."[22]

This fear of vulnerability has already surfaced when her father whipped her, as a sixteen-year-old, for running away to Boston; Cathy's fear-driven response is to exude repentance while meticulously planning her parents' murder and her own escape. And again this fear arises during the birth of Aron and Caleb, the agony of which causes her to disclose her real self to Adam's friend, Samuel Hamilton. In this most vulnerable of circumstances, in which her "innocent" demeanor transforms to pure "hatred" as she tears at Samuel's hand like "a terrier worries a sack," Cathy's true nature surfaces. Her hatred of Samuel for looking "into" her and her wish to "have killed him if . . . [she] could" is really a reaction to her own fears of vulnerability toward the "forest of enemies" that surround her.[23]

Hence, it is paranoia that primarily moves Cathy to use the sexual "impulses in others . . . for her own gain," for Cathy had "learned that by the manipulation and use of this one part of people she could gain and keep power over nearly anyone"[24] and thus protect herself against them. Cathy's power over others, an essential aspect of her cruelty, is likely a way of coping with or denying her own fear, for cruelty—in its attempt to subjugate another's will to one's own— becomes the ultimate salve to a fragile psyche. Indeed, the malevolent person's sense of superiority over his victim depends upon this denial of fear, which is made possible as the more consuming emotion of hatred takes center stage. As Judith Shklar contends concerning "the universal cognitive situation of all human beings," we tend to see others as "things" or from the paradigm of "victims and victimizers." Some people, "to escape this uneasy subjugation, turn to sadism" and "become the fear they inspire. They see themselves as they have forced others to see them, as cruel," and this act of deception and of running "from oneself"[25] works for a time, for to be cruel is to be powerful and afraid of nothing. Kate, in her manipulation of men's sexual impulses, revels in this power.

But the power that comes with cruelty, with maiming another person's dignity and enjoying his suffering, only temporarily relieves the driving fear of someone like Kate because the underlying terrors remain unresolved. At the end of *East of Eden*, Cathy/Kate becomes an example of this insufficiency within the power dynamics of cruelty. Having lost her beauty, and hence much of her sexual power, she can no longer personally tempt men into her web of depravity. She has also begun to lose control over her employees (as evidenced by Joe Valery's secret mutiny), and thus resorts more and more often to hiding in her little gray room. Pained with arthritis and with no one to turn to, Kate finds herself "cold and desolate," "a sick ghost, crooked and in some way horrible." Upon finally admitting to herself that she may not be inherently superior to others, that they may indeed have had "something she lacked," she can no longer avoid her inner psychological horrors; her only escape becomes swallowing the little "capsule" around her neck that says to her, "Eat me." But even this brings no relief, for suicide, in many ways, is the ultimate act of surrender and loss of control. As Steinbeck writes, the once powerful and manipulating madam leaves this world shaking with "nausea" and staring "about in terror,"[26] unable to escape the fears that have driven her her whole life.

Thus, while Hallie marks the dependence of cruelty upon an imbalance of power, an underlying reason for the cruel person's seeking of power seems to be irrational fear. Kate's violent reactions against those whom she perceives as threatening—her parents, Mr. Edwards, Samuel, Adam, and men in general—belie her arrogant facade. In reality, Kate's ability to destroy others, appropriately symbolized in the sordid pictures of councilmen and clergy which she can mail at any time, is an indirect measure of her own terror at being seen into, controlled, and/or destroyed. Fear is the more fundamental component at work here, not power, for it is this emotion that drives her need for power, an essential prerequisite for cruelty. In this way, as Steinbeck maintains, "cruelty" is one of the products or "children" of "fear."[27]

Yet fear, in and of itself, is not sufficient to provoke cruelty. Many people deal with their fears through other means than seeking power over others, such as withdrawing from society rather than engaging it. And many who do seek power, as G. Rothman notes, are "free from any signs of cruelty."[28] Simply having irrational fears, or even using one's power to mitigate those fears, does not make one a cruel person. Nor is the possibility of cruelty without fear denied; in *East of Eden* Steinbeck's initial proposal that Kate is a monster "born without kindness or the potential of conscience"[29] may be true. Perhaps some people are inherently cruel and just enjoy the pleasure (sick as it may be) that comes from causing others pain and treating them as objects. Then again, perhaps people are also born with a susceptibility for irrational emotions, which idea returns fear to the center of cruelty's origin. Kate, at times, seems to have such an inbred tendency for fear.

Whatever the case may be, in those instances of cruelty where fear is an underlying factor, the awful exercise of power to humiliate and torture another being seems to require hatred as well. This connection between fear and hatred has been noted already by scholars, with June Callwood observing that our "fears [often] congeal into hatred" as a protective device against our own "in-adequacy,"[30] and Richard Taylor noting the frequent connection between hatred and cruelty; indeed, Taylor uses these terms interchangeably when he writes of "the irrationality of malice," a virulent form of hatred, lying in its *pointless* but deliberate infliction of suffering," a common definition for cruelty. Taylor sees hatred and cruelty, if not as near synonyms, at least as intricately intertwined entities. Furthermore, he argues that hatred is the primary motivation for com-mitting cruel acts: "The moral perception goes straight to the heart, to the incen-tive that produced and was indeed aimed at producing those evils, and the one thing it sees, overriding everything else, is malice."[31] However, contrary to Tay-lor's contention concerning cruelty's pointlessness, the infliction of suffering has a very definite, albeit warped, purpose for the malicious person. Here, the competitive nature of hatred again comes into play, for a cruel act, in its at-tempted degradation of another, signifies to the hater the ultimate victory or proof of superiority—a "game" between hater and hated which the sadist is de-termined to win. In this way, as a competitive response, hatred is frequently the immediate motivation (more so than fear or anger) behind cruelty. It is this competitive, and hence insecure, aspect of hatred that demands "those evils" that rational people find so abhorrent.

Moreover, hatred not only *moves* a person toward cruelty in many instances (both in action and character development), it also *enables* cruelty or makes such cruel actions possible given its blinding impact upon one's ability to rea-son, feel, and perceive clearly and deeply.[32] Hatred, in combination with fear and anger, drowns out the appeal for kindness and humanity that most people, with a balanced range of emotional and mental capabilities, are able to hear. In its place, this most consuming of emotions leaves only the kind of "contempt" that Kate feels even toward her own parents and the adoring school teacher, James Grew. As she reveals to Adam:

> When I was a little girl I knew what stupid lying fools they were—my own mother and father pretending goodness. And they weren't good. I knew them. I could make them do whatever I wanted. I could always make people do what I wanted. When I was half-grown I made a man kill himself. He pretended to be good too, and all he wanted was to go to bed with me—a little girl. . . . He was a fool.[33]

Such open disdain for others and for humankind in general would seem to arise out of Kate's fear, anger, and hatred, all of which prevent her, at least to some extent, from truly knowing these "people" despite her protesting other-wise. Rather, as Steinbeck points out, Cathy really only "knows one part very well," human weakness and depravity, "and can't conceive the other parts" even though they exist. Such a blinding "hatred"—as that which later shines "in Kate's eyes" and audibly surfaces in "a long and shrill animal screech"—thus makes possible the objectification of the other that occurs in acts of cruelty: the labeling of all men as "liars,"[34] of Jews as a subhuman race, of blacks as "niggers" and Italians as "wops." As Emmanuel Levinas maintains, "cruelty," in its attempt to "integrate . . . the other" into the dominant person's designs, "ignores the Other" or speaks *to* him rather than "*with* him," and thus denies the infinite aspects of the other or those parts of her that cannot be subsumed within a mere definition or totalization.[35] Hatred, by coloring what the cruel person sees and distorting what he thinks or feels, may play the immediate and primary role in this reduction of others to mere objects.

And yet, ironically, cruelty also requires its victim to be human as well as subhuman, subject in being aware of the cruelty and object in receiving it, active in an observing sense and passive in one's inability to escape the cruel person's designs. Or, as Hallie perceives, cruelty demands a kind of participating "awareness" upon the part of the victim—"[t]here is no cruelty without consciousness"[36]—while also paralyzing and rendering "her even more passive than she was before. It enchants, enthralls her, makes the will of another her law."[37] In this way, cruelty, as motivated and enabled by a sustained state of hatred, becomes the ultimate act of irrationality, for as with hatred cruelty "is satisfied precisely when it is not satisfied, since the Other satisfies it only by becoming an object, but can never become object enough, since at the same time as his fall [or degradation], his lucidity and witness are demanded." Hence, "the logical absurdity of [both] hatred" and cruelty.[38]

It is this "irrationality" that produces what Taylor describes as the "acute and revolting ugliness" of cruelty, for "the *pointless* but deliberate infliction of suffering"[39] makes no sense to the compassionate individual. Adam Trask, when confronted with his former wife's brutality toward men—her use of "sex as an instrument of torment"[40]—cannot understand her evil, although he does discern her motivation: "You [Kate] hate something in them you can't understand. . . . You hate the good in them you can't get at." Adam can find only revulsion in Kate's horrible blackmail pictures, as well as in her animalistic ecstacy over them: "'No one has ever escaped,' she said softly. Her eyes were flat and cold but her fingernails were tearing at the upholstery of the chair, ripping and fraying the silk."[41]

Likewise, Kate's first employer, Faye, a kindly and trusting madam whose whorehouse was once "the refuge of young men puling in puberty" and "the reassurer of misbegotten husbands,"[42] cannot comprehend the evil that Kate represents. When, in a drunken moment, her "daughter" confesses her delight in fixing "the gray slugs that come in here and dump their nasty little loads," Faye can only weep in disbelief: "'Kate,' she said, 'don't talk like that. You're not like that. You're not like that.'" But contrary to the sweet image she presents, Kate *is* like that, and the enormity of her cruelty surfaces despite Faye's protestations:

> "Dear Mother, sweet fat Mother, take down the pants of one of my regulars. Look at the heelmarks on the groin—very pretty. And the little cuts that bleed for a long time. Oh, Mother dear, I've got the sweetest set of razors all in a case—and so sharp, so sharp." Faye struggled to get out of her chair. Kate

pushed her back. "And do you know, Mother dear, that's the way this whole house is going to be. The price will be twenty dollars, and we'll make the bastards take a bath. We'll catch the blood on white silk handkerchiefs—Mother dear—blood from the little knotted whips."[43]

The cruelty represented in *East of Eden*'s Kate, far from being a mere literary aberration, has its real-life counterpart in those forms of hatred "acted out sexually" in one's "cruelty toward the opposite sex," particularly in acts of sadomasochism and rape. In the former category of sexual perversion, the masochist "seeks humiliation and punishment . . . by provoking . . . a sadist into behaving hatefully and sexually at the same time" (as in the naked state senator who enjoys whips or the minister with a "match under his skinny flank"), while the sadist "acts out hate by being cruel and degrading to the masochist" (Kate's pleasure in "heelmarks on the groin" and "little knotted whips"). Here, cruelty serves as a vehicle for the masochist's self-hatred and the sadist's gender hatred, as well as a means of denial for their irrational fear of the opposite sex. As Gerald Schoenewolf observes, "This ritual becomes a veiled, incestuous gratification for both . . . [participants, a temporary] overcoming of" one's fears of the other sex—either of "castration" or "annihilation"—that ultimately "does not resolve the underlying conflicts, but rather reinforces them by gratifying the sexual fantasies."[44] The codependency of sexual sadomasochism, with its complementary elements of submission and domination, make this form of cruelty especially degrading, for as Robert Morsberger notes, "Kate's [willing] customers are almost as depraved as she."[45]

Moreover, cruelty is also represented in *East of Eden* in acts of rape, what Schoenewolf describes as "the most hateful form of perversion, an extreme, sociopathic brand of sexual sadism." While such acts do occur from men to women, as in the suggested violation of Lee's mother by the crazed Canton men, Steinbeck provocatively describes those acts of "psychic rape" that women such as Cathy inflict when they play with a man's sexual desires and then reject him, or engage in sex and then disparage his performance, all in an attempt to destroy his sense of worth as a masculine being.[46] Cathy Ames is a master of such tactics, having "always been able to shovel into the mind of any man and dig up his impulses and . . . desires," taunting him with sexual delights and then slamming his male ego. Such sexual manipulation is likely what drove her Latin teacher, James Grew, to suicide. A "quiet young man" who already carried within him a "sense of failure" for being rejected "in divinity school,"[47] James would have been the perfect candidate for Cathy's cruelty: naive, vulnerable, and madly in love. It is certainly psychic rape that Cathy commits against Mr. Edwards as she uses his own emotions to tear him "to quivering fragments." As the narrator explains:

In their sexual relations she convinced him that the result was not quite satisfactory to her, that if he were a better man [sexually] he could release a flood of unbelievable reaction in her. Her method was to keep him continually off balance. She saw with satisfaction his nerves begin to go, his hands take to quivering, his loss of weight, and the wild glazed look in his eyes. And when she delicately sensed the near approach of insane, punishing rage, she sat in his lap and soothed him and made him believe for a moment in her innocence. She could convince him.[48]

At the heart of this cruelty, this desire to denigrate a man's sexuality and destroy the male ego, seems to be a virulent form of gender hatred. And underlying this animosity toward men and the power they possess, both physically and socially, is fear: cold, chilling, unspeakable terror of the other sex and the vulnerability that engaging with that sex in any intimate relationship would bring. This is why, as Beth Everest and Judy Wedeles argue, Kate "punishes men simply for their maleness,"[49] because their "maleness" represents (to Kate) not only depravity but also power, the kind of power that almost kills her when she underestimates Mr. Edwards and feels his rage firsthand. This denied terror of men is also a likely explanation for why Kate cannot enjoy sex with a man and has "very little of the impulse herself," for to enjoy intimate relations one must be willing to be vulnerable and dependent upon another—something that Cathy will not, or cannot, do. Rather, the only indication in the novel of Cathy enjoying sex is when she betrays Adam by sleeping with his brother, and here no real vulnerability arises, for Charles (as Cathy reminds Adam) is "like . . . [her] in a way," incapable of romantic intimacy or emotional openness with another human being. Charles' warm reception of Cathy, in his words a "bitch" and a "slut,"[50] is to him but another night of whorehouse rutting.

I would argue that Cathy Ames avoids her terror of vulnerability by hating that which she fears, and that her hatred motivates and makes possible her cruelty, her maiming of "the fresh and young and beautiful . . . so . . . that they can never be whole again."[51] By objectifying others she makes her depraved actions acceptable, for if men really are disgusting animals, her whips and razors and toilet water are quite justified. Hate, by subsuming fear and finding expression in cruelty, makes Cathy/Kate feel powerful and superior to those that threaten her. The frequent result of indulging this most caustic of emotions, however, seems to be the development of a taste for cruelty or the formation of a cruel nature, a state of near permanent hatred and fear.

Kate has this long-term character trait or vice; she is what we call a cruel person, someone who uses other people, deliberately causes them pain, and then sits back and enjoys her handiwork. For example, while effecting Faye's demise by taking advantage of her affection for her, Kate stretches like a cat, yawns luxuriously, and then slowly runs her hands along her body while smiling the faintest of smiles. She clearly enjoys manipulating this woman who has taken her under her wing and now calls her daughter; indeed, as her sensuality suggests, cruelty seems to take the place of sex in its satisfaction for Kate. And earlier, upon learning of her teacher's suicide by blowing his brains out with a shotgun, Cathy takes special pleasure in having made this "man kill himself." Upon hearing the news that James had frantically come to her house the night before but was turned away by her father, "Cathy wiped her mouth, and when she laid the napkin on her lap she was smiling."[52] Such pleasure, as Taylor notes, in what normal people would find horrible is clearly one of the features of cruelty that make this vice so incomprehensible.

And, yet, at least part of the enjoyment that cruel people experience by tormenting and humiliating their victims can be explained by cruelty's roots in fear and hatred. Cruelty, as the ultimate act of depraved power over another, can be extremely exhilarating because it temporarily relieves one's underlying fears of vulnerability and/or inferiority. The power to control and even destroy another person's life provides a temporary respite from one's deepest insecurities, a moment of sheer freedom as the cruel person abandons all that normally constrains us as humans. Caleb Trask experiences this exhilaration, for a short time, when he contemplates and then executes the deliberate destruction of Aron by taking his naively idealistic brother to see his mother, Kate. Cal's enjoyment over this devastating revelation, his laughter and "fulfilled cruelty" at what eventually spurs Aron to enlist and die in battle, has at its core this avoidance of his own fear that his father does not love him and will always prefer his "blond and beautiful" brother.[53] Like a powerful narcotic, cruelty subdues the pains within by providing a temporary diversion without.

Furthermore, some of cruelty's pleasure also seems to arise in its sheer venting of the hatred that often (and perhaps always) motivates and enables such acts. While never resolving the underlying causes of such displays of depravity,[54] and thus never really resolving the hatred, cruelty nevertheless allows this emotion a form of expression or release—a sort of "orgasm" to maintain the sexual analogy—which is surely a part of the sadistic person's pleasure. In addition, the competitive aspect of hatred finds rich satisfaction as the sadist proves himself superior or at least able to bring the other down to his own level.[55] Kate's delight in causing James Grew's death is surely linked to these acts proving her own power and worth. Again, in these characters we see the dynamic interconnections and interplay between irrational fear and hatred, which frequently comprise the emotional core, the real substance, of cruelty.

However, the pleasure inherent in cruelty in the end brings no lasting enjoyment or peace. In the case of Cal Trask, who at heart is not cruel and really loves his brother, his laughter and "look of . . . fulfilled cruelty" quickly turn into remorse for what he has done. As Steinbeck writes, "Cal had never drunk before, had never needed to. But going to Kate's had been no relief from pain and his revenge had been no triumph." The same can be said of Kate, who ultimately cannot escape her driving inner fears and dies sick and alone, a picture of isolation and nihilism: "And then her eyes closed again and her fingers curled as though they held small breasts. And her heart beat solemnly and her breathing slowed as she grew smaller and smaller and then disappeared—and she had never been." Even Steinbeck himself, as a character within his own novel, admits his regret as a boy from his cruel words to Mr. Fenchel, an immigrant that the whole town of Salinas persecuted during World War I. He remembers with "shame" his sister Mary and he approaching Mr. Fenchel, standing at attention, and saying "in unison, 'Hoch der Kaiser!'" He also recalls the man's face, "his startled innocent blue eyes" and his quiet "sobbing," as he and his sister turned around and marched back to their yard.[56] Cruelty, while offering immediate satisfaction, ultimately brings only pain and degradation to its perpetrators and, in many instances, merely continues the awful cycle of fear, hatred, and suffering.

But such need not be. Contrary to the often cited contention "that cruelty is [an] inexplicable" vice,[57] an understanding of the fears and hatred that drive the cruel person, the sadist or rapist, may very well be the first step in addressing many of the awful cruelties committed today. If, as argued in this analysis of Cathy Ames, cruelty toward the other sex frequently has at its core an intense fear of that gender, then we can work to avoid those things that only serve to alienate the sexes further. Whether it be social conventions denigrating women's abilities or college demonstrations pronouncing all men rapists, we must address any actions or attitudes demeaning to the other sex and thus indirectly promoting cruelty among the most insecure and hate-filled. On a more fundamental level, the proper and healthy upbringing of children may be the most important preventative measure. Steinbeck, a man who took the ethical development of his own sons, Thom and John IV, very seriously, traces in *East of Eden* the emotional pathway to moral and psychological dysfunction through his frequent mouthpiece, the Chinese servant Lee:

> The greatest terror a child can have is that he is not loved, and rejection is the hell he fears. . . . And with rejection comes anger, and with anger some kind of crime in revenge for the rejection, and with the crime guilt—and there is the story of mankind. . . . [T]his old and terrible story [of Cain and Abel] is important because it is the chart of the soul—the secret, rejected, guilty soul.[58]

As shown in the example of Caleb Trask, the cruel revelation of Kate to his brother Aron would have never occurred had Cal been more secure in the love of his father, Adam.[59]

Rather, as Philip Hallie contends in *The Paradox of Cruelty*, what is needed to break the cycle of fear, hatred, and cruelty is "for the victim and her allies . . . to find a way to power that will not provoke new responsive cruelties by creating new victims, but will end the long history of cruelties by upsetting the hierarchy of power and forcing human beings to face each other with a little fear and with much respect."[60] Such a healthy use of "power"—largely untainted with irrational fear, anger, and hatred—can approach cruelty without succumbing to its seductive offer of freedom from fear, its indulgence in the pain of others so that "one's own suffering appears to diminish."[61] This use of power must be a virtuous expression of courage and compassion, of reaching out to the "enemy" with respect rather than giving in to one's hatred and attacking them to quell one's own fears.[62]

Symbolically, this is what Adam Trask does when he finally confronts Kate in all her cruelty; despite being repulsed by what she has become, Adam is able to remain "detached and free" from Kate's "will" by refusing to give in to his fear and hatred. When Kate throws her final dagger at him, revealing to Adam that the real father of Cal and Aron is his brother Charles, Adam is staggered by the attack. But in response he shows a level of virtue that only maddens Kate more. As the narrator observes, "Adam closed his eyes and his head reeled with the rum. He opened his eyes and shook his head violently. 'It wouldn't matter [if Charles was the father of Cal and Aron]—even if it were true,' he said. 'It wouldn't matter at all.' And suddenly he laughed because he knew that this was so."[63]

In this way, by responding to Kate's cruelty with virtue and understanding, Adam avoids the awful cycle of pain that Kate tempts him with when she beckons, "And now, my love, take off your clothes. And I will show you what else I can do."[64] By refusing Kate's offered degradation and accepting Cal and Aron as his sons, Adam—although still a flawed father—answers his former wife's hatred with love and a certain nobility. Ultimately, as Richard Taylor concludes and Steinbeck's epic novel shows, this may be the only way to effectively respond to such evil, for "it is [only] a compassionate heart that manages to overcome [cruelty's] fear" and "hatred."[65] As the selfless example of Adam Trask suggests, the appeals to power offered by this most terrible of all vices seem too strong to be countered in any other way.

Notes

1. Judith N. Shklar, *Ordinary Vices* (Cambridge: Belknap, 1984), 37.

2. "Violence," *Webster's New World Dictionary of the American Language*, 1986 ed., 1585.

3. John Steinbeck, *East of Eden* (New York: Penguin, 1992), 236.

4. Ibid., 72, 184.

5. In one of the most insightful recent studies, Justin Oakley (*Morality and the Emotions*, Routledge, 1992) concludes that the emotions are central to such virtues as wisdom and compassion, for they provide a sympathy and understanding impossible in the emotionally deficient person "characterized by insensitivity, apathy, listlessness, and detachment" (48-49). In the same way, and as this essay argues, destructive and irrational emotions seem integral to the development of the vices, particularly as enabling and motivating entities.

6. Mike W. Martin, *Everyday Morality* (Belmont, Calif.: Wadsworth, 1989), 141.

7. Martha C. Nussbaum, *Love's Knowledge: Essays on Philosophy and Literature* (New York: Oxford University Press, 1990), 19.

8. Shklar, 8.

9. Phillip Hallie, *The Paradox of Cruelty* (Middletown, Conn.: Wesleyan University Press, 1969), 26.

10. Richard Taylor, "Compassion," in *Vice & Virtue in Everyday Life*, ed. Christina Hoff Sommers (San Diego: Harcourt, 1985), 43.

11. Robert DeMott, "Cathy Ames and Lady Godiva: A Contribution to *East of Eden*'s Background," *Steinbeck Quarterly* 14, no. 3-4 (Summer-Fall 1981): 83.

12. Philip Hallie, "From Cruelty to Goodness," in *Vice & Virtue in Everyday Life*, 5th ed., eds. Christina Sommers and Fred Sommers (San Diego: Harcourt, 2001), 7-8, 10.

13. John McKenzie noted over four decades ago (*Guilt: Its Meaning and Significance*, Abingdon, 1962) that the time is far overdue for psychologists to "realize that ethical theory cannot be reduced to a psychology of morals, and [for] ethics and theology to acknowledge that human behavior is always within a psychological field" (176). This essay, while admitting essential epistemological differences, will nonetheless seek to blend these two disciplines.

14. G. Rothman, *The Riddle of Cruelty* (New York: Philosophical Library, 1971), 14.

15. Steinbeck, *East of Eden*, 161.

16. Hallie, "From Cruelty to Goodness," 7-8, 10.

17. Steinbeck, *East of Eden*, 502; emphasis added.

18. Hallie, *The Paradox of Cruelty*, 26.

19. Jeffrie G. Murphy and Jean Hampton, *Forgiveness and Mercy* (Cambridge: Cambridge University Press, 1988), 69.

20. Steinbeck, *East of Eden*, 322-23.

21. Irrational emotions are defined here as inherently destructive entities which tend to promote deviant character dispositions. In an admitted over-simplification, irrationality may be determined by using a standard similar to Aristotle's concept of the "mean," namely: 1) is the emotion extreme or deficient in its intensity given its provocation, and 2) is the emotion directed at the right object? Hence, rational fear would represent a "mean" between too much and too little fear, as "the intelligent person would define" such a mean (*Nicomachean Ethics*, 44), and would be directed at its proper cause, while irrational fear would fail on one or both counts.

22. Steinbeck, *East of Eden*, 74, 98, 121, 320.

23. Ibid., 192-93, 320, 551.

24. Ibid., 75.

25. Shklar, 20.

26. Steinbeck, *East of Eden*, 552-54.

27. John Steinbeck, *Once There Was a War* (New York: Viking, 1958), xx.

28. Rothman, 14.

29. Steinbeck, *East of Eden*, 72.

30. June Callwood, *Emotions* (Garden City, N.Y.: Doubleday, 1986), 97.

31. Taylor, 43, 50.

32. Oakley perceives the powerful motivational and enabling features of the emotions when he defines them not as mere feelings over which we have little or no control but rather as complexes involving "cognition, desire, and affectivity" which play a crucial role in our achieving clear perception, judgment, and understanding, and in motivating us to act in accordance with our values (34, 53).

33. Steinbeck, *East of Eden*, 321.

34. Ibid., 322-23, 325.

35. Emmanuel Levinas, *Totality and Infinity: An Essay on Exteriority*, trans. Alphonos Lingis (Pittsburgh: Duquesne University Press, 1969), 52; emphasis added.

36. Hallie, "From Cruelty to Goodness," 7.

37. Hallie, *The Paradox of Cruelty*, 83.

38. Levinas, 239.

39. Taylor, 50.

40. Robert E. Morsberger, "Steinbeck's Happy Hookers," *Steinbeck Quarterly* 9, no. 3-4 (Summer-Fall 1976): 112.

41. Steinbeck, *East of Eden*, 322-23.

42. Ibid., 220.

43. Ibid., 236.

44. Gerald Schoenewolf, *The Art of Hating* (Northvale, N.J.: Jason Aronson, 1991), 63, 70-71.

45. Morsberger, 112.

46. Schoenewolf, 72-73.

47. Steinbeck, *East of Eden*, 79, 161.

48. Ibid., 94.

49. Beth Everest and Judy Wedeles, "The Neglected Rib: Women in *East of Eden*," *Steinbeck Quarterly* 14, no. 1-2 (Winter-Spring 1988): 20.

50. Steinbeck, *East of Eden*, 75, 123, 324.

51. Ibid., 306.

52. Ibid., 81, 230, 321.

53. Ibid., 548.

54. Schoenewolf, 71.

55. Murphy and Hampton, 62, 75-76.

56. Steinbeck, *East of Eden*, 518, 554, 566.

57. Rothman, 16.

58. Steinbeck, *East of Eden*, 270-71.

59. The role of parenting, particularly concerning fathers, in the emotional and moral development of children has received a great deal of attention in the past decade. By far one of the best studies is sociologist David Popenoe's *Life Without Father* (Martin Kessler Books, 1995), which concludes that the influence of strong fathers and stable marriages is essential for the healthy development of children.

60. Hallie, *The Paradox of Cruelty*, 84.

61. Rothman, 15.

62. A concept very similar to Christianity's confronting evil while also "turning the other cheek."

63. Steinbeck, *East of Eden*, 322, 325.

64. Ibid., 325.

65. Taylor, 51.

"No Sanctuary": Reconsidering the Evil of Cathy Ames Trask

SARAH APPLETON AGUIAR
Murray State University

Created for what John Steinbeck considered his finest novel, Cathy Ames Trask remains one of the most irredeemable and inhumane characters in American literature. *East of Eden*'s narrator leaves no room for conjecture as he describes Cathy (later known as Kate): "I believe there are monsters born in the world to human parents."[1] Cathy lies, cheats, and murders, and her special field of expertise is perverse sexuality, although Cathy's vocation of sadistic prostitute is belied by her appearance as she is described as having "a face of innocence" and a "child's figure." The narration asserts that Cathy is possessed of an inexplicable and innate knowledge of depravity that has no known source; perhaps, however, such an absolute assertion needs reconsideration. There are several possible explanations for Cathy's mentality and conceptions (or lack thereof) of morality; examinations of the novel's Biblical theme as well as Cathy's interaction with Lewis Carroll's children's novel, *Alice in Wonderland*, offer insight into the nature of her character.

Situated within a novel that explores ideas of free will and the possibilities of breaking out of the absolutes of good and evil, the character of Cathy—as an apparently fixed character with no free will—has perplexed a number of critics. Louis Owens asks, "Is Cathy . . . a genetically misshapen monster who is simply predetermined to be evil because of something she lacks?"[2] Recently, Carol L. Hansen has argued that Cathy "falls into a triploid of familiar associations: an amoral monster, a satirical fantasy, and a genetic mutation,"[3] and Kyoko Ariki concludes that "Cathy is the product of a mutation which is destined to become extinct."[4] These critics assert that Cathy is an amoral creature, exempt from the dilemma of good and evil that possesses the majority of the novel's characters. Yet, although this assertion holds much validity, Cathy, stripped to her barest essence, could be read as a type of prelapsarian individual barred from the luxury of morality as she must be concerned with a primal sense of self-preservation.

In 1958, Peter Lisca in *The Wide World of John Steinbeck* observed that in his fiction Steinbeck's "women do not have a place, but they seem to be condemned to choose between homemaking and whoredom."[5] In *East of Eden*, this opposition seems firmly in place: Faye, Jenny, and Ethel are relegated to the role of whore while "good plain cook" Liza Hamilton and "deep scrubber and corner-cleaner" Alice Trask are definitive wife characters.[6] Yet the binary distinction fails to account for women such as Dessie Hamilton, Abra Bacon and, it seems, Cathy Trask, who cannot be thus characterized. In addition, in Steinbeck's fiction he often refuses to ascribe traditional archetypal characteristics to the women; in other words, there are far too many examples of wicked wives and mothers and heart-of-gold whores in his work to invoke the basic stereotypes of good and evil to his female characters based on their sexuality. Thus, Cathy's fixed status as wholly and irredeemably evil is an anomaly in Steinbeck's traditional characterization.

Indeed, the often paradoxical natures of *East of Eden*'s characters serve to underscore the novel's central problem: the definition of good and evil and how those definitions relate to *timshel*, the novel's ultimate assertion of free will. As the male and female characters struggle with and contradict edenic notions of good and evil, the impossibility of such absolute assertions becomes increasingly evident. For example, Adam's essential "goodness" is flatly contradicted by his failure at fatherhood, and Charles's fundamental evil is likewise challenged by his later attempts to love his brother. Similarly, Abra, the dutiful daughter and representative of redemptive femininity, ultimately chooses the "bad" Cal over the "good" Aron. Therefore, if Cathy Ames Trask is, as Robert E. Morsberger asserts, Steinbeck's "one wholly evil character,"[7] her characterization negates one of the novel's most basic contentions: that good and evil are not, in fact, absolute qualities, that a clinging to unchanging fictions of morality is often detrimental.

A brief summation of Cathy's journey through the text reveals her depravity. The narrative of Cathy's childhood is laden with insinuations of unnatural intellect and carnality. The narrator implies that Cathy possesses an elemental knowledge of depravity; she uses her sexuality at an almost impossibly early age to ruin several lives. For example, while still a child, Cathy apparently suggests that two teenage boys pay her for the privilege of removing her underwear. They are later charged with molesting her even as they swear that she was the instigator. At the age of sixteen, she attempts to flee from her childhood home, and after having been detained by her naïve parents, Cathy murders them. She then willingly proceeds to her seemingly inevitable profession: whore. It is only upon a miscalculation in her ability to handle alcohol that whoremaster Mr. Edwards finally recognizes how truly corrupt she is and beats her to the brink of death.

Cathy crawls her way to the farm of Charles and Adam Trask, two brothers whose destiny is to repeat the story of Cain and Abel. Adam, quintessentially innocent, seems marked for favor while Charles, bewildered by his own mark of evil, struggles with his unfulfilled yearnings for acceptance and deliverance from rage. Motherless Adam and father-neglected Charles are both ill-equipped to deal with a complex world, as Adam recognizes only the illusions of a romantic existence and Charles is likewise blinded by a cynical recognition of man's failings. Therefore, Adam's nurturing instincts fail to allow him insight into Cathy's nature while Charles's perceptions condemn Cathy: "She's just a two bit whore. I wouldn't trust her with a bit piece—why, that bitch, that slut!" Cathy understands Charles—"She had respected Charles—and Charles would probably kill her if he could"[8]—but she marries Adam for protection in the novel's first hint that Cathy is not nearly as self-sufficient as she appears.

Cathy never understands Adam's tender nature, and, just as damning, Adam is unable to comprehend Cathy as well. The narrator notes,

> Perhaps Adam did not see Cathy at all, so lighted was she by his eyes. Burned in his mind was an image of beauty and tenderness, a sweet and holy girl, precious beyond thinking, clean and loving, and that image was Cathy to her husband, and nothing Cathy did or said could warp Adam's Cathy. She said she did not want to go to California and he did not listen, because *his* Cathy took his arm and started first.[9]

Cathy does accompany Adam to the Salinas Valley, bears the twins she had tried to abort and who could be fathered by either Adam or Charles or both, and prepares to leave. When Adam tries to stop her, Cathy shoots him with cool indifference. She then resumes her profession, eventually murdering the "grandmotherly" madam Faye to inherit the brothel's ownership. After turning the whorehouse into a specialty shop for sadomasochistic perversion and fetishism, Cathy ultimately commits suicide after being confronted by the one individual— her son Aron—whom she may care for.

If Cathy's evil is particularly incarnate in her choice of profession, the depiction of Cathy contradicts many other portrayals of prostitutes in Steinbeck's work. In *Cannery Row*, for example, the narrator contends that whores can be regarded "through another peephole" as "angels."[10] Rose and Maria Lopez in *The Pastures of Heaven* consider their prostitution as "encouragement" for their Mexican restaurant's male customers, and Fauna, the Madam in *Sweet Thursday*, gives her employees lessons in etiquette, ultimately arranging a marriage for a protégé. Morsberger comments that in these novels, "Whoring seems positively wholesome."[11] Indeed, even in *East of Eden* Steinbeck rhapsodizes upon the virtues of the whorehouse: "the whorehouse was an accepted if not openly discussed institution. It was said that its existence protected decent women. An unmarried man could go to one of these houses and evacuate the sexual energy which was making him uneasy and at the same time maintain the popular attitudes about the purity and loveliness of women." Later the narrator equates churches with brothels, maintaining that both "took a man out of his bleakness for a time."[12] However, in contrast to those figures of prostitution, Cathy Trask is purely malevolent. In fact, potential customers are often warned against patronizing Kate/Cathy's establishment.

If Cathy is to be viewed as more than merely a one-dimensional character, certain aspects of her nature must be examined to determine the makeup of her psyche. *East of Eden*'s male narrator reflects, "there was a time when a girl like Cathy would have been called possessed by the devil. She would have been exorcised to cast out the evil spirit, and if after many trials that did not work, she would have been burned as a witch for the good of the community."[13] Barbara Heavilin argues that Cathy has chosen to "follow a life of perversion,"[14] yet does not articulate any cause for that choice. A logical conclusion to the question of Cathy's nature could be found in contemporary theories of psychology that might deduce that Cathy is a psychopath. Absent of empathy, psychopaths have neither conscience nor remorse; they are concerned only with themselves. However, although Cathy is manipulative, cold, and superficially charming—characteristics associated with the psychopath—she differs in one critical area: Cathy's acts of evil are usually not designed for her personal pleasure or satisfaction. In fact, Cathy's malevolent nature tends to present itself only when she is feeling cornered or trapped. For example, Cathy plans and carries out the murder of Faye only after having dropped her guard with yet another bout of alcohol; the novel implies that Cathy may have waited for the natural death of Faye to inherit the whorehouse.[15] Cathy also lacks the necessary narcissism of the psychopath. Although she is definitely self-absorbed, she demonstrates such emotions as fear and loneliness; she apparently never experiences pleasure but only satisfaction when her perceptions of humanity are proven true. Nor is her behavior obsessive through most of the novel; her primary goal appears to be self-protection.[16]

Surprisingly, *East of Eden* metaphorically associates Cathy with Eve as she is the mother of Caleb and Aron, the Cain and Abel characters. Eve's crime, assisting in (or, even, instigating) the fall of man, arises from her piqued desire to possess knowledge; thus Cathy's scorn for Adam Trask as representing the biblical Adam is revealed by Steinbeck to be a paradoxical fear of the unknown: her own inability to learn from the tree of knowledge. If Cathy/Eve, then, has failed to learn the knowledge of both evil and good, she must necessarily remain in a prelapsarian state, unable to distinguish a pervasive and uncompromising morality. And, most importantly, she is denied access to the most powerful principle of the novel: *timshel*. That is, without the basic ability to discern between good and evil, she—as a pre-fallen Eve—is barred from evoking free will: she lacks the power to choose. Cathy discerns that she has no choice; when Cathy comes upon evidence of human nature that does not correspond with her preconceptions that humanity is basically evil and fraudulent, she is confused because, as the novel states, "Cathy had always been able to shovel into the mind of any man and dig up his impulses and his desires."[17]

More than symbolically representing Eve, however, Cathy is often compared to an animal rather than a human. Nowhere in the novel is this more apparent than in the narrator's description of Cathy's labor: "there was no scream—only a series of grunting squeals." At one point, Samuel Hamilton, who is acting as midwife, threatens to muzzle her like a "collie bitch."[18] In fact, Cathy's physical description endows her with the appearance and nature of a serpent, corresponding with the idea, as Nel Noddings in *Women and Evil* notes that "the association of woman, snake and demonic power persists in contemporary literature."[19] Cathy herself denies her affiliation with humanity; she asks Adam, "Do you think I want to be a human? . . . I'd rather be a dog than a human. But I'm not a dog. I'm smarter than humans."[20]

If Cathy's psyche contains primal characteristics of survival untainted by human artifice and sophistication, perhaps her strongest instincts are those of self-preservation. For example, Cathy tells lies to save herself from punishment; she kills only as a last resort—to escape imprisonment; she even refrains from indulging in substances which would dull her survival instincts. On the level of the most fundamental natural instincts, Cathy's "immoral" strategies are invoked whenever she is cornered or her freedom of identity is challenged. Even Cathy's murder of Faye can be read as a means of acquiring a safe and strongly armed fortress. Cathy only commits suicide when she feels that she has been exposed by her son Cal's undeniable revelation of her nature. Thus, although Cathy's actions appear to have the hallmarks of free will and choice, she is behaving instinctually rather than logically or morally; that is, her deeds are dictated by survival and not by higher faculties that measure actions by freely considered values.

Late in the novel both Adam and Cal accuse Cathy of "lacking something," and this lack is implied to be the virtues of compassion and love. Many critics agree that Cathy is a study in human omission,[21] yet Cathy finds no use for what she sees as the luxury of caring for others. That is, because Cathy is consumed by her need to protect herself, she has no decisive ability to sacrifice for others unless it is to her benefit. Thus, if she is, in fact, a representative of Eve, her bite of the apple has not endowed her with the knowledge of good and evil. She is only capable of a childlike egocentricity, an almost desperate need to isolate herself against encroachment, to protect her self at all costs. She feels herself to be "cold and desolate, alone and desolate,"[22] and also beyond the moral world.

From early childhood, Cathy has realized with a precocious intellect and ensuing cynicism that the world is not interested in who she is but only with the appearance she presents. Even her parents are unwilling to penetrate beneath her constructed veneer and become responsible for her moral training. Cathy tells Adam, "When I was a little girl I knew what stupid lying fools [people] were— my own mother and father pretending goodness. And they weren't good. I knew them. I could always make them do whatever I wanted." Cathy contends that she does not feel hatred toward others, but only "contempt." She laments, "I remember how they talked. 'Isn't she a pretty little thing, so sweet, so dainty?' And no one knew me." Cathy believes that the world is populated with liars and hypocrites. When Adam asks her, "Do you mean that in the whole world there's only evil and folly," she responds, "That's exactly what I mean."[23]

Conventional aspects of self-sacrificing morality are completely untenable for Cathy. Cathy has penetrated beneath the veil of what she perceives as false and shallow morality to a core of depravity. As Cathy has consistently fooled all of those about her with her appearance, she adapts herself into an agent of self-protection. Seeing only evil and depravity in others, she develops the means to shield herself from becoming a helpless part of the world she fears. Yet in the final hours of her existence, we learn that she had early on fostered a fantasy involving *Alice in Wonderland*; in particular, Cathy has imagined that she may shrink herself to avoid the gaze and ways of the world. This fantasy is startling because it is not the fantasy of a power-hungry and destructive woman; rather, it is the fantasy of a frightened child.

Of all the childhood figures she might have had at her disposal to emulate, the question then remains: Why Alice? Alice, both in Wonderland and through the looking glass, confronts false worlds. The characters inhabiting these places seem to find their world to be a place of normalcy; however, Alice knows the truth. For example, Alice is perfectly capable of discerning that the Mad Hatter's tea party is a travesty of the ceremonial good manners expected at such affairs. Cathy, then, associates with Alice because, like Alice, Cathy is certain that she knows the truth. Cathy views her own world as one of hypocrisy, adamant in her assessment that humanity is comprised of liars. And in the text of *Alice in Wonderland*, Alice too views the place she has fallen into as one that is compromised in the areas of truth and morality.

In the children's novel, Alice initially desires entrance into "the loveliest garden" with "beds of bright flowers and . . . cool fountains."[24] However, no matter what Alice tries, she finds her way into the garden blocked by circumstances that she is unable to control. Throughout her journey Alice repeatedly attempts to correct miscommunication and educate Wonderland's inhabitants, yet no one seems interested in correction. The citizens of Wonderland, in one form of elaborate charade or another, cling to hypocrisy and insist that all others agree with their fallacies. For example, although it is well known that none of the subjects whom the Queen orders to be decapitated are actually punished with this sentence, all the croquet players act as if the Queen's commands actually have power. In fact, the Gryphon assures Alice, "It's all [the Queen's] fancy, that they never execute nobody, you know." Ultimately Alice learns to conform, to pretend. She lies to the Queen to flatter her, patiently waits for the boring Mock Turtle to tell his tale of woe, and outwardly accepts his preposterous explanation of school curriculum (Ambition, Distraction, Uglification, and Derision), while inwardly questioning its meaning. Alice learns to present the image that is most acceptable to Wonderland. It is only when she grows large enough to feel safe that she contradicts the court, accusing the participants of being ridiculous. Just before waking she has the satisfaction of saying to the Queen, "Who cares for *you*?"[25] Likewise, Cathy's ambition is to grow large enough financially to move to New York in anonymity. As Carol Hansen notes, like Alice, Cathy believes she "is not culpable but is instead an observer of the true monsters—the mad hatters, the queens and kings of hearts."[26] Cathy, in all of her dealings with people, has never found anyone to "love her and trust her" as she imagines Alice does.[27]

In the preface to *Alice in Wonderland*, Lewis Carroll contends that the child—and thus Alice—is a "spirit fresh from God's hands, on whom no shadow of sin . . . has yet fallen."[28] Cathy believes that inside her self she is not "soiled"; she is "clean and bright."[29] She reasons that humanity's duplicity has caused her to resort to extreme measures to survive. And, like Alice, who may employ less than moral standards to negotiate her way through Wonderland,[30] Cathy too justifies her behavior as necessary.

Cathy is fascinated by and admires her "good" son Aron, whom she dares not approach, yet she speaks about him with familiarity with the troubled Cal. Indeed, she recognizes Cal with his knowledge of evil; however, instead of identifying with Cal, she seems to share something with Aron beyond the physical similarities, and that something might be the fear she senses within Aron. Aron's rigidity and insistence on control is a similar manifestation of his mother's fear. Aron's dreams center on "purity and peace"; he wishes to "hide from the ugliness"—a wish he shares with Cathy.[31] Aron's younger fantasies revolved around a mythical mother figure who would envelop and protect him; similarly, Cathy's fantasies center upon a tiny friend who teaches her the means to shrink and disappear. On the day of her suicide, Cathy remembers her younger self:

> Most of the time she knew she was smarter and prettier than anyone else. But now and then a lonely fear would fall upon her so that she seemed surrounded by a tree-tall forest of enemies. Then every thought and word and look was aimed to hurt her, and she had no place to run and hide. And she would cry in panic because there was no escape and no sanctuary.[32]

When Cal exposes Cathy to Aron, Aron reacts with "mad shock" and "ugly words aimed not so much at her as at himself."[33] Cathy could be feeling remorse for the first time in her life as she prepares to kill herself; however, in looking upon her "blond and beautiful" son's face, she may in fact be seeing only herself. Just as Aron has constructed an inviolate life, separating himself from his family and Abra, Cathy has retreated as well.

Thus, it is possible that the character of Cathy Ames Trask, a uniquely prelapsarian creation, should not be judged through the lens of traditional morality. In fact, in Cathy's own conception of herself (at least throughout most of her story), she is the most moral character of all. In examining her society as she perceives it, she believes herself to be pure. Her justification centers on her needs for self-preservation in a world of hypocrisy. Yet the irony remains that although Cathy has attempted—fiercely—to protect herself, in the end she finds no sanctuary.

Notes

1. John Steinbeck, *East of Eden* (New York: Viking, 1952), 82.

2. Louis Owens, "The Mirror and the Vamp: Invention, Reflection, and Bad, Bad Cathy Trask in *East of Eden*" in *Writing the American Classics*, eds. James Barbour and Tom Quirk (Chapel Hill: University of North Carolina Press, 1990), 251.

3. Carol L. Hansen, "Beyond Evil: Cathy and Cal in *East of Eden*," in *Beyond Boundaries: Rereading John Steinbeck*, eds. Susan Shillinglaw and Kevin Hearle (Tuscaloosa: University of Alabama Press, 2002), 221-22.

4. Kyoko Ariki, "Cathy in *East of Eden*: Indispensable to the Thematic Design," in *Beyond Boundaries: Rereading John Steinbeck*, eds. Susan Shillinglaw and Kevin Hearle (Tuscaloosa: University of Alabama Press, 2002), 241.

5. Peter Lisca, *The Wide World of John Steinbeck* (New Brunswick, N.J.: Rutgers University Press, 1958), 207.

6. Steinbeck, *East of Eden*, 13, 18.

7. Robert E. Morsberger, "Steinbeck's Happy Hookers," *Steinbeck's Women: Essays in Criticism*, ed. Tetsumaro Hayashi (Muncie, Ind.: The Steinbeck Society of America and Ball State University, 1979), 45.

8. Steinbeck, *East of Eden*, 141, 586.

9. Ibid., 152.

10. John Steinbeck, *Cannery Row* (New York: Viking, 1945), 1.

11. Morsberger, 47.

12. Steinbeck, *East of Eden*, 104, 249.

13. Ibid., 83.

14. Barbara A. Heavilin, "Steinbeck's Exploration of Good and Evil: Structural and Thematic Unity in *East of Eden*," *Steinbeck Quarterly* 26, no. 3-4 (Summer-Fall 1993): 94.

15. After Cathy reveals her sadistic nature to Faye, the novel notes that Cathy feels "dread" and "panic" when she realizes what she has said and done under the influence of alcohol (337).

16. The text states, "[Cathy] never hurried. If a barrier arose, she waited until it disappeared before continuing. She was capable of complete relaxation between the times for action" (340).

17. Steinbeck, *East of Eden*, 261.

18. Ibid., 221-22.

19. Nel Noddings, *Women and Evil* (Berkeley: University of California Press, 1989), 54. Interestingly enough, in *Alice in Wonderland* the heroine also experiences herself as a snake, frightening a pigeon that is protecting its nest.

20. Steinbeck, *East of Eden*, 372.

21. See, for example, Owens's essay.

22. Steinbeck, *East of Eden*, 632.

23. Ibid., 370-71.

24. Lewis Carroll, *Alice's Adventures in Wonderland & Through the Looking Glass* (New York: Macmillan, 1966), 6.

25. Ibid., 91, 94, 122.

26. Hansen, 224.

27. Steinbeck, *East of Eden*, 589.

28. Carroll, xi.

29. Steinbeck, *East of Eden*, 586.

30. For example, Alice is rude to her elders in Wonderland, steals concoctions to regulate her growth, and ultimately terrorizes the Queen's court.

31. Steinbeck, *East of Eden*, 584.

32. Ibid., 631.

33. Ibid., 635.

Business, Sex, and Ethics in *The Wayward Bus*

JOSEPH ALLEGRETTI
Siena College

Most critics consider *The Wayward Bus*, published in 1947, an inferior book, evidence of Steinbeck's alleged artistic decline after his great works of the 1930s. Warren French, for example, claims that the book is "loaded with hokey symbolism" and is "disappointingly banal."[1] Jackson Benson calls the characters "among [Steinbeck's] least lifelike and convincing."[2] Roy Simmonds sums up the scholarly criticism by concluding that *The Wayward Bus* is a book of "stereotyped characters and . . . worn-out themes that completely fail to address the problems and preoccupations of the times."[3]

Whatever the defects of *The Wayward Bus*, it deserves a more careful reading than it usually receives. In fact, Simmonds is wrong to criticize the book for not addressing the problems of postwar America. Peter Lisca is closer to the mark when he notes that *The Wayward Bus* (along with *Cannery Row* and *The Pearl*) represents "an examination of the underlying assumptions of modern civilization."[4] Howard Levant makes a similar point when he calls the novel "a trenchant, accurate portrayal of the darker side of the American dream."[5]

The Wayward Bus is a sustained attack on the morals of postwar America, particularly postwar American business. Steinbeck uses the novel to address some of the most important issues of the time, issues that remain important today: questions of business ethics, the difference between good work and immoral work, and the relationship between business and sexuality. In the wake of the Enron collapse and other recent business ethics scandals, Steinbeck's critique of business, ethics, and American culture has, if anything, become more relevant and worthy of attention.

Business and Ethics

One of the passengers on Steinbeck's bus is Elliot Pritchard, a company president who looks "like Truman and like the vice-presidents of companies and like certified public accountants."[6] Although he had dabbled in radical politics as a youth (even voting for Eugene Debs), he has long since retreated into a colorless conservatism. He is a new Babbitt for a new era. He wants to fit in, be part of the crowd:

> He was never alone. His business was conducted by groups of men who worked alike, thought alike, and even looked alike. . . . Wherever he went he was not one man but a unit in a corporation, a unit in a club, in a lodge, in a church, in a political party. His thoughts and ideas were never subjected to criticism since he willingly associated only with people like himself. . . . He did not want to stand out from his group. He would like to have risen to the top of it and be admired by it; but it would not occur to him to leave it.[7]

Pritchard has little self-composure or self-confidence. He lives in a constant state of anxiety because his values come from outside himself, and he knows that at any moment he might slip up and betray the group: "It was just that people in his group watched one another. Any variation from a code of conduct was first noted, then discussed. A man who varied was not a sound man, and if he persisted no one would do business with him."[8] He lives a life characterized by self-deception and hypocrisy, both revealed in his dealings with the other passengers. Pritchard's dealings with Ernest Horton, in particular, allow Steinbeck to cast a critical eye on the world of business and business ethics. Ernest Horton is a traveling salesman for the Little Wonder Company who sells trinkets and practical-joke gadgets. He has none of the self-delusion that characterizes Pritchard. He is open and honest—"earnest"—about himself and the business world.

Horton has an idea for an invention that would transform a business suit into a tuxedo. Pritchard is impressed by Horton's "get-up and go."[9] He thinks it's a wonderful idea, a sure moneymaker, but Horton quickly disabuses him of the notion, assuring him that the big tuxedo manufacturers would never allow such an invention to succeed. "Mr. Pritchard nodded gravely. 'Yes, I can see the point. They have to protect themselves and their stockholders.'"[10] Pritchard, who believes passionately in a free market economy unfettered by government or unions, is oblivious to the irony.

Later, when the two men return to the topic of Horton's invention, Pritchard's hypocrisy is highlighted, because his real reason for talking to Horton is to be closer to the sexy Camille Oaks. Pritchard now suggests that they pool their resources. He will handle the merchandising of the product for a percentage of the profits. When Horton says again that the tuxedo manufacturers aren't interested in putting themselves out of business, Pritchard reveals his real scheme: to scare the manufacturers into buying out Horton's and Pritchard's company. Pritchard's desire for Camille Oaks is now transmuted into another kind of desire, the lust for profits:

> He had forgotten Camille. "Look ahead a little further," he said. "When we sell and dissolve the company we only pay a capital gain tax on the profits."
> "That's smart," said Ernest excitedly. "Yes sir, that's very smart. That's black-mail and a very high-class blackmail. Yes sir, nobody could touch us."
> . . . Mr. Pritchard said, "I hope you don't think it's dishonest. I've been in business thirty-five years and I've climbed to the head of my company. I can be proud of my record."[11]

Horton punctures Pritchard's illusions of business rectitude. He immediately drives the point home by casually mentioning how much better he will feel as soon as his letter registering his invention reaches the patent office in Washington. Pritchard is insulted and replies, "You don't think for one minute . . ."[12] His protestation may or may not convince Horton, but not the reader, for one page earlier Pritchard had been wondering whether registration by mail would hold up in court. He had decided that it would be better to work with Horton than to steal the idea, not because of moral scruples, but because "[o]nly the really big fellows could afford to lift an invention whole."[13]

Horton sees Pritchard more clearly than the corporation president sees himself. When Horton suggests that they meet in Los Angeles, where Horton has two women waiting, Pritchard replies, disingenuously, "Maybe we could talk a little business."[14] Horton won't let him off the hook, referring again to the women, understanding only too well that Pritchard is hiding both his personal and professional immorality under a veneer of bourgeois respectability. Rather than accept his own moral faults, however, Pritchard redoubles his efforts to prove to Horton that he is not the kind of person who would steal another's idea or have an affair. He offers Horton his own idea for a kind of spring-loaded cuff link. Horton, ever the realist, asks him what he wants. Pritchard replies that he wants nothing, but immediately he is plagued by the fear that Horton might make a million dollars off the idea. When Horton thanks him and hands him the address where he'll be staying in Los Angeles, Pritchard pockets it nervously. He decides to throw it away as soon as he can—but not before memorizing the number.

Pritchard's one attempt to do a good deed is reduced in the end to nothing but another shabby business deal. With a clarity of vision that Pritchard, trapped in his veil of self-deception, does not have, Horton knows when business becomes blackmail and is not afraid to say so. Later, when Pritchard ruminates about the feelings of cynicism that are infecting younger people, Horton explains that his father had faith in two things: honesty and thrift. Horton's father had thought that if a man worked hard enough he could protect himself. But those days are gone. Pritchard, as usual, totally misunderstands Horton's point and says that people aren't thrifty anymore because of high taxes, which destroys ambition. It's the returning veterans, he says, that are the problem: "They think the government owes them a living and we can't afford it."[15] Horton, a decorated veteran, responds in words that surely echo Steinbeck's own thoughts:

> "I read in the papers about our best men. They must be our best men 'cause they got the biggest jobs. I read what they say and do, and I've got a lot of friends that you might call bums, and there's awful little difference between them. I've heard some of the bums get off stuff that sounded even better than the stuff that the Secretary of State gets off—Oh, what the hell!"[16]

Horton's reference to "bums" underscores a major point for understanding Steinbeck's treatment of business and ethics in *The Wayward Bus*. The "best men" are no better than—indeed, less moral than—"bums." In Elliot Pritchard we have the mirror image of Mack and the boys from *Cannery Row*, and there can be no doubt on which side Steinbeck's sympathies lie. As Richard Astro explains, "[T]he main difference between the two works is that in *Cannery Row* the leading characters are wholly natural men who resist the growing threat posed by the acquisitive brand of American, while in *The Wayward Bus* various representatives of this type become the leading characters and dominate the novel's action."[17] Peter Lisca puts it succinctly: "*The Wayward Bus* is a pitiless examination of the civilization which Mack and the boys reject."[18]

Pritchard is the epitome of this "acquisitive brand of American." But his incessant drive to acquire and control hides a nagging sense of failure and inadequacy at the core of his being. After the bus breaks down, Horton challenges Pritchard to admit that he knows nothing about the car he drives or about how to survive in the wild. After a fight with his wife, Pritchard feels "the sudden lonely sorrow that came so often" and remembers his childhood, when he had always felt a "little dirty and noisy and unworthy and his mother was always busy. And then the cold loneliness had fallen on him . . . that still came to him sometimes, that came to him now."[19] Pritchard's tragedy is that he cannot accept the hollowness of his existence but takes comfort in silly dreams of a time when Bob Taft will be President, buying everyone happiness.

Forced to confront his own inadequacies, Pritchard takes refuge in Hollywood-like fantasies, dreaming of killing a cow and feeding the passengers.[20] In this dream, Camille Oaks asks him if it is proper to kill the cow, which belongs to someone, and Pritchard responds, "Expediency knows no law. The law of survival comes first."[21] His answer to Camille, coming in a dream, may be the most truthful and revealing statement he makes in the book. For this is his business motto, his creed of moral irresponsibility and non-accountability: *Expediency knows no law*. Business is a jungle and only the strong survive. Pritchard has no "sins" in his business life, justifying his immoral actions as a "necessity and responsibility to the stockholders."[22] He is like those business executives who attempt to justify illegal or unethical conduct by claiming they are only doing their job.[23]

It is tempting to see Ernest Horton as the antitype to Elliot Pritchard because he is a decorated war veteran with a modest job who is struggling to find success. We have already seen his honesty and clear vision when it comes to business and business ethics, with his honesty extending beyond business to sexual relationships when he has more success with Camille Oaks than Pritchard has. And Horton is kind to Norma when she claims to be Clark Gable's cousin, playing along with her fantasy rather than ridiculing her. But despite his good qualities, Horton does not represent the model of the good businessman in contrast to Pritchard.

For one thing, Horton is happy to go along with Pritchard's scheme for blackmailing the tuxedo manufacturers. Immediately after Pritchard broaches the idea, Horton answers with a proposal of his own—that Pritchard join him in Los Angeles for some fun with "a couple of very luscious dames."[24] Beyond that, as Robert Morsberger notes, Horton is flawed by his irresponsibility.[25] Although Horton tells Pimples that he would love to have a home and that his wife is dead, in reality he admits to himself that "he didn't want a home. He loved moving around and seeing different people. He would run away from a home immediately. Once he had been married, and the second day he had walked out."[26] When he found out later that his wife was arrested for marrying five Army men, he was impressed, even admiring. Honest he may be, and, to a degree, "earnest" and kind—but Horton is no model of either the ethical businessman or the ethical person.

Does Steinbeck leave us with no models of good work and sound ethics? Should we take his portraits of Pritchard and Horton as a blanket condemnation of American work and business in the postwar period? Are we left with only "petty struggles, insignificant power-plays and foolish self-deceptions"?[27] The answer comes in Steinbeck's treatment of Juan Chicoy, the bus driver, and in his relationship with his assistant, Pimples or Kit Carson. Steinbeck here provides an alternative to the immorality, selfishness, and irresponsibility of Pritchard and Horton. Good and moral work, according to Steinbeck, seems to be marked by two qualities—*community* and *responsibility*.

Early in the book, Juan and Pimples work on the bus, with each working together with meticulous care, collaboratively and competently in what John Ditsky calls a "communion of work."[28] Work strengthens the bond between the two men, creating a "sense of comradeship" between them that is underscored at the end of the scene when Pimples asks Juan to agree not to call him Pimples anymore.[29] Juan agrees, and begins to call him Kit, in honor of his distant ancestor, the trailblazer Kit Carson. As Ditsky notes, this change in name is "a recognition of [Kit's] passage from adolescence to manhood."[30] The two men are now equals in some sense.

This scene also highlights the significance of apprenticeship and mentoring. Horton is a young man on his own, a traveling salesman, and subject to flights of irresponsibility. Juan, however, initiates Kit into the adult world of work and manhood. Perhaps we are to see Pritchard's fumbling attempts to forge a relationship with Horton as a counterexample—the hypocritical and self-deceived Pritchard tries to mentor the irresponsible Horton, but their conversation inevitably degenerates into talk of business blackmail and sexual escapades. Furthermore, there is no trust between Pritchard and Horton; Horton suspects the older man of scheming to get the better of him. Without trust a relationship of mentor and apprentice is impossible. In contrast, Juan and Kit like and trust each other, and this trust is the precondition for the experience of good work done communally.

Good work is also work done responsibly. While on the trip, Juan daydreams about leaving Alice and the bus and running away. He fantasizes about going back to Mexico and living the carefree life, perhaps in Mexico City where he can conduct tours and make more money. He'll simply leave his passengers to fend for themselves: "Juan could take care of himself and he was going to start doing it too."[31] As Ditsky notes, Juan seems much more interested in the welfare of his bus than his passengers. [32]

Tempted by the siren call of irresponsibility, Juan even makes a deal with the Virgin of Guadalupe, whose small metal statue sits atop his dashboard. If the bus breaks down, he will leave; if not, he will stay. Juan refuses to take responsibility for running away from his commitments. Instead, he shifts the burden of choice to the Virgin: "And now I am about to put a decision in your hands. I cannot take the responsibility for running away from my wife and my little business. When I was younger I could have done it, but I am soft now and weak in my decisions. And I am putting this in your hands."[33]

The bus does get stuck—with some help from Juan, whose face wore a "fierce grin" as he deliberately dug the wheels in deeper.[34] Interestingly, only his apprentice notices what Juan has done. Kit, however, trusts that his mentor must have a good reason for his actions. Juan knows that he has "cheated" on his deal with the Virgin, but he leaves anyway, telling the passengers that he will walk ahead and find a phone. Once again, only his apprentice knows what Juan is really up to: "Pimples knew he was running out. Juan didn't feel good about it now. Not the way he thought he would. It didn't seem as good or as pleasant or as free."[35] Juan knows that by running away he is violating the bonds between himself and Kit; he knows that he is doing something wrong.

As he walks away, thoughts of Alice and Kit come into his mind. He has responsibilities to both. He tries to convince himself that he'll get over his feelings for Alice—his love for her is just a habit, a trap. And eventually he'll get in touch with Pimples and explain his reasons for leaving. A vision of Pimples's "trusting face" comes to him, and he realizes that few others had trusted him. Note the telling detail—now that he has abandoned Kit, Juan returns to calling him Pimples, the name he had used before initiating the younger man into adulthood. Juan's joy at leaving dissipates as he considers his responsibilities to his wife and apprentice, and misery replaces the original sense of freedom.

When Mildred Pritchard, who meets Juan in the deserted barn, also dreams of running away and never coming back, they have a brief sexual encounter. She asks him to take her with him to Mexico, but Juan's flirtation with irresponsibility has ended. When Mildred asks him what to do now, he responds simply, "Go back and dig out the bus and drive to San Juan."[36] Juan can be tempted by irresponsibility and can even surrender to it for a short time, but, ultimately, he knows that he must return to the world of personal and professional obligations. He is honest with himself. As Levant puts it, "A return to the past is impossible, an affair is simply good luck, hence the real world is the moral call to duty."[37]

"The real world is the moral call to duty." To responsibility. To the everyday world of wife and work. Juan returns to take care of his passengers. He leaves the world of fantasy and reenters the world of commitment and caring. He does not love his passengers, he does not even like most of them, but he has duties towards them, and these duties prove stronger than any dreams of escape. As Astro notes, "To be sure, Juan, like many Steinbeck heroes, is masculine, strong, and a good workman from the beginning, but until he overcomes his personal fantasies and cares for rather than disdains his fellow men, he suffers from the same kind of illusions and motives of self-interest as the rest of the travelers."[38]

Compare Juan to Pritchard. Juan knows that he is responsible for his actions; in the end he cannot abdicate that responsibility or deny his moral accountability. Work is not separate from or divorced from the moral life. Pritchard, on the other hand, lives by the business creed that expediency knows no law and business has no sins, "for the cruelties there were defined and pigeonholed as necessity and responsibility to the stockholders."[39] Juan comes to know what Pritchard never admits—there are few necessary cruelties, only choices.

When he returns to the bus, Juan calls Kit by the old name of Pimples, as if to underscore that their relationship has been damaged and that the bond of communion between them has been weakened.[40] Pimples throws himself into the work of freeing the bus and destroys his shoes and clothes in the process. When Juan sees what Pimples has done, the ties between them are restored, with Juan's responsible act of returning to the bus restoring the communion between them. In *The Wayward Bus*, community and responsibility define good work, and self-deception and irresponsibility lead to bad work, and bad ethics.

Business, Sex, and Power

Steinbeck's critique of American business and business ethics is intensified by the subtle way he weaves together threads of business, sexuality, and power. In an examination of *The Wayward Bus*, Bobbi Gonzales and Mimi Gladstein argue that the novel's misogyny can be traced to Steinbeck's troubled marriage to Gwendolyn Conger. Whereas Brian Railsback has rebutted the charge of misogyny, these critics agree that sexual relationships in *The Wayward Bus* are loveless and often brutal. As Gonzales and Gladstein write:

> The relationships between men and women in the novel are never honest
> searches to establish contact on the basis of human interconnectedness. Every
> male/female relationship is seen as a power struggle, one in which the primary
> weapons are sex or brutality, and often a combination of both.[41]

Consider the relationship between Elliot and Bernice Pritchard. Although he
is a successful businessman, Elliot is clearly dominated by his manipulating
wife. Bernice is "handicapped by what is known as a nun's hood, which pre-
vented her from experiencing any sexual elation from her marriage." She uses
her frigidity as a weapon to control her husband:

> Her husband's beginning libido she had accepted and then gradually by faint
> but constant reluctance had first molded and then controlled and gradually
> strangled, so that his impulses for her became fewer and fewer until he himself
> believed that he was reaching an age when such things did not matter.[42]

At home, Bernice prepares bland meals and avoids spices because of their pur-
ported aphrodisiac effects. Bernice's "body and her mind were sluggish and
lazy."[43] Her only passion is for material things. Indeed, the closest she ever
comes to sexual arousal is when she eavesdrops on Camille's telling Norma the
story of how her friend Loraine manipulated a boyfriend into punching her so
that she could get a mink coat. As she listens, "Mrs. Pritchard's face was glowing. She breathed very rapidly. Her skin tingled, and there was an aching itching
feeling in her legs and stomach."[44]

Bernice has also used headaches as another weapon in her sexual arsenal;
her husband and daughter live in constant fear of these headaches. Mildred,
more insightful than her father, realizes that the headaches are used as a weapon
to govern and punish the family. Bernice governs the family, then, as her husband Elliot might govern his business—using every controlling tactic at her
command.

Elliot's reaction to his wife's power plays is instructive. He has a brother-
sister relationship with her, with his blocked sexual life leading to physical ail-
ments: "His nerves, his bad dreams, and the acrid pain that sometimes got into
his upper abdomen he put down to too much coffee and not enough exercise."[45]
And he sometimes attends stag parties where "naked girls danced on the tables
and sat in great glasses of wine."[46] He considers Bernice's headaches a fitting
punishment for his personal sins: "For Mr. Pritchard had gradually come to depend on the headaches. They were in a way a justification to him. They were a
punishment on him and they gave him sins to be atoned for. Mr. Pritchard
needed sins."[47] It is clear that Pritchard needs his *personal* sins because he has
convinced himself that there are none in his business life.

But this is another example of Pritchard's self-deception. His business life
is full of "sins," as Ernest Horton is so quick to realize. Pritchard's immorality in
the business world is mirrored by his unhealthy sexual relationships, for he lives
by "the controlled robbery and perverse sexuality that a [perverse] business ethic

permits and encourages."[48] That is why "he considered the young women who danced naked at stags depraved, but it would never have occurred to him that he who watched and applauded and paid the girls was in any way associated with depravity," just as it would never have occurred to him that his business practices are in any way immoral.[49]

The link between business and sexuality is made most explicit in the events leading up to Pritchard's vicious rape of his wife. Challenging Pritchard's business ethics, Horton concludes the conversation with an offer to do business and slips into Pritchard's hand the address of two gorgeous women. Pritchard next has a business proposition for Camille. Like the rest of the male passengers, Elliot has been sexually attracted to her from the start. He has struggled throughout the journey to recall just where he had seen her before. Elliot now offers her a job as a receptionist, but Camille has no illusions about what is really being offered and immediately penetrates Elliot's facade of conservative rectitude:

> Now let me talk a little bit. You couldn't ask a girl outright. You'd have to go around about that. But there's only two ways, mister. You either fall in love or you make a business proposition. If you'd said, "Here's the way it is. So much for an apartment and so much for clothes," why, I could have thought it out and I could have come to a conclusion, and it might have worked.[50]

Even more devastating is Camille's clear insight into the link between Bernice's control of the Pritchards' marriage and the world of business: "You say your wife doesn't run your business, but I say she does. You and your business and everything about you."[51] Bernice's tactics for controlling her husband make her well suited for success in the business world; indeed, as Camille implies, Bernice does in fact have a career in business, for she controls her husband at work, not just at home. Steinbeck again drives home the link between sexuality and business.

Finally, Camille reveals that she is the girl whom Elliot has ogled at his stag parties. Although she may have been forced to shed her clothes for money, it is Elliot and his friends who are the perverse ones. What they do isn't "pretty"—at their parties and, we might add, at their offices.[52] Following his talks with Horton, Camille's comments force Elliot to drop his mask of respectability, and his long-suppressed passions erupt. Imagining the naked Camille, he is overcome by sexual desires, entering the cave where Bernice is resting and brutally raping her. Yet, despite Elliot's brutal assertion of power over his wife, Bernice remains in charge. After Elliot leaves, she slashes her face with her fingernails, as Gonzales and Gladstein indicate, "to assure Elliot's guilt, a guilt that will result in his building her the orchid house she has been wanting."[53] As the novel closes, Elliot has achieved a painful insight into the sickness and immorality at his core. He asks himself, "Oh, God, . . . how do I get into these things? Why can't it be me here, dying, instead of this old man [the passenger Van Brunt]? He's never going to have to go through anything again."[54]

A brief examination of some other characters in *The Wayward Bus* reveals a similar link between work and sexuality. Louie, the bus driver, tries to steal the money that George finds in the bus. He calls girls "pigs" and is sexually attracted to Camille but at the same time "wanted to slap her face with his open hand."[55] Although he dreams of taking control of Camille, he realizes that he will never have her, and when she rebuffs his overtures, he blames a noisy old woman who has been bothering him. Once again, a lack of business ethics equates with an immature, violent, and depraved sexuality. Loraine, Camille's friend, is a prostitute who uses sex not only as a profession but also as a weapon. She needles her boyfriend until he hits her and parleys his guilt into a new mink coat. Bernice, who hears Camille tell the story, is shocked at its vulgarity—but, of course, Loraine is just a small-time version of herself, using the same weapons to get what she wants.

It is surely no coincidence that Camille and Ernest Horton, who are frank and open about the immorality of business, are two of the most well-adjusted characters sexually. Camille rebuffs all the men except Ernest, and they part with the understanding that they might get together for dinner in Hollywood. Finally, Juan Chicoy is one who has a healthy attitude towards his work—and towards sex. Although tempted by irresponsibility, he returns to his duties. Railsback concludes: "Juan and Mildred use each other and know it; both seem satisfied. She leaves free, and in a sense, still becoming. Juan goes back to his bus."[56]

We are left to reflect upon the complex tie between sexuality and business. In *The Wayward Bus,* both business and sex deal with the buying and selling of commodities. Sex becomes an extension of business—and business an extension of sex. Business morality corresponds to sexual morality. Those characters that are manipulative and dishonest in their approach to business are manipulative and dishonest in their approach to sexuality. As Howard Levant says, Elliot Pritchard is "imprisoned by the defects of his sexual and moral life."[57] The two go hand in hand; each implies the other. In *The Wayward Bus* morality cannot be pigeonholed. It is not possible, it seems, to be a good person in one's personal life and a bad person at work, or vice versa. The effort to be one person at work and another at home leads only to what Solomon calls "a fragmentation of the self."[58] For Steinbeck, wholeness or integrity is the hallmark of the good person.[59]

Whatever its flaws, *The Wayward Bus* is a rich and rewarding look at the morals of postwar America. Nothing has happened since its publication in 1947 to diminish its relevance. Indeed, in today's post-Enron environment, with almost daily revelations of business fraud and corruption, *The Wayward Bus* assumes even more significance. We need more, not less, reflection on questions of business ethics and the difference between good work and bad work. And Steinbeck may have something to teach us as well in his forthright treatment of the link between sexual and business morality, a link that is rarely acknowledged or explored even today.

Notes

1. Warren French, *John Steinbeck's Fiction Revisited* (New York: Twayne, 1994), 108.

2. Jackson J. Benson, *The True Adventures of John Steinbeck, Writer* (New York: Viking Press, 1984), 583.

3. Roy Simmonds, *A Biographical and Critical Introduction to John Steinbeck* (Lewiston, N.Y.: Edwin Mellen Press, 2000), 143.

4. Peter Lisca, *The Wide World of John Steinbeck*, New ed. (New York: Gordian Press, 1981), 232.

5. Howard Levant, *The Novels of John Steinbeck: A Critical Study* (Columbia: University of Missouri Press, 1974), 233.

6. John Steinbeck, *The Wayward Bus* (New York: Penguin, 1995), 30.

7. Ibid., 31-32.

8. Ibid., 32.

9. Ibid., 128.

10. Ibid., 62.

11. Ibid., 131.

12. Ibid.

13. Ibid., 130.

14. Ibid., 132.

15. Ibid., 231.

16. Ibid.

17. Richard Astro, "Steinbeck's Post-War Trilogy: A Return to Nature and the Natural Man," *Twentieth Century Literature*, Volume 16, Issue 2 (April 1970): 114.

18. Lisca, 232.

19. Steinbeck, 229.

20. It is worth pausing to consider Pritchard's dream in which he sees himself as the hero in a Hollywood movie. Most of the other characters in the book are also allured by Hollywood. Camille Oaks looks like one of the calendar girls, takes her name from a Camel advertisement on the wall, treats all the men she meets as sex objects, and earns a living as a stripper. Norma lives in a dream world in which she is Clark Gable's cousin. Pimples is addicted to sweets and takes a correspondence course to learn how to be a radar operator. *The Wayward Bus* clearly represents a full-scale broadside against the world of falsehood and advertising symbolized by Hollywood.

21. Steinbeck, 233.

22. Ibid., 177-78.

23. For a discussion of rationalization and business ethics, see Solomon and Martin, especially chapter 8, "'It's Not My Problem': The Concept of Responsibility" (*Above the Bottom Line: An Introduction to Business Ethics*, 2004). And see George's "'The Disintegration of a Man': Moral Integrity in *The Winter of Our Discontent*" in this book for a thoughtful examination of how Steinbeck deals with the problem of rationalization in his final novel.

24. Steinbeck, 132.

25. Robert E. Morsberger, "*The Wayward Bus*," in *A Study Guide to Steinbeck (Part II)*, ed. Tetsumaro Hayashi (Metuchen, N.J.: Scarecrow Press, 1979), 220.

26. Steinbeck, 125.

27. Astro, 115.

28. John Ditsky, "Work, Blood, and *The Wayward Bus*," in *After* The Grapes of Wrath: *Essays on John Steinbeck in Honor of Tetsumaro Hayashi*, eds. Donald V. Coers, Paul D. Ruffin, and Robert J. DeMott (Athens: Ohio University Press, 1995), 137.

29. Patrick K. Dooley, "Human Dignity, Work, the Need for Community and 'The Duty of the Writer to Lift Up': John Steinbeck's Philosophy," *Steinbeck Studies* (Fall 2002): 24.

30. Ditsky, 137.

31. Steinbeck, 195.

32. Ditsky, 143.

33. Steinbeck, 184.

34. Ibid., 197.

35. Ibid., 201.

36. Ibid., 242.

37. Levant, 222.

38. Astro, 117-18.

39. Steinbeck, 177-78.

40. When Juan leaves, Pimples makes a half-hearted effort to force himself on Norma, which perhaps signifies that he has lost his sense of masculine maturity and slipped back into adolescent irresponsibility.

41. Bobbi Gonzales and Mimi Gladstein, "The Wayward Bus: Steinbeck's Misogynistic Manifesto?" *Rediscovering Steinbeck—Revisionist Views of His Art, Politics and Intellect*, ed. Cliff Lewis and Carroll Birch (Lewiston, N.Y.: Edwin Mellen Press, 1989), 161; likewise, Railsback, in "*The Wayward Bus*: Misogyny or Sexual Selection," finds the novel grotesque in its use of the Darwinian theory of sexual selection to portray repressed and perverted sex.

42. Steinbeck, 51.

43. Ibid., 52.

44. Ibid., 212.

45. Ibid., 53.

46. Ibid., 32.

47. Ibid., 177-78.

48. Levant, 218.

49. Steinbeck, 50.

50. Ibid., 238.

51. Ibid., 237.

52. Ibid., 239.

53. Ibid., 165-66.

54. Ibid., 255.

55. Ibid., 86.

56. Brian Railsback, "*The Wayward Bus*: Misogyny or Sexual Selection?" in *After* The Grapes of Wrath: *Essays on John Steinbeck in Honor of Tetsumaro Hayashi*, eds. Donald V. Coers, Paul D. Ruffin, and Robert J. DeMott (Athens: Ohio University Press, 1995), 130.

57. Levant, 219.

58. Robert C. Solomon, *A Better Way to Think About Business: How Personal Integrity Leads to Corporate Success* (New York: Oxford University Press, 1999), 41.

59. According to George, moral integrity and its loss is the central theme of *The Winter of Our Discontent*. Perhaps we can see *The Winter of our Discontent* as Steinbeck's effort to deal comprehensively with the questions of integrity that had concerned

him in *The Wayward Bus* and other novels. In this sense, *Winter* builds upon and extends *The Wayward Bus*.

"The Disintegration of a Man": Moral Integrity in *The Winter of Our Discontent*

STEPHEN K. GEORGE
Brigham Young University-Idaho

> Without integrity, and the identity-conferring commitments it assumes, there would be nothing to fear the loss of, not because we are safe but because we have nothing to lose.
>
> —Lynne McFall in "Integrity"

> "Only in a single man alone [is there a difference]—only in one man alone. There's the only power. . . . Can't depend on anything else."
>
> —Cap'n Hawley, *The Winter of Our Discontent*

Moral integrity or, more precisely, "the difficulty of an individual's maintaining [such] . . . integrity in an avaricious and devious world," is *the* central theme of John Steinbeck's *The Winter of Our Discontent*.[1] John Steinbeck's last novel is more about a loss of integrity, however, than a complete lack of it, for Ethan Hawley, a middle-aged descendant of New England Puritans/pirates, begins this story as a man of conscience: a war hero, faithful husband, dutiful father, honest employee. His childhood friend, Danny Taylor, remembers Ethan as "the kid with the built-in judge,"[2] a man who has always taken his commitments seriously and who has based his life, up to this point, on certain principles and standards of conduct. In many ways Ethan is the literary foil to the author himself, who possessed an extraordinary measure of integrity; as Jackson Benson affirms, Steinbeck would "insist on his own beliefs and maintain them regardless of the many pressures to conform" to the "tastes" and "values" of others.[3]

This essay is an in-depth, philosophical exploration of Ethan Hawley's struggle to hold on to his ideals amid the pressures, internal and external, urging him to conform. It will also examine the thought processes that enable and justify his fall, as well as the disastrous personal consequences of Ethan's loss of integrity. A foundation for this study can be laid by reviewing some basic definitions and qualifications of integrity, a virtue once regarded as the backbone of all the other virtues given its ability to "strengthen" one's commitment to "honesty, fidelity, trustworthiness, sensitivity, courage, and temperance." Mark Halfon broadly defines moral integrity as "a consistent commitment to do what is best—especially under conditions of adversity." Such a virtue allows one to revise or reassess one's moral commitments but not to compromise them; the former action still maintains a consistent and honest determination to do what is best, while the latter includes the belief that one is "pursuing a morally unjustified course of action" and is therefore a violation of one's integrity.[4]

Jeffrey Blustein further defines integrity but does so in terms of the concept of coherence. For Blustein, one has integrity when there is "coherence between principle and action (for the case of a single commitment)" and "coherence within one's set of commitments (for the case of multiple commitments)." This idea of coherence demands that commitments—which may be to principles or people—be prioritized, that we "find some way of ordering or integrating [our] commitments" in a meaningful and moral way.[5]

Moreover, in order to consistently do what is best and find a coherence among the many demands of one's commitments, integrity requires a keen self-awareness and commitment to the truth, whether it be about oneself or the nature of one's commitments. As Gabriele Taylor argues, the person of integrity must possess some degree of "self-detachment" in order to accurately assess his or her desires, as well as the moral situation at hand. To have integrity means being able to value and act consistently concerning certain commitments (such as to the principle of fairness or to your spouse) which may not always represent what one most strongly desires at the time. Indeed, the person of integrity "is in control of his desires" and thus able to reason among competing demands and "identify with a desire which is less strong than its competitors" because it is morally preferable.[6] Hence, integrity requires the ability to honestly assess one's desires, to reject certain desires, and to will other desires effective because they are consistent with one's commitments.

But these commitments must be important commitments, or at least ones that a reasonable person would recognize as important, given their ties to our sense of identity and self-worth. Clearly some commitments are so essential to our concepts of our "selves" that to break them would mean "self-betrayal and personal disintegration" because they comprise our "core" and make "us who we are." Without adherence to such essential commitments "we could not 'live with' ourselves; we would not be the persons we thought we were."[7] It is here, in the realm of personal identity, that the concepts of lack of integrity and loss of self-respect meet. The person without integrity inevitably ends up identifying with conflicting desires, thus thwarting any consistent sense of identity. Indeed, lack of integrity "means the mutual undermining of identifications" so that the weak-willed or hypocritical or self-deceived individual eventually has no set of core values or commitments to identify with. And without any such core, without the unified identity that comes from acting on commitments that embody one's highest values, "values" that make one's "life worthwhile," self-respect becomes impossible.[8] As Lynne McFall's epigraph suggests, without integrity there really is no self to respect, for the self itself becomes morally fragmented.

Some people lack integrity simply because they are hypocritical or weak-willed, not necessarily because of outside pressures. Such people have nothing to lose. A loss of integrity, however, may require strong opposition, given its presumption of some substantial integrity in the first place. This opposition, or "the pressures above" and "below" that eventually change Ethan Hawley's moral "shape,"[9] is pervasive in the seaside community of New Baytown, a place where "the meanings of . . . good and evil" are "reversed"[10] and where "selling one's soul has become the norm."[11] In this world of upside-down moral values, money equals respect, the end justifies the means, and virtue and idealism are liabilities. As Ethan wryly observes concerning his father, "a gentle, well-informed, ill-advised, sometimes brilliant fool, . . . it wasn't depression or hard times that wiped us out"—it was his father's inability to adjust to the realities of a harsh, dog-eat-dog environment. Earlier generations of Allens and Hawleys, "a hard-bitten surviving bunch of monkeys," had prospered and gained a substantial fortune in the process.[12] Ethan, like his idealistic father before him, has not.

It is this fallen world that comes knocking on Ethan's door on Good Friday, the day commemorating Christ's crucifixion. Scarcely before he leaves his house, Ethan is met by Joey Morphy, the street-wise bank teller who has "the inside dope on everything" and who gives Ethan his "six bits" lecture on how to rob a bank. As Morphy sees it, being a success in this world depends on following a few simple rules, such as money makes money, always refuse the first offer, and a thing's value is worth what someone is willing to pay. Morphy's advice makes sense to him, given its obvious success in New Baytown, but Ethan is still repulsed by Joey's lack of principle and his reduction of everything to monetary terms.[13]

The temptations continue when Ethan meets Mr. Baker, his long-time friend and banker. In many ways Mr. Baker is Ethan's mentor: the perfect example of how to appear decent and respectable while simultaneously using any means available to advance his own interests. On this day Mr. Baker applies real pressure on Ethan to become an active participant in New Baytown's future, insisting that he is "letting down the memory of old Cap'n Hawley" if he lets this opportunity to advance pass him by.[14] With the departure of Mr. Baker, another temptation enters in the pert form of Margie Young-Hunt, a silky smooth, tightly-dressed woman whom Ethan recognizes as "a predator, a huntress, Artemis for pants." Seduction is the game here, with Margie sweetly asking Ethan to teach her about men, perhaps at her apartment "some evening." Margie, whose looks are beginning to fade and whose alimony is in jeopardy because of an ex-husband's failing health, sees Ethan as her future meal ticket. She also sets his fall in motion by predicting a change for the better in Ethan's financial future and then daring him "to live up to it."[15]

Finally, the external pressures upon Ethan reach a climax with the appearance of his boss, Marullo, and the drummer from B.B.D. and D., Mr. Biggers. Marullo, an Italian immigrant who learned the hard way how to make a buck, criticizes Ethan, whom he calls "kid," for trimming too much off the vegetables, for paying too much for meat, and for allowing people to charge on credit. As he tells Ethan, "Business is money. Money is not friendly. Kid, maybe you too friendly. . . . Money got no friends but more money."[16] Later, after Marullo departs and Ethan is left feeling a "darkness [descend] on the world," Mr. Biggers slithers in the door to offer him a cut on whatever he is willing to buy from his company. When Hawley offers to turn over the discount to Marullo if the quality is comparable, Biggers replies, "You don't get it. I don't want Marullo. This five per cent could be in cash . . . just clean green cabbage from my hand . . . to your pocket." The bribe is complete when Biggers slides a billfold over to Ethan with his initials on the outside and twenty dollars within. His parting words—"Don't be a fool. Everybody does it. . . . Everybody!"—leave Ethan more desolate than ever.[17]

Such are the pressures that urge Ethan, in the space of a few hours, to capitulate to the corrupt standards of New Baytown. As Raymond Sargent observes, "Ethan's growth of consciousness is rather a reversal of the moral and philosophical movement experienced by other Steinbeck characters: Joseph Wayne, George Milton, Tom Joad, Doc, Kino, Juan Chicoy, and Cal Trask." These characters all move, to some degree, from a state of moral confusion to moral clarity and strength. However, in portraying this reversal, the author shows how such a change "is more typical," given "the times that Steinbeck is presenting" and "the extent to which this 'new morality' or amorality is prevalent."[18] Moreover, this "new morality" is so accepted by its practitioners that even to question it provokes a righteous indignation, as when Morphy tells Ethan to "go and screw" himself for even suggesting that he would tell him to "do anything dishonest."[19] Ethan's moral resistance is clearly weakened as he closes the store and moves wearily along his way home. His earlier opening of the store's doors to a green and gold day has foreshadowed a future opening of himself to the values of this money-obsessed world.

Perhaps this forsaken man could withstand his own Gethsemane if it were not for additional pressures from his family. His son Allen has already bought into New Baytown's corrupt values and would "sure like to cut in on some of that loot" if only he could find a "gimmick." His daughter Ellen is likewise "sick of being poor," while his wife Mary, although a patient and supportive woman, longs for the day when Ethan will be a success. As she confesses to Ethan, "No, I don't love money. But I don't love worry either. I'd like to be able to hold up my head in this town." The ultimate blow comes when Mary attacks Ethan for "wallowing" in his "failure" by clinging to his "old-fashioned fancy-pants ideas"; in a nod to New Baytown's standard for respect, she exclaims, "Everybody's laughing at you. A grand gentleman without money is [still] a bum."[20]

Undoubtedly these words sting Ethan; they bring a sense of shame to Mary as well. But they also represent a conflict of interest between Ethan's commitment to live by certain principles or virtues and his equally important commitment to his family's welfare. As some feminist philosophers have noted, there is a problem in taking a purely abstract and impersonal approach to issues of morality. In this case,

Ethan's commitments to his family are real, and they indeed have legitimate needs that Ethan rightly desires to meet. However, taking a purely personal approach likewise has problems, as Blustein notes, for "the notion of an ethic founded on caring alone, dissociated from justice, [is also not very] appealing," given that some qualities, such as loyalty and devotion, are virtues only insofar as they encourage moral actions.[21] Perhaps the conflict between Ethan's principles and his family is not so stark since his family, even Mary to a degree, seems to have sold out to New Baytown's values. While the ends may be good, the means to those ends (which Mary does not really want to know about) are certainly suspect. And for Steinbeck, who saw life itself as a process, the means are just as important because, in the final analysis, no real difference exists—"the ends are the means."[22]

As Ethan is being "nudged and jostled . . . in a direction contrary to . . . [his] normal one," a life (in his eyes) of "failure" and "responsibilities" and repressive "habits and attitudes,"[23] even his once proud heritage as a Hawley beckons him to rethink his principles and character. True, old Cap'n Hawley and Aunt Deborah stand as symbols of moral solidity within a sea of change. For the Captain there were things that you had to do and other things that you could never do, such as burn a ship for the insurance money, a crime old Cap'n had suspected of Mr. Baker's father. And with Aunt Deborah, religion and morality were living, breathing things, as when "every Easter, Jesus really rose from the dead, an explosion, expected but nonetheless new."[24] But at the same time, Ethan acknowledges that most of his ancestors, although commissioned during wartime to raid enemy ships, were really as much pirates as patriots, and it was this raiding that started the Hawley fortune. His own ambiguous heritage leaves him little to stand on as Ethan, "feeling the blighting loneliness of the Crucified,"[25] finds himself being forced in a direction contrary to his deepest values. At one point in the novel, Ethan describes these pressures to conform as largely external: "The structure of my change was . . . pressures from without, Mary's wish, Allen's desires, Ellen's anger, Mr. Baker's help." But little has been said of the internal forces, the "pressures" from "below,"[26] that play an essential role in Ethan's loss of integrity, and perhaps in the loss of integrity of people generally. For *Winter* not only shows an environmental factor in the disintegration of a person's principles and commitments, it also reveals how Ethan's personal emotional state moves and enables him to embrace his "bold new world." As much as anything else, Ethan's fear, shame, and anger cause his loss of integrity.

Ethan Hawley is a man torn by powerful emotions—even the novel's opening pages resound with Ethan's shame at being nothing more than "a goddam grocery clerk" and with his anger at his inferior status to Marullo, to whom he must constantly "kowtow" and whose "mice" he would catch if so ordered. At the heart of this shame and anger is his fear that he has failed both his family and his family name by being nothing more than a "clerk . . . in a town they used to own."[27] Ethan's identity as a provider and Hawley is at stake, and he hungers for dignity and security, at the same time terrified that he will lose his job, which he hates. Because of the inner doubts about himself and his family's future, Ethan's confidence has slowly eroded, thus making him hesitant to take a chance in the business world again. Working in the store that used to be his own, located near the "half a block of real estate [he had to sell] to stock it,"[28] Ethan has his failure as a man constantly before his eyes.

Yet Ethan's fears over his personal worth are largely irrational, given their basis in New Baytown's corrupt standards. On this Easter weekend Ethan is in the process of accepting the tenet that a "gentleman without money is a bum," that money, given enough time, inevitably conveys respectability.[29] He is unable to assess his worth on more important aspects of his life, such as his adherence to moral principles, his fidelity to his wife, and his example to his children and the community, an example that later leads Marullo to see Ethan as a symbol of all that is good in the American Dream even though Ethan has inwardly forsaken his ideals. These acts of integrity could provide another moral standard to live by, as well as a strong foundation for self-respect.   But Ethan, in embracing a moral standard "alien" to his being, has instead come to feel a "false shame" which, although unjustified, has nonetheless inflicted a very real "injury to [his] self-respect." The pressures without, when combined with the effects of his fear and shame within, have made Ethan vulnerable. His extreme emotions exert a pressure upon him to be a self which conflicts with his earlier values and commitments, and hence a self which is not genuine.[30] And they also serve to distort his thinking, judgments, and perceptions, as reflected by Ethan's clearer, albeit brief, vision of Marullo's dignity when "his rage [was] all leaked away," thus leading Ethan to question, "If I've missed this, what else have I failed to see?"[31]

As the novel shows, Ethan fails to see a great deal. And it is under these conditions and pressures that Ethan makes a conscious decision to reevaluate his values, principles, commitments, and character by retiring to his "quiet, secret place" along the harbor, a "place where soul-shivers can abate, where a man is one and can take stock of it."[32] Influenced and/or blinded to some degree by these forces internal and external—his fears, his false shame, his family's desires, his peers' opinions— Hawley begins to lose his integrity by changing his own beliefs, values, and actions in order to accommodate the world that he now perceives, a world where one can temporarily trade "a habit of conduct and attitude for comfort and dignity," and then just as easily take it back again.[33] Before, Ethan had believed that certain attitudes and actions were not a part of his nature, but no longer. The new Ethan Hawley hungrily eyes Margie's assets, holds out for more money from Bigger, goes along with others' follies for his own use, and then scrubs the day's business off his hands with a little soap. Hawley has begun a rebirth during this Easter season that "is the reverse of Christ's," for while "Christ dies to sin, . . . Ethan's sinless life dies."[34] Ethan returns from his secret place willing to sacrifice almost anything, be it people or principles, in order to be successful.

Three elements, or what could be loosely called thought processes, mark this moral disintegration. Specifically, Ethan's loss of integrity is made possible largely by his self-deception and rationalizations, which echo those of Mr. Baker, Joey, Bigger, and Marullo. Moreover, these rationalizations arise from Hawley's acceptance of a code of extreme ethical relativity, which supports his rationalizations and encourages mental play with principles and relations that once comprised his core identity. For the sake of emphasis, these elements may be labeled "the three Rs of Ethan's fall": rationalization, relativity, and recreation. Not only does Ethan succumb because of the influence of outside pressures and inner emotional turmoil, his very way of thinking about and seeing the world must change in order for him to forsake his previous moral self.

The first element marking Ethan's loss of integrity, his tendency to rationalize, is a process by which "plausible and acceptable reasons for situations, actions, thoughts, or impulses" are created in order "to hide the real explanations from oneself."[35] As Michael Meyer notes, "rationalization" is also the means by which "corruption [is] . . . transformed into righteousness" in *Winter* as Ethan attempts to defend his various betrayals.[36] Ethan's peers are some of the best at this game of calling good evil and evil good. For example, Mr. Baker justifies his involvement in throwing out the old town leadership by insisting that the takeover is for the good of New Baytown; as he puts it, "A good businessman owes it to his town to help it develop." Likewise, Joey Morphy, a sort of John the Baptist who prepares the "way" for Ethan's transformation, is acknowledged by Ethan as "the best teacher I had ever had." Joey's rationalization that Hawley should take Bigger's offer because he needs it and no one "gets hurt" conveniently ignores the impact to the original company when B.B.D. and D. takes its business. Joey's (and Bigger's) appeal to morality by majority—"Don't be a fool. Everybody does it"—is a rationalization that sticks with Ethan, given his own spotted ancestry.[37]

However, Ethan's primary rationalization for temporarily laying aside his principles and commitments comes from his analogy (shaky at best) between business and war, both of which, as he maintains, are worlds based on survival of the fittest. For Ethan "there is no doubt that business is a kind of war" and money a necessary evil, an objective to be won in order to provide peace and security for himself and his family. In war Ethan was required to kill in order to survive and was even decorated for his daring and "wildness"; as he relays to Mary, "I was a goddam good soldier, potkin—clever and quick and merciless, an effective unit for wartime." Given his linking of war and business, with war as a condition in which the normal rules of morality are temporarily suspended for a larger objective, the next step in Ethan's reasoning is clear: why can't he "be an equally efficient unit in this time"? If with money, as in war, "the ordinary rules of conduct take a holiday," what is stopping Ethan from waging "all-out war [in the business arena] in pursuit of peace"? If, indeed, the times demand ruthlessness and he is being fitted into yet another role in order to survive, why not play that role for a time, regain his fortune and dignity, and then reassume his former character? If "war did not make a killer of" Ethan, how could the business war that raged around him do so?[38]

Such rationalizations help Ethan to avoid, at least initially, moral responsibility for his own actions. Instead of assuming blame for turning Marullo in to immigration and giving Danny money so he will drink himself to death and leave Ethan his property, Hawley is able, at least superficially, to depict the victims of his actions as "casualties . . . of a process." Indeed, Ethan's analogy between war and business enables him to see himself as caught up in a process in which the decision to forsake his commitments has been made for him by "a faceless jury" in his subconscious, leaving Ethan as "the last to know" of this change. It is by rationalizing his actions as necessary, as no different than those of other respectable people, and as part of a larger and uncontrollable process, that Ethan is able to justify his rise to the top. As he himself reflects, "In business and in politics a man must carve and maul his way through men to get to be King of the Mountain. Once there, he can be great and kind—but he must get there first."[39]

This reduction of all business affairs to a sort of jungle warfare is encouraged by the second element of Ethan's loss of integrity: the transition of his moral foundation from a belief in certain absolute standards of morality to an acceptance of a code of extreme ethical relativity. Such relativity not only encourages Ethan to see his world in a purely naturalistic or Darwinian light—a world of "the eaters and the eaten"—it also enables him to question whether "the eaters [are any] more immoral than the eaten," for "in the end all are eaten—all—gobbled up by the earth, even the fiercest and the most crafty."[40] Ethan begins this shift to ethical relativity in his first visit to his secret place. Here he begins to question his own character and the reality of virtue itself, which may in fact only be "a weakness" in human affairs. As Ethan puts it:

> They [Marullo, Joey, Mr. Baker] all told it straight. Why did it revolt me and leave a taste like a spoiled egg? Am I so good, or so kind, or so just? I don't think so. Am I so proud? Well, there's some of that. Am I lazy, too lazy to be involved? There's an awful lot of inactive kindness which is nothing but laziness, not wanting any trouble, confusion, or effort.[41]

Such questioning of his own conscience and moral conduct eventually leads to a questioning of all matters of conscience and morality; as Ethan observes, "If the laws of thinking are the laws of things, then morals are relative too, and manner and sin—that's relative too in a relative universe. Has to be. No getting away from it."[42] This shift in Ethan's moral "point of reference" allows him to make sense of his family's ambiguous status as patriotic pirates and of a business world where virtue is construed to be "weakness." In reality, as Ethan concludes, there is no virtue or vice, but only things that people do in order to survive. It is money, not one's character or commitments, that brings respectability, and thus one can abolish all rules of conduct in order to gain money and then reassume one's "virtue as easily as changing . . . [one's] shirt." Indeed, the only real vice, if one wanted to call it that, is failure, for "strength and success . . . are above morality, above criticism." Rather, no internal check or punishment exists within men—"the only punishment is for failure" and "no crime is committed unless a criminal is caught."[43]

This denial of any ultimate or metaphysical existence of good and evil, virtue and vice, underlies Ethan's naturalistic world view and his subsequent loss of integrity, a virtue that by definition depends on more permanent values and commitments for it to have any meaning. Without the assumption of extreme ethical relativity, human existence could not be so easily reduced to that of animals or soldiers, nor could one's moral accountability be so quickly denied and forsaken. In a world of fixed moral standards, shirts cannot be changed so easily.

Moreover, just as relativity can justify rationalizations, even becoming the ultimate rationalization for depravity ("There are no fixed morals so it doesn't matter what I do"), so do the brutal consequences of rationalizations serve to support relativity ("See, we really are like brutes, quite amoral"). With awful circularity, Ethan's insistence that "the laws of thinking are the laws of things" justifies his betrayals of Danny, Marullo, Mr. Baker, and his family, while his own depravity, his own changed nature, confirms his assumption that nothing is absolute, not even good and evil. Furthermore, out of Ethan's conversion to relativity and his comforting self-deceptions comes the third element of his fall, which may have been there all along as an instrumental element in his acceptance of extreme ethical relativity. This third element is Ethan's new willingness to test the moral limits by mentally toying with ideas and conduct that before would have been unthinkable—a sort of recreation with morality (or immorality) that eventually bridges the gap between his inner change and his outer behavior.

This perverse recreation, encouraged by the view that morals are but playthings anyway, takes many forms with Ethan. It surfaces as a game with Mr. Biggers to see whether he can get six per cent instead of five, as a toying with Marullo to find out his immigration status, and as a flirtation with Margie lined with undertones of infidelity. Even Ethan's betrayal of his childhood friend for the land that will be New Baytown's future airport has a game at its center; as Danny Taylor observes when Ethan comes with money supposedly for his cure in an alcohol rehabilitation program, "This is fun, Eth. This isn't chess, it's poker." The fallen Ethan, who sees his world with playful "new eyes," can now flirt with crime and immorality, or (as he calls it) engage in "a game of imagining," because there is really no such thing as morality anymore.[44] Ultimately, this recreation serves to move Ethan away from playing with crime to participating in it, as he himself reveals concerning his plan to rob Mr. Baker's bank:

> If my plan had leaped up full-grown and deadly I would have rejected it as nonsense. People don't do such things, but people play secret games. Mine began with Joey's rules for robbing a bank. Against the boredom of my job I played with it and everything along the way fell into it. . . . As a game I timed the process, enacted it, tested it. But gunmen shooting it out with cops—aren't they the little boys who practiced quick draws with cap pistols until they got so good they had to use the skill? I don't know when my game stopped being a game.[45]

Saying or believing that there is no good or evil is one thing; living as if there were none is another. Despite Ethan's rationalizations, his playing with morality, and his belief that he can adjust to anything, just as "rack and pincers must be just a job when one gets used to it,"[46] Ethan's actual experience with evil proves different. Contrary to his earlier assumptions, he finds he cannot just reassume his discarded virtues and habits of conduct as easily as he put them down, nor can he stop the process of his change at will. Rather, a "frightening conviction" grows within him "that such a process may become a thing in itself, a person almost, having its own ends and means and quite independent of its creator." A "fission in the soul"[47] begins within Ethan as he finds himself torn between two conflicting and mutually destructive identities: the ruthless businessman, who would betray even his best friend for the power and respect he craves, and the loving and upright husband and father who represents certain virtues to his family. Ethan becomes, as the novel progresses, a curious mixture of incompatible qualities: smooth in taking advantage of Marullo, adamant in reprimanding Allen's dishonesty; coldly calculating in his dealings with Mr. Baker for control of New Baytown, sweetly sensitive to Mary's needs during their weekend getaway just prior to his takeover. Such contradictions only confirm Mr. Baker's observation as he discerns the "new" Ethan who stands before him: in the moral transformation of Ethan Allen Hawley, we are indeed watching "the disintegration of a man."[48]

Evidence of this disintegration, the result of Ethan's loss of integrity, surfaces as Ethan finally finds that "there is no solid core of either goodness or badness for him to tap into," that his "soul seems to have become amorphous."[49] Eventually Ethan even begins to lose his memory of his ancestors, symbolic of his own loss of virtue since they—his father and Aunt Deborah and old Cap'n Hawley—are the ones who had always represented such ideals. Hawley excuses the loss of their once vivid "outlines" as being the process of an aging mind, saying, "I couldn't hold them forever," but their loss is nonetheless disturbing. Ethan, at least subconsciously, senses that drastic changes are occurring to his core identity as he is pulled between incompatible visions of himself. His breaking point occurs when Allen, caught in his own duplicity, accuses his father of taking "some" in his own "time, because they all do."[50] In this dreadful epiphany, Ethan realizes the fundamental disparity between his personal and public selves and the values that each demands. With crushing force, Allen's words reveal Ethan to himself; his own lack of principle and commitment becomes undeniable.

With this revelation comes an immediate suicidal response, a reaction quite understandable given the fact that an "effort to live a morally unified life is the basis for proper self-respect."[51] Ethan Hawley, whose moral life stands in ruin around him, finds himself with little basis for self-respect. Rather, his depraved actions and fragmented identity confirm the truth of Allen's words, leaving his "self" fully open to the disgust and self-hatred that have been building for some time. As evidenced by the fading memory of his ancestors, Ethan no longer respects himself and has instead been actively seeking "something to hate" in an effort "to take the heat off"[52] and avoid his own self-hatred. It is this self-hatred, encouraged all along by his extreme fear and shame, that drives Ethan to his secret place along the harbor with a package of razor blades in his pocket.

However, Ethan Hawley has also been moved during the novel by rational feelings of shame and guilt, especially concerning what he calls "the real crimes . . . against men,"[53] such as his betrayals of Danny and Marullo. These normal and healthy emotions, while being evidence of some lack of integrity on his part, also reveal Ethan's inner struggle to maintain his integrity, given that "the focus of guilt . . . is on the creation, maintenance, and repair of boundaries, within society and within ourselves."[54] In particular, Ethan's "dreams, nightmares, imagination, and memory are essential indicators of . . . personal struggle,"[55] as when he imagines he sees the limping form of Danny outside his restaurant window and pictures himself running after him, calling, "Danny! Danny! Give me back the money. . . . Don't take it. It's poisoned. I poisoned it!"[56] Contrary to his belief that he can live with what he has done, walling it off like a piece of shrapnel, Ethan's frequent episodes of guilt suggest that some of his integrity remains intact. Like the *Belle-Adair*, the Hawley vessel which is "not all dead if her keel's alive,"[57] Ethan's remorse is a sign that his moral life may yet be revived.

The end of *Winter*, although somewhat sudden and stilted, supports this possibility of renewal, for Ethan refuses the easy answer of suicide and instead accepts personal responsibility for what he has done, thus making "him a free moral agent in the fullest sense."[58] When Ethan finds the family talisman, a magical "translucent stone" representing intuitive ways of knowing that was placed in his pocket by his loving daughter, he reconsiders his decision "for a decent, honorable retirement, . . . a warm bath and an opened vein." Although he believes his own "light is out" and asserts that "there's nothing blacker than a wick," he also acknowledges Ellen's dependence upon him as an example of good, or at least of not giving up in the conflict between good and evil. Ethan finally decides to fight his way out of the surf so that he may "return the talisman to its new owner. Else another light might go out."[59] Such a selfless choice, based on Ethan's "intuition rather than on empirical cognition,"[60] indicates that Ethan's own light may yet still flicker. Integrity, then, as developed in following one's conscience or inner light, is a virtue that may be redeemed as well as lost.

Finally, we should note that this analysis of moral integrity would be impossible without Steinbeck's careful characterizations and use of narrative point of view. By telling most of the story from a first person perspective, the author shows the downfall of a man's character in a way that is impossible in real life, for we not only have access to what Ethan says and does, we also know his dreams, his memories, his internal conflicts, and his deepest moral ponderings. Moreover, through Steinbeck's detailed description of the circumstances surrounding Ethan's fall, we are able to distinguish several elements that in all likelihood accompany a general loss of integrity—irrational emotions, self-deception, distorted reasoning, belief in ethical relativity, and a willingness to play with morality, all combined with intense societal pressures to conform to corrupt moral standards. Such pressures seem to have only increased since *Winter*'s publication in 1961. As Sissela Bok argues:

> The very stress on individualism, on competition, on achieving material success which so marks our society [today] also generates intense pressures to cut corners. To win an election, to increase one's income, to outsell competitors—such motives impel many to participate in forms of duplicity they might otherwise resist. The more widespread they judge these practices to be, the stronger will be the pressures to join, even compete, in deviousness.[61]

Old Cap'n Hawley's belief that only a single man or woman can make a difference is perhaps the only real answer to what Steinbeck once described as an "all pervading, nerve-gas of immorality which starts in the nursery and does not stop before it reaches the highest offices. . . ."[62] Halfon concludes his book on integrity with the observation that the "authority of morality may [ultimately] reside in the judgments of" people with moral integrity, who are "entitled to a privileged moral perspective." For such people there is no need to "justify their moral point of view," not because they cannot, but because they already exact upon themselves the highest standards for moral judgment.[63] In the end, such committed people seem to be all that can be counted on, for rules, laws, and principles mean very little unless they can be applied by individuals possessing moral strength and wisdom.

Such an observation is only reaffirmed in *Winter*, which represents the pendulum swing in Steinbeck from his early focus on the group's moral potential (*In Dubious Battle, The Grapes of Wrath*) to the lone individual. Clearly, a mature Steinbeck now views society's redemption as dependent on the moral character of each person within that society, a philosophical shift that explains the preoccupation with moral integrity in this, his last novel. If John Steinbeck is correct in *Winter* that each "community of light" is really a collection of individual lights, where "everyone carries his own, his lonely own,"[64] then the essential worth of integrity to the modern world cannot be denied. As illustrated in the disintegration and rebirth of Ethan Allen Hawley, Steinbeck's Everyman, the virtue of integrity may be the only force standing between us and a world of complete moral darkness.

Notes

1. Warren French, "Steinbeck's Winter Tale," *Modern Fiction Studies* 11 (1965): 68.

2. John Steinbeck, *The Winter of Our Discontent* (New York: Penguin, 1989), 153.

3. Jackson J. Benson, *The True Adventures of John Steinbeck, Writer* (New York: Viking, 1984), 636.

4. Mark S. Halfon, *Integrity: A Philosophical Inquiry* (Philadelphia: Temple University Press, 1989), 8, 100, 162.

5. Jeffrey Blustein, *Care and Commitment: Taking the Personal Point of View* (New York: Oxford University Press, 1991), 11-12, 80, 94.

6. Gabriele Taylor, *Pride, Shame, and Guilt: Emotions of Self-Assessment* (Oxford: Clarendon, 1985), 112-13.

7. Lynne McFall, "Integrity," *Ethics* 98 (1987): 11, 13.

8. Taylor, 129, 137.

9. Steinbeck, *The Winter of Our Discontent*, 111.

10. Tetsumaro Hayashi, "Steinbeck's *Winter* as Shakespearean Fiction," *Steinbeck Quarterly* 12, no. 3-4 (Summer-Fall 1979): 111.

11. Michael Jon Meyer, "Steinbeck's *The Winter of Our Discontent* (1961)," in *A New Study Guide to Steinbeck's Major Works, With Critical Explications*, ed. Tetsumaro Hayashi (Metuchen, N.J.: Scarecrow, 1993), 255.

12. Steinbeck, *The Winter of Our Discontent*, 47-48.

13. Ibid., 8, 11, 34, 71.

14. Ibid., 19.

15. Ibid., 21-23.

16. Ibid., 29.

17. Ibid., 29-32.

18. Raymond Matthews Sargent, *Social Criticism in the Fiction of John Steinbeck* (Ann Arbor, Mich.: University Microfilms, 1981), 284-85.

19. Steinbeck, *The Winter of Our Discontent*, 34.

20. Ibid., 42-43, 91, 95.

21. Blustein, 7.

22. Jackson J. Benson, "Through a Political Glass, Darkly: The Example of John Steinbeck," *Studies in American Fiction* 12 (1984): 47.

23. Steinbeck, *The Winter of Our Discontent*, 111.

24. Ibid., 66.

25. Ibid., 45.

26. Ibid., 111, 116.

27. Ibid., 4.

28. Ibid., 17.

29. Ibid., 43, 73.

30. Taylor, 134, 140.

31. Steinbeck, *The Winter of Our Discontent*, 27-28.

32. Ibid., 57.

33. Ibid., 257.

34. Meyer, "Steinbeck's *The Winter of Our Discontent* (1961)," 253.

35. Linda L. Davidoff, *Introduction to Psychology*, 3rd ed. (New York: McGraw, 1987), 352.

36. Michael Jon Meyer, *Darkness Visible: The Moral Dilemma of Americans as Portrayed in the Early Short Fiction and Later Novels of John Steinbeck* (Ann Arbor, Mich.: University Microfilms, 1986), 424.

37. Steinbeck, *The Winter of Our Discontent*, 32-34, 140, 278.

38. Ibid., 73-74, 117, 129, 257.

39. Ibid., 109, 113, 195, 258.

40. Ibid., 60.

41. Ibid., 59, 72.

42. Ibid., 72.

43. Ibid., 117, 239.

44. Ibid., 153, 169-70.

45. Ibid., 275.

46. Ibid., 147.

47. Ibid., 197, 238.

48. Ibid., 333.

49. Bradd Burningham, "Relation, Vision, and Tracking the Welsh Rats in *East of Eden* and *The Winter of Our Discontent*," *Steinbeck Quarterly* 15, no. 3-4 (Summer-Fall 1982): 86.

50. Steinbeck, *The Winter of Our Discontent*, 245, 354.

51. Mike W. Martin, *Everyday Morality: An Introduction to Applied Ethics* (Belmont,

Calif.: Wadsworth, 1989), 75.

52. Steinbeck, *The Winter of Our Discontent*, 317.

53. Ibid., 275.

54. Roger W. Smith, *Guilt: Man and Society* (Garden City, N.Y.: Doubleday, 1971), 20.

55. Robert DeMott, "The Interior Distances of John Steinbeck," *Steinbeck Quarterly* 12, no. 3-4 (Summer-Fall 1979): 90.

56. Steinbeck, *The Winter of Our Discontent*, 194.

57. Ibid., 325.

58. Douglas L. Verdier, "Ethan Allen Hawley and the Hanged Man: Free Will and Fate in *The Winter of Our Discontent*," *Steinbeck Quarterly* 15, no. 1-2 (Winter-Spring 1982): 50.

59. Steinbeck, *The Winter of Our Discontent*, 357-58.

60. DeMott, 91.

61. Sissela Bok, *Lying: Moral Choice in Public and Private Life* (New York: Vintage, 1989), 244.

62. John Steinbeck, "Our 'Rigged' Morality," *Coronet* 47 (1960): 146.

63. Halfon, 167.

64. Steinbeck, *The Winter of Our Discontent*, 357.

Bibliography

Alcoff, Linda. "Cultural Feminisms Versus Post-Structuralism." 295-306 in *Feminist Theory in Practice and Process*, edited by Micheline R. Malson. Chicago: University of Chicago Press, 1989.

Allegretti, Joseph G. "Can Legal Ethics Be Christian?" 453-69 in *Christian Perspectives on Legal Thought*, edited by Michael W. McConnell, Robert F. Cochran, Jr., and Angela C. Carmella. New Haven: Yale University Press, 2001.

———. "Shooting Elephants, Serving Clients: An Essay on George Orwell and the Lawyer-Client Relationship." *Creighton Law Review* 27 (1993): 1-23.

American Library Association. www.ala.org (January 4, 2004).

Anderson, Travis. "Drawing Upon Levinas to Sketch Out a Heterotopic Poetics of Art and Tragedy." *Research in Phenomenology* 24 (1994): 69-96.

Ariki, Kyoko. "Cathy in *East of Eden*: Indispensable to the Thematic Design." 230-42 in *Beyond Boundaries: Rereading John Steinbeck*, edited by Susan Shillinglaw and Kevin Hearle. Tuscaloosa: University of Alabama Press, 2002.

Aristotle. *The Nicomachean Ethics*. Trans. D. P. Chase. New York: Dover Publications, 1998.

———. *The Nicomachean Ethics*. Trans. F. H. Peters. London: Kegan Paul, Trench, Trubner & Co., 1891. In *Ethics: Selections from Classical and Contemporary Writers*. 4th ed., edited by Oliver A. Johnson. New York: Holt, Rinehart, and Winston, 1978. 63-92.

———. *The Nicomachean Ethics*. Trans. W. D. Ross. Ed. Richard McKeon. New York: Random House, 1941.

Arts & Entertainment Television Networks. *Biography. John Steinbeck: An American Writer*. New York: New Video Group, 1998.

Astro, Richard. *John Steinbeck and Edward F. Ricketts: The Shaping of a Novelist*. Minneapolis: University of Minnesota Press, 1973.

———. "Steinbeck's Post-War Trilogy: A Return to Nature and the Natural Man." *Twentieth Century Literature* 16, no. 2 (April 1970): 109-122.

Beach, Joseph Warren. *American Fiction, 1920-1940*. New York: Russell & Russell, 1960.

Beauchamp, Tom L., and Norman E. Bowie, eds. *Ethical Theory and Business*. 6th ed. Upper Saddle River, N.J.: Prentice-Hall, 2001.

Beegel, Susan F., Susan Shillinglaw, and Wesley N. Tiffney, Jr., eds. *Steinbeck and the Environment: Interdisciplinary Approaches*. Tuscaloosa: University of Alabama Press, 1997.

Bennett, Jonathan. "The Conscience of Huckleberry Finn." *Philosophy* 49 (1974): 123-34.

Benson, Jackson J. "The Favorite Author We Love to Hate." 8-22 in *The Steinbeck Question*, edited by Donald R. Noble. Troy, N.Y.: Whitston, 1993.

———. *The Short Novels of John Steinbeck*. Durham, N.C.: Duke University Press, 1990.

———. "Through a Political Glass, Darkly: The Example of John Steinbeck." *Studies in American Fiction* 12 (1984): 45-59.

———. *The True Adventures of John Steinbeck, Writer*. New York: Viking Press, 1984.

Bentham, Jeremy, and John Stuart Mill. *The Utilitarians*. Garden City, N.Y.: Anchor Press, 1973.

Bloom, Harold. "Introduction." 1-5 in *Modern Critical Interpretations:* The Grapes of Wrath, edited by Harold Bloom. New York: Chelsea House Publishers, 1988.

Blustein, Jeffrey. *Care and Commitment: Taking the Personal Point of View*. New York: Oxford University Press, 1991.

Bly, Carol. *Changing the Bully Who Rules the World: Reading and Thinking About Ethics*. Minneapolis, Minn.: Milkweed Editions, 1996.

Bok, Sissela. *Lying: Moral Choice in Public and Private Life*. New York: Vintage Books, 1989.

Booth, Wayne C. *The Company We Keep: An Ethics of Fiction*. Berkeley: University of California Press, 1988.

Buchler, Justus. *The Main of Light: On the Concept of Poetry*. New York: Oxford University Press, 1974.

Buell, Lawrence. "In Pursuit of Ethics." *PMLA* 114 (January 1999): 7-19.

Burningham, Bradd. "Relations, Vision, and Tracking the Welsh Rats in *East of Eden* and *The Winter of Our Discontent*." *Steinbeck Quarterly* 15, no. 3-4 (Summer-Fall 1982): 77-90.

Burress, Lee. *Battle of the Books: Literary Censorship in the Public Schools, 1950-1985*. Metuchen, N.J.: Scarecrow Press, 1989.

Callwood, June. *Emotions*. Garden City, N.Y.: Doubleday, 1986.

Carpenter, Frederick I. "The Philosophical Joads." 7-15 in *Modern Critical Interpretations:* The Grapes of Wrath, edited by Harold Bloom. New York: Chelsea House Publishers, 1988.

Carroll, Lewis. *Alice's Adventures in Wonderland & Through the Looking Glass*. New York: McMillan, 1966.

Carson, Thomas L. "Corporate Moral Agency: A Case from Literature." *Journal of Business Ethics* 13, no. 2 (1994): 155-56.

Cohen, Richard A. "Translator's Introduction." 1-15 in *Ethics and Infinity: Conversations with Philippe Nemo*, translated by Richard A. Cohen. Pittsburgh: Duquesne University Press, 1985.

Coles, Robert. *The Call of Stories: Teaching and the Moral Imagination.* Boston: Houghton Mifflin, 1989.

Culler, Jonathon. *On Deconstruction: Theory and Criticism After Structuralism.* Ithaca, N.Y.: Cornell University Press, 1982.

Davidoff, Linda L. *Introduction to Psychology.* 3rd ed. New York: McGraw, 1987.

DeMott, Robert. "Cathy Ames and Lady Godiva: A Contribution to *East of Eden*'s Background." *Steinbeck Quarterly* 14, no. 3-4 (Summer-Fall 1981): 72-83.

———. "The Interior Distances of John Steinbeck." *Steinbeck Quarterly* 12, no. 3-4 (Summer-Fall 1979): 86-99.

De Waal, Frans. *Good Natured: The Origins of Right and Wrong in Humans and Other Animals.* Cambridge: Harvard University Press, 1996.

Ditsky, John. "Ritual Murder in Steinbeck's Dramas." *Steinbeck Quarterly* 11, no. 3-4 (Summer-Fall 1978): 72-76.

———. "Work, Blood, and *The Wayward Bus*." 136-47 in *After* The Grapes of Wrath: *Essays on John Steinbeck in Honor of Tetsumaro Hayashi*, edited by Donald V. Coers, Paul D. Ruffin, and Robert J. DeMott. Athens: Ohio University Press, 1995.

Dooley, Patrick K. "Human Dignity, Work, the Need for Community, and 'The Duty of the Writer to Lift Up': John Steinbeck's Philosophy." *Steinbeck Studies* 15 (Fall 2002): 21-25.

Emerson, Ralph Waldo. "Nature." 384-412 in *The Norton Anthology of American Literature*, edited by Nina Baym, et al. 3rd ed. shorter. New York: W. W. Norton and Company, 1989.

Everest, Beth, and Judy Wedeles. "The Neglected Rib: Women in *East of Eden*." *Steinbeck Quarterly* 21, no. 1-2 (Winter-Spring 1988): 13-23.

Fensch, Thomas, ed. *Conversations with John Steinbeck.* Jackson: University of Mississippi Press, 1988.

Ferrell, O. C., John Fraedrich, and Linda Ferrell. *Business Ethics: Ethical Decision Making and Cases.* 5th ed. Boston: Houghton Mifflin, 2002.

Fogel, Robert W. *The Four Great Awakenings and the Future of Egalitarianism.* Chicago: University of Chicago Press, 2000.

Fontenrose, Joseph. *John Steinbeck: An Introduction and Interpretation.* New York: Rinehart and Winston, 1963.

Frankl, Viktor. *Man's Search for Meaning: An Introduction to Logotherapy.* New York: Simon and Schuster, 1959.

French, Warren. *John Steinbeck.* Revised 2nd ed. Boston: Twayne, 1975.

———. *John Steinbeck's Fiction Revisited.* New York: Twayne, 1994.

———. "Steinbeck's Winter Tale." *Modern Fiction Studies* 11 (1965): 66-74.

George, Stephen K. "'The Disintegration of a Man': Moral Integrity in *The Winter of Our Discontent*." 93-111 in *Steinbeck Yearbook:* The Winter of Our Discontent, edited by Barbara A. Heavilin. Lewiston, N.Y.: The Edwin Mellen Press, 2000.

———. *John Steinbeck: A Centennial Tribute*. Westport, CT: Praeger, 2002.

Girard, Rene. *A Theatre of Envy: William Shakespeare*. New York: Oxford University Press, 1991.

Gladstein, Mimi R. "The Indestructible Woman: Ma Joad and Rose of Sharon." 115-27 in *Modern Critical Interpretations:* The Grapes of Wrath, edited by Harold Bloom. New York: Chelsea House Publishers, 1988.

———. "Steinbeck and the Woman Question: A Never-Ending Puzzle." 107-114 in *John Steinbeck: A Centennial Tribute*, edited by Stephen K. George. Westport, Conn.: Praeger, 2002.

Gonzales, Bobbi, and Mimi Gladstein. "*The Wayward Bus*: Steinbeck's Misogynistic Manifesto?" 157-73 in *Rediscovering Steinbeck: Revisionist Views of His Art, Politics and Intellect*, edited by Cliff Lewis and Carroll Birch. Lewiston, N.Y.: The Edwin Mellen Press, 1989.

Guerin, Wilfred L., et al. *A Handbook of Critical Approaches to Literature*. 4th ed. New York: Oxford University Press, 1999.

Hadella, Charlotte Cook. Of Mice and Men*: A Kinship of Powerlessness*. New York: Twayne Publishers, 1995.

Halfon, Mark S. *Integrity: A Philosophical Inquiry*. Philadelphia: Temple University Press, 1989.

Hallie, Philip. "From Cruelty to Goodness." 5-20 in *Vice & Virtue in Everyday Life: Introductory Readings in Ethics*, 5th ed., edited by Christina Sommers and Fred Sommers. San Diego: Harcourt College Publishers, 2001.

———.*The Paradox of Cruelty.* Middletown, Conn.: Wesleyan University Press, 1969.

Hansen, Carol L. "Beyond Evil: Cathy and Cal in *East of Eden*." 221-29 in *Beyond Boundaries: Rereading John Steinbeck*, edited by Susan Shillinglaw and Kevin Hearle. Tuscaloosa: University of Alabama Press, 2002.

Hardimon, Michael O. "Role Obligations." 396-401 in *Morality and the Market: Ethics and Virtue in the Conduct of Business*, edited by Eugene Heath. New York: McGraw-Hill, 2002.

"Harried Potter." *The Arizona Republic.* September 28, 2002: 2.

Hart, Richard E. "The Concept of Person in the Early Fiction of John Steinbeck." *Personalist Forum* 3, no. 1 (Spring 1992): 67-73.

———. "Steinbeck and Agrarian Pragmatism." 269-78 in *The Agrarian Roots of Pragmatism*, edited by Paul B. Thompson and Thomas C. Hilde. Nashville: Vanderbilt University Press, 2000.

———. "Steinbeck on Man and Nature: A Philosophical Reflection." 43-52 in *Steinbeck and the Environment: Interdisciplinary Approaches*, edited by

Susan Beegel, Susan Shillinglaw, and Wesley N. Tiffney Jr. Tuscaloosa: University of Alabama Press, 1997.

Hayashi, Tetsumaro. "Steinbeck's *Winter* as Shakespearean Fiction." *Steinbeck Quarterly* 12, no. 3-4 (Summer-Fall 1979): 107-115.

Heavilin, Barbara A. "Steinbeck's Exploration of Good and Evil: Structural and Thematic Unity in *East of Eden*." *Steinbeck Quarterly* 26, no. 3-4 (Summer-Fall 1993): 90-100.

Herbert, T. Walter. "Mozart, Hawthorne, and Mario Savio: Aesthetic Power and Political Complicity." *College English* 57 (1995): 397-409.

Higdon, David L. "Dionysian Madness in Steinbeck's 'The Chrysanthmums,'" *Classical and Modern Quarterly* 11, no. 1 (September 1990): 59-63.

Hughes, R. S. *John Steinbeck: A Study of the Short Fiction*. New York: Twayne Publishers, 1989.

Iser, Wolfgang. *Prospecting*. Baltimore: The Johns Hopkins University Press, 1989.

Jackson, Joseph Henry. Introduction. *The Short Novels of John Steinbeck: Tortilla Flat, The Red Pony, Of Mice and Men, The Moon Is Down, Cannery Row, The Pearl*. By John Steinbeck. New York: Viking, 1953. vii-xiii.

Johnson, Oliver A., ed. *Ethics: Selections from Classical and Contemporary Writers*. 4th ed. New York: Holt, Rinehart, and Winston, 1978.

Kant, Immanuel. *Critique of Practical Reason and Other Writings in Moral Philosophy*. Trans. Lewis White Beck. Chicago: University of Chicago Press, 1949.

Karolides, Nicholas, Margaret Bald, and Dawn B. Sova. *100 Banned Books: Censorship Histories of World Literature*. New York: Checkmark Books, 1999.

Kazin, Alfred. *On Native Grounds*. (1942) New York: Doubleday Anchor Books, 1956.

Kennedy, Ellen J., and Leigh Lawton. "Business Ethics in Fiction." *Journal of Business Ethics* 11 (1992): 187-95.

Kreeft, Peter, and Ronald K. Tacelli. *Handbook of Christian Apologetics*. Downers Grove, Ill.: InterVarsity Press, 1994.

Levant, Howard. "The Fully Matured Art: *The Grapes of Wrath*." 35-62 in *Modern Critical Views: John Steinbeck*, edited by Harold Bloom. New York: Chelsea House Publishers, 1987.

———. *The Novels of John Steinbeck: A Critical Study*. Columbia: University of Missouri Press, 1974.

Levinas, Emmanuel. *Ethics and Infinity: Conversations with Philippe Nemo*. Trans. Richard A. Cohen. Pittsburgh: Duquesne University Press, 1985.

———. "Signature." 289-95 in *Difficult Freedom: Essays on Judaism*, edited by Emmanuel Levinas. Baltimore: Johns Hopkins University Press, 1990.

———. *Time and the Other and Additional Essays*. Trans. Richard A. Cohen. Pittsburgh: Duquesne University Press, 1987.

————. *Totality and Infinity*. Trans. Alphonso Lingis. Boston: Martinus Nijhoff,
    1979.

————. *Totality and Infinity*. Trans. Alphonso Lingis. Pittsburgh: Duquesne
    University Press, 1969.

Lisca, Peter. *The Wide World of John Steinbeck*. New Brunswick, N.J.: Rutgers
    University Press, 1958.

————. *The Wide World of John Steinbeck*. New ed. New York: Gordian Press,
    1981.

MacIntyre, Alasdair. *After Virtue*. 2nd ed. Notre Dame, Ind.: University of Notre
    Dame Press, 1984.

Marcus, Mordecai. "The Lost Dream of Sex and Childbirth in 'The Chrysan-
    themums.'" *Modern Fiction Studies* 14 (Spring 1965): 54-58.

Martin, Mike W. *Everyday Morality: An Introduction to Applied Ethics*. Bel-
    mont, Calif.: Wadsworth, 1989.

McAdams, Tony, and Roswitha Koppensteiner. "The Manager Seeking Virtue:
    Lessons from Literature." *Journal of Business Ethics* 11 (1992): 627-634.

McCarthy, Paul. *John Steinbeck*. New York: Unger, 1980.

McFall, Lynne. "Integrity." *Ethics* 98 (1987): 5-20.

McKay, Nellie Y. "'Happy (?)-Wife-Motherdom': The Portrayal of Ma Joad in
    John Steinbeck's *The Grapes of Wrath*." 47-69 in *New Essays on* The
    Grapes of Wrath, edited by David Wyatt. New York: Cambridge University
    Press, 1990.

McMahon, Elizabeth. "'The Chrysanthemums': A Study of a Woman's
    Sexuality." *Modern Fiction Studies* 14 (Winter 1968): 953-58.

McWilliams, Carey. *Factories in the Field: The Story of Migratory Farm Labor
    in California*. Boston: Little, Brown and Company, 1939.

Meyer, Michael Jon. *Darkness Visible: The Moral Dilemma of Americans as
    Portrayed in the Early Short Fiction and Later Novels of John Steinbeck*.
    Ann Arbor, Mich.: University Microfilms, 1986.

————. "Steinbeck's *The Winter of Our Discontent* (1961)." 240-73 in *A New
    Study Guide to Steinbeck's Major Works, With Critical Explications*,
    edited by Tetsumaro Hayashi. Metuchen, N.J.: Scarecrow Press, 1993.

————. "Traveling with John: My Journey as a Steinbeck Scholar." 147-52 in
    John Steinbeck: A Centennial Tribute, edited by Stephen K. George. West-
    port, Conn.: Praeger, 2002.

Miller, Arthur. "Steinbeck." 64-67 in *John Steinbeck: Centennial Reflections
    By American Writers*, edited by Susan Shillinglaw. San Jose, Calif.: Center
    for Steinbeck Studies, San Jose State University, 2002.

Miller, William V. "Sexual and Spiritual Ambiguity in 'The Chrysanthemums.'"
    Modern Fiction Studies 20 (Summer 1972): 3-9.

Mitchell, Marilyn L. "Steinbeck's Strong Women: Feminine Identity in the
    Short Stories." *Southwest Review* 61 (Summer 1976): 304-15.

Morsberger, Robert E. "Steinbeck's Happy Hookers." *Steinbeck Quarterly* 9, no.
    3-4 (Summer-Fall 1976): 101-115.

————. "Steinbeck's Happy Hookers." 36-48 in *Steinbeck's Women: Essays in Criticism*, edited by Tetsumaro Hayashi. Muncie, Ind.: The Steinbeck Society of America and Ball State University, 1979.

————. *"The Wayward Bus."* 210-31 in *A Study Guide to Steinbeck (Part II)*, edited by Tetsumaro Hayashi. Metuchen, N.J.: Scarecrow Press, 1979.

Murphy, Jeffrie G., and Jean Hampton. *Forgiveness and Mercy.* Cambridge: Cambridge University Press, 1988.

Noble, Donald R., ed. *The Steinbeck Question: New Essays in Criticism.* Troy, N.Y.: Whitston, 1993.

Noddings, Nel. *Women and Evil.* Berkeley: University of California Press, 1989.

Nussbaum, Martha. "The Literary Imagination." 355-65 in *Falling Into Theory: Conflicting Views on Reading Literature*, 2nd ed, edited by David H. Richter. Boston: Bedford/St. Martin's Press, 2000.

————. *Love's Knowledge: Essays on Philosophy and Literature.* New York: Oxford University Press, 1990.

Owens, Louis. "Deadly Kids, Stinking Dogs, and Heroes: The Best Laid Plans in Steinbeck's *Of Mice and Men.*" *Steinbeck Studies* (Fall 2002): 1-8.

————. The Grapes of Wrath*: Trouble in the Promised Land.* New York: Twayne, 1996.

————. *John Steinbeck's Re-Vision of America.* Athens: University of Georgia Press, 1985.

————. "The Mirror and the Vamp: Invention, Reflection, and Bad, Bad Cathy Trask in *East of Eden.*" 235-57 in *Writing the American Classics*, edited by James Barbour and Tom Quirk. Chapel Hill: University of North Carolina Press, 1990.

Parini, Jay. *John Steinbeck: A Biography.* New York: Holt, 1995.

Pellow, Kenneth. "'The Chrysanthemums' Revisited." *Steinbeck Quarterly* 22, no. 1-2 (Winter-Spring 1989): 8-16.

Pritchard, H. A. *Moral Obligation.* Oxford: Oxford University Press, 1950.

Railsback, Brian. *"The Wayward Bus*: Misogyny or Sexual Selection?" 125-35 in *After* The Grapes of Wrath*: Essays on John Steinbeck in Honor of Tetsumaro Hayashi*, edited by Donald V. Coers, Paul D. Ruffin, and Robert J. DeMott. Athens: Ohio University Press, 1995.

Renner, Stanley. "The Real Woman Behind the Fence in 'The Chrysanthemums.'" *Modern Fiction Studies* 31 (Summer 1985): 305-17.

Ricketts, Edward F. *The Outer Shores: Part 2—Breaking Through,* edited by Joel W. Hedgpeth. Eureka, Calif.: Mad River Press, 1978.

Ricoeur, Paul. *Oneself as Another.* Trans. Kathleen Blamey. Chicago: University of Chicago Press, 1992.

Rorty, Richard. *Contingency, Irony and Solidarity.* Cambridge: Cambridge University Press, 1989.

Rosaldo, Michelle Zimbalist. *Women, Culture, Society.* Stanford: Stanford University Press, 1978.

Rosenstand, Nina. *The Moral of the Story: An Introduction to Ethics*. 4th ed. Boston: McGraw Hill, 2003.

Rothman, G. *The Riddle of Cruelty*. New York: Philosophical Library, 1971.

Sargent, Raymond Matthews. *Social Criticism in the Fiction of John Steinbeck*. Ann Arbor, Mich.: University Microfilms, 1981.

Schlosser, Eric. "In the Strawberry Fields." *The Atlantic Monthly*, November 1995: 80-108.

Schoenewolf, Gerald. *The Art of Hating*. Northvale, N.J.: Jason Aronson, 1991.

Shillinglaw, Susan. *John Steinbeck: Centennial Reflections by American Writers*. San Jose, Calif.: Center for Steinbeck Studies, 2002.

Shklar, Judith N. *Ordinary Vices*. Cambridge: Belknap, 1984.

Simmonds, Roy. *A Biographical and Critical Introduction to John Steinbeck*. Lewiston, N.Y.: The Edwin Mellen Press, 2000.

————. "The Original Manuscript of Steinbeck's 'The Chrysanthemums.'" *Steinbeck Quarterly* 7, no. 3-4 (Summer-Fall 1974): 102-111.

Sims, Ronald R., and Johannes Brinkman. "Enron Ethics (Or: Culture Matters More than Codes)." *Journal of Business Ethics* 45 (2003): 243-56.

Smith, Roger W. *Guilt: Man and Society*. Garden City, N.Y.: Doubleday, 1971.

Solomon, Robert C. *A Better Way to Think About Business: How Personal Integrity Leads to Corporate Success*. New York: Oxford University Press, 1999.

Solomon, Robert C., and Clancy Martin. *Above the Bottom Line: An Introduction to Business Ethics*. 3rd ed. Belmont, Calif.: Wadsworth/Thompson Learning, 2004.

Spellmeyer, Kurt. *Common Ground: Dialogue, Understanding, and the Teaching of Composition*. Englewood Cliffs, N.J.: Prentice Hall, 1993.

Steinbeck, Elaine, and Robert Wallsten, eds. *Steinbeck: A Life in Letters*. (1975) New York: Penguin Books, 1989.

Steinbeck, John. "About Ed Ricketts." vii-lxxvii in *The Log from the Sea of Cortez*. New York: Penguin Books, 1986.

————. *America and Americans*. New York: Viking Press, 1966.

————. *America and Americans and Selected Nonfiction*, edited by Susan Shillinglaw and Jackson Benson. New York: Viking Press, 2002.

————. *Cannery Row*. (1945) New York: Penguin Books, 1994.

————. *East of Eden*. (1952) New York: Penguin Books, 1992.

————. Foreword. *Tortilla Flat*. New York: Modern Library, 1937.

————. *The Forgotten Village* (Book). New York: Photogravure and Color Co., 1941.

————. *The Grapes of Wrath*. (1939) New York: Penguin Books, 1976, 1992.

————. *The Harvest Gypsies: On the Road to the Grapes of Wrath*. (1936) Berkeley: Heyday Books, 1988.

————. *In Dubious Battle*. New York: Penguin Books, 1992.

————. *Journal of a Novel: The* East of Eden *Letters*. New York: Penguin Books, 1969.

————. "Leader of the People." 2101-2112 in *The Norton Anthology of American Literature*, edited by Nina Baym, et al. 3rd ed. shorter. New York: W. W. Norton and Company, 1989.

————. *The Log from the Sea of Cortez.* (1951) New York: Penguin Books, 1986.

————. *The Long Valley.* (1938) New York: Viking Press, 1956.

————. *Of Mice and Men.* (1937) New York: Penguin Books, 1994.

————. *Once There Was A War.* New York: Viking Press, 1958.

————. "Our 'Rigged' Morality." *Coronet* 47 (1960): 146.

————. *Sea of Cortez.* New York: Viking Press, 1941.

————. *The Short Novels of John Steinbeck:* Tortilla Flat, The Red Pony, Of Mice and Men, The Moon Is Down, Cannery Row, The Pearl. New York: Viking Press, 1953.

————. *Sweet Thursday.* New York: Viking Press, 1954.

————. *Tortilla Flat.* New York: Modern Library, 1937.

————. *Travels with Charley in Search of America.* (1962) New York: Penguin Books, 2002.

————. *The Wayward Bus.* (1947) New York: Penguin Books, 1995.

————. *The Winter of Our Discontent.* (1961) New York: Penguin Books, 1989, 1996.

————. *Working Days: The Journals of* The Grapes of Wrath, edited by Robert DeMott. New York: Penguin, 1989.

Stout, Jeffrey. *Ethics after Babel: The Languages of Morals and Their Discontents.* Boston: Beacon Press, 1988.

Sullivan, Ernest. "The Cur in 'The Chrysanthemums.'" *Studies in Short Fiction* 16 (1975): 215-17.

Sweet, Charles. "Ms. Elisa Allen and Steinbeck's 'The Chrysanthemums.'" *Modern Fiction Studies* 21 (Fall 1974): 211-15.

Taylor, Gabriele. *Pride, Shame, and Guilt: Emotions of Self-Assessment.* Oxford: Clarendon Press, 1985.

Taylor, Richard. "Compassion." 40-52 in *Vice & Virtue in Everyday Life: Introductory Readings in Ethics*, edited by Christina Sommers. San Diego: Harcourt Brace, 1985.

Tedlock, E. W., Jr., and C. V. Wicker, eds. *Steinbeck and His Critics: A Record of Twenty-Five Years.* Albuquerque: University of New Mexico Press, 1957.

Thoreau, Henry David. *Walden,* edited by J. Lyndon Shanley. Princeton, N.J.: Princeton University Press, 1971.

Timmerman, John H. "John Steinbeck: An Ethics of Fiction." 99-106 in *John Steinbeck: A Centennial Tribute*, edited by Stephen K. George. Westport, Conn.: Praeger, 2002.

————. *John Steinbeck's Fiction: The Aesthetics of the Road Taken.* Norman: University of Oklahoma Press, 1986.

————. "John Steinbeck's Use of the Bible: A Descriptive Bibliography of the Critical Tradition." *Steinbeck Quarterly* 21, no. 1-2 (Winter-Spring 1988): 24-39.

Tompkins, Jane. *Sensational Designs: The Cultural Work of American Fiction, 1760-1860*. New York: Oxford University Press, 1985.

Trevino, Linda K., and Katherine A. Nelson. *Managing Business Ethics: Straight Talk About How To Do It Right*. 2nd ed. New York: John Wiley & Sons, 1999.

Valesquez, Manuel P. *Business Ethics: Concepts and Cases*. 5th ed. Upper Saddle River, N.J.: Prentice-Hall, 2002.

Verdier, Douglas L. "Ethan Allen Hawley and the Hanged Man: Free Will and Fate in *The Winter of Our Discontent*." *Steinbeck Quarterly* 15, no. 1-2 (Winter-Spring 1982): 44-50.

Walhout, Clarence. "The End of Literature: Reflections on Literature and Ethics." *Christianity and Literature* 47 (1998): 459-76.

Wasserstrom, Richard. "Lawyers as Professionals: Some Moral Issues." *Human Rights* 5 (1975): 1-15.

Watkins, Floyd C. "Flat Wine from *The Grapes of Wrath*." 57-66 in *Modern Critical Interpretations:* The Grapes of Wrath, edited by Harold Bloom. New York: Chelsea House Publishers, 1988.

Watt, F. W. *John Steinbeck*. New York: Grove Press, 1962.

West, Ray B., Jr., *The Short Story in America: 1910-1950*. Chicago: Henry Regnery, 1952.

Wilkens, Steve. *Beyond Bumper Sticker Ethics: An Introduction to Theories of Right & Wrong*. Downers Grove, Ill.: InterVarsity Press, 1995.

Index

Alice in Wonderland, 145, 150-53
Allen, Elisa, ("The Chrysanthemums"), 35, 90-105
America: future, 17-18, 180; greed, xii, 34, 53, 57; heritage, 46-47; moral decline, 13-18, 34, 50, 155, 172; racism, 16-17, 115
America and Americans, xi, 17-18, 49
American dream, 3-5, 13, 69, 155
applied ethics, vii
Aristotle, vii, xiv, 4, 18, 38, 62, 74-77, 83, 87-89

Bentham, Jeremy, 41, 62
Bible, xi, 37, 124
Booth, Wayne C., xiv, 39, 48, 88. *See also* narrative ethics
business ethics, 21-30, 155-67; and role morality, 22, 25-29; sex and power, 161-64; sex and work, 164

Campbell, Joseph, 121
Camus, Albert, vii, 63
Cannery Row, xii, 45, 147, 155, 158
Casy, Jim, (*The Grapes of Wrath*), 44-45, 115-21
charity, 11-12
Christianity, xii, 41, 46-47, 54, 115-117, 119, 124-25
"The Chrysanthemums," 90-102
classroom experiences with Steinbeck, 81, 91-92
communism, 41, 110. *See also* Marxism
compassion, xiii, 18, 75-76, 81-83, 101, 131, 149

conformism, 50
consequentialist ethics. *See* utilitarian ethics
Constitution, 46-47
Crane, Stephen, 111
Crooks, (*Of Mice and Men*), 68-70
cruelty, 131-42
Cup of Gold, 41
Curley's wife, (*Of Mice and Men*), 5, 64-67, 70, 79

Darwin, Charles. *See* evolution; naturalism
deconstruction, 88, 123, 129
deontological ethics, 6-9, 36-37, 39, 44-46, 62, 77
dignity. *See* self-respect
Dust Bowl, 74, 81-82
duty. *See* deontological ethics

East of Eden, xi-xiii, xiv, 45, 131-42, 145-51
Eastern philosophy, xi-xii
Eliot, T. S., xi
Emerson, Ralph Waldo, xii, 41, 120-21. *See also Nature*
emotions, 8, 34, 74-75, 101, 132-43, 173-74, 178-79. *See also* moral philosophy, emotions; Steinbeck, John, sentimentality
Enron, xii, 155, 164
environment, 15, 62
environmental ethics, xii, 62
Epictetus, xi
epistemology, 121
eros, 123

ethical criticism, 88-90
ethical entrapment, 89-90, 92-93
ethical relativity, 55, 62, 175-77
ethics. *See* moral philosophy. *See also*
    applied ethics; business ethics;
    deontological ethics; environmental
    ethics; existential ethics; extrinsic
    ethics; intrinsic ethics; narrative
    ethics; normative ethics; personal
    ethics; postmodern ethics; rationalist
    ethics; social ethics; theological
    ethics; utilitarian ethics; virtue ethics
ethos, 25, 87
euthanasia, 79
Everyman, 52
evolution, 41, 176
existential ethics, 35, 49-57, 67
extrinsic ethics, 37-39

family, 5, 56-57, 121-27, 144, 172-73
Fascism. *See* Holocaust
Faulkner, William, xi, 57, 122
femininity, 90, 96-97, 100-101, 105
feminism, 88, 103, 172
Fitzgerald, F. Scott, xi
"Flight," 38
The Forgotten Village, 73, 111-12
Frankl, Victor E., 49-51, 53, 56-57
free will, 65, 67, 145-46, 148-49.
    See also naturalism
Freudian psychology, 51-52, 88

Gardner, John, vii
generosity, 9-11
The Grapes of Wrath, xii, 5-13, 22-29,
    44-45, 73-77, 81-84, 110-27
Great Awakenings, 46
Great Depression, 13, 21. *See also* Dust
    Bowl
group man. *See* phalanx theory

happiness, 4, 13, 17-18, 41-42, 45-46,
    88
Hawley, Ethan Allen, (*The Winter of
    Our Discontent*), 50-57, 169-80
Heidegger, Martin, 35, 108
Hemingway, Ernest, xi, 57, 122, 127
Hollywood, 158, 165
Holocaust, 49, 79, 108

Horton, Ernest, (*The Wayward Bus*),
    156-60
Husserl, Edmund, 108

In Dubious Battle, xii, 25, 37, 43-44
integrity, 164, 167, 169-80
intrinsic ethics, 35-37

Jeffersonian agrarianism, 41
Joad, Ma, (*The Grapes of Wrath*), 7-11,
    27-28, 122-23
Joad, Tom, (*The Grapes of Wrath*),
    114, 120
Journal of a Novel: The East of Eden
    Letters, 18
Jungian psychology, 122

Kant, Immanuel, xi, 36-37, 77. *See also*
    deontological ethics
Kazin, Alfred, 61
Kennedy, John F., 17
King Jr., Martin Luther, 17

Lawrence, D. H., xi
Levinas, Emmanuel, 48, 108-10, 113-
    16, 118-21, 123, 126-27, 137
The Log from the Sea of Cortez, 31, 39
logos, 56
London, Jack, 111
loneliness, 65-69,
The Long Valley, 37

marriage, 53-54, 123-24, 162-63
Marxism, 37, 62, 88
Mill, John Stuart, 41, 62
Milton, George, (*Of Mice and Men*),
    76-81
minorities. *See* Steinbeck, John,
    portrayals of minorities
The Moon Is Down, xii
moral experience, 62-63, 70
moral philosophy, vii, 62, 107-8; and
    aesthetics, 33, 107, 112, 179;
    emotions, 19, 74-75, 142-43;
    literature, vii-viii, 21-22, 33-34, 38-
    39, 46, 48, 63, 71, 74, 89-90;
    psychology, 141-44, 148
moral reasoning, 21, 87-88
Morte d' Arthur, 34

multiculturalists, 88

narrative ethics, xiii-xiv, 39
naturalism, 41, 108, 111, 176
Nature, 120-21
Nazism. *See* Holocaust
New Criticism, 88-89
New Historicism, 88
Nietzsche, Friedrich, vii, 108
nihilism, 50
non-teleological thinking, 39, 63, 107-
    9, 113
normative ethics, 64
Nussbaum, Martha, vii, 48, 71

Oaks, Camille, (*The Wayward Bus*),
    163-64
Of Mice and Men, xii, 4-5, 44, 63-70,
    76-81, 83-84
Once There Was a War, xii
ontology, 108

paisanos, 42-43
The Pastures of Heaven, 147
The Pearl, xiii, 38, 155
personal ethics, xii
phalanx theory, 25, 115-17, 119, 125
phenomenology, 108
Plato, vii, xi, 62, 87
postmodern ethics, 107-10
pragmatism, xii, 41
Pritchard, Elliot, (*The Wayward Bus*),
    156-58
Puritanism, 46, 103, 108, 169

racism, 67-70. *See also* America,
    racism
rape, 138-39, 163
rationalist ethics, 35
rationalization, 52-55, 158, 174-77
realism, 41, 111, 121
recreation with morality, 175, 177
Ricketts, Edward F., xi, 107-8, 121
role morality. *See* business ethics
romanticism, 41, 46
Rose of Sharon, (*The Grapes of
    Wrath*), 18, 76-78, 81-83, 124-26

sadomasochism, 138-39

Sartre, Jean-Paul, vii, 35, 63
The Sea of Cortez, xi, xii, 37
self-respect, 12, 170-71
sentiment. *See* emotions
September 11, 2001, 57
Sexism, 64-67, 69-70, 92, 123, 164. *See
    also* feminism; Steinbeck, John,
    portrayals of women
Small, Lennie. *See* Milton, George
social ethics, xii-xiii, 35
*Speech Accepting the Nobel Prize for
    Literature*, 83
Spinoza, Benedict, xi
Steinbeck, John: and America, viii, 34,
    57; artistry, 34-35, 179; censorship,
    73-74, 82, 126; the common man, 3-
    4, 14; literary critics/criticism, 45-
    46, 61; moralists, 107; Nobel Prize,
    3; philosophy, viii, xi-xiv, 33-39,
    41-42, 45-47, 61-64, 83, 107-8:
    portrayals of minorities, xiii, 114-15;
    portrayals of women, 65, 122-23,
    146-48; religion, xii; sentimentality,
    34, 57, 61, 112
Sweet Thursday, 45, 147

Tao Teh Ching, xi
teleology, 38-39
theological ethics, 35-36, 39
Thoreau, Henry David, 4-6
timshel. *See* free will
To a God Unknown, xii, 35
Tortilla Flat, xii-xiii, 37, 42-43
totalitarianism, 50, 115-16, 123
transcendentalism, 41, 115, 117-18,
    120-21, 125. *See also* Emerson,
    Ralph Waldo; Thoreau, Henry
    David
Trask, Cathy/Kate, (*East of Eden*), 131-
    42, 145-51
*Travels with Charley in Search of
    America*, xi, 13-17

Uncle Tom's Cabin, 112
utilitarian ethics, 41-47, 62
utopia, 4-5, 13, 18

virtue ethics, 62, 74-77

The Waste Land, 54
The Wayward Bus, 155-65
Whitman, Walt, 41
will-o'-the-wisp, 91-93, 96

The Winter of Our Discontent, xi-xii,
49-58, 167, 169-80
work, 12-13, 19-20, 159-61
World War II, 13

About the Contributors

Sarah Appleton Aguiar (Ph.D., University of Connecticut, 1995) is an associate professor in the Department of English and Philosophy at Murray State University in Murray, Kentucky, where she teaches courses in women's and contemporary literature. Her publications include *The Bitch Is Back: Wicked Women in Literature* (Southern Illinois University Press, 2001) as well as numerous scholarly articles, and she is the coeditor of *He Said, She Says: An RSVP to the Male Text* (Fairleigh Dickinson University Press, 2001).

Joseph Allegretti is professor of business and religious studies at Siena College in Loudonville, New York. Professor Allegretti received his B.A. from Colgate University, his J.D. from Harvard Law School, and his M.Div. from Yale Divinity School. His research and writing interests are in professional ethics, the intersection of law and religion, and the relationship between literature and ethics. He is the author of two books and over fifty scholarly articles and chapters on a variety of topics in law, religion, ethics, and literature.

Richard Astro is distinguished university professor at Drexel University and chief academic officer for the National Consortium for Academics and Sports at the University of Central Florida. Formerly the provost of Drexel University, Dr. Astro co-directed with Tetsumaro Hayashi the first major Steinbeck conference in 1970 at Oregon State University and is best known in Steinbeck circles for his groundbreaking *John Steinbeck and Edward F. Ricketts: The Shaping of a Novelist*. Dr. Astro is considered by many to be the leading authority on Steinbeck and ecology, particularly Ricketts's early influence on the writer's philosophical worldview.

Patrick K. Dooley, Board of Trustees Distinguished Professor of Philosophy at St. Bonaventure University, received his B.A. (in philosophy and Latin) from St. Thomas College and his M.A. and Ph.D. (in philosophy) from the University of Notre Dame. From 1996-1999 Professor Dooley was distinguished visiting professor of philosophy and English at the United States Air Force Academy. He has published three books and more than sixty articles and book chapters in the general area of philosophy and American culture. He is also the bibliographer for *Stephen Crane Studies* and editor of the *Society for the Advancement of American Philosophy Newsletter*.

Terry Gorton received his B.A. and M.A. in English from Brigham Young University and his Ph.D. in English from Stony Brook University in New York. He served on the editorial board for *John Steinbeck: A Centennial Tribute* (2002), is a co-director for the 2006 "Steinbeck and His Contemporaries" conference, and has been published in such venues as *A Centennial Tribute* and *The Steinbeck Review*. Dr. Gorton currently teaches literature and composition at Brigham Young University-Idaho.

John J. Han (Ph.D., Nebraska) is professor of English at Missouri Baptist University, where he teaches American, world, and minority literature. Dr. Han has also taught at Kansas State University, the University of Nebraska-Lincoln, and Nebraska Wesleyan University. He has written scholarly publications on Flannery O'Connor, Andrew Marvell, and Christian issues within higher education, and serves as founding editor of *Intégrité: A Faith and Learning Journal*. Dr. Han received the Emerson Electric Excellence in Teaching Award in 2000 and the Parkway Distinguished Teaching Award in 2001.

Michael D. Hansen is a freelance scholar currently living in Chapel Hill, North Carolina. He received his M.A. in English from Brigham Young University in 1997. He has also pursued graduate studies at Duke University and the University of North Carolina-Chapel Hill, where he taught composition and literature courses. He has presented papers on literature and postmodern ethics at several conferences, including the 1997 "Literature and the Law" conference at the University of Southern California.

Richard E. Hart is Cyrus H. Holly Professor of Applied Ethics at Bloomfield College in Bloomfield, New Jersey. He has written and lectured on various aspects of Steinbeck and philosophy, with essays in *The Steinbeck Review, Steinbeck Studies, The Personalist Forum, The Agrarian Roots of Pragmatism*, and *Steinbeck and the Environment: Interdisciplinary Approaches*. Professor Hart is also the editor or coeditor of *Ethics and the Environment* (1992), *Plato's Dialogues: The Dialogical Approach* (1997), and *Philosophy in Experience: American Philosophy in Transition* (1997).

Barbara A. Heavilin, associate professor of English at Taylor University in Upland, Indiana, is co-editor-in-chief of the scholarly journal *The Steinbeck Review*. Dr. Heavilin received her A.B. in English and Spanish from Indiana Wesleyan University, her M.A. in English from Virginia Polytechnic Institute, and her Ph.D. in English from Ball State University. She is the former editor of the *Steinbeck Yearbook* and the author of *The Critical Response to John Stein-*

beck's The Grapes of Wrath (2000), *John Steinbeck's* The Grapes of Wrath: *A Reference Guide* (2002), and *The Quaker Presence in America* (2002). In addition, she has published articles and reviews on Margaret Fell Fox, William Wordsworth, and James Thurber.

Luchen Li (Ph.D., Oregon) is a professor of humanities at Kettering University. Professor Li has served on the editorial boards for *John Steinbeck: A Centennial Tribute* (2002) and *The Moral Philosophy of John Steinbeck.* His publications appear in *Steinbeck Studies, The Steinbeck Review, John Steinbeck: A Centennial Tribute* (edited by M. A. Syed, 2004*)*, and the forthcoming *Steinbeck Encyclopedia.* He recently completed *John Steinbeck* (a DLB documentary volume, 2005) and is currently coauthoring *A Critical Companion to John Steinbeck.* His dissertation, *Between Society and Nature: A Rhetoric of John Steinbeck's Aesthetics*, has been widely cited and referenced. Dr. Li is also editor of the MCEA (Michigan College English Association) newsletter.

Allene M. Parker, an assistant professor of humanities at Embry-Riddle Aeronautical University in Prescott, Arizona, teaches courses in writing, literature, business communications, comparative religions, science and religion, and ethics. She received her D.A. from Idaho State University and recently presented papers on Steinbeck at "John Steinbeck's Americas: A Centennial Conference" in Hempstead, New York, and at the RMMLA annual meeting in Scottsdale, Arizona, in October 2002.

John H. Timmerman, professor of English at Calvin College in Grand Rapids, Michigan, has published two books on Steinbeck—*John Steinbeck's Fiction: The Aesthetics of the Road Taken* (1986) and *The Dramatic Landscape of Steinbeck's Short Stories* (1990)—as well as numerous essays and book chapters. In the past decade Professor Timmerman has authored *T. S. Eliot: The Poetics of Recovery, Jane Kenyon: A Literary Life*, and *Robert Frost: The Ethics of Ambiguity.* He has also published twenty short stories in such journals as *The Texas Review, Western Humanities Review, Critic*, and *The Steinbeck Review.*

About the Editor

Stephen K. George is a professor of English at Brigham Young University-Idaho, where he teaches courses in American Literature, ethical criticism of literature, Steinbeck, Shakespeare, composition, and ethics. He received his B.A. and M.A. in English from Brigham Young University and his Ph.D. in English from Ball State University. With Barbara Heavilin, Dr. George is co-editor-in-chief of the premier scholarly journal in Steinbeck studies, *The Steinbeck Review*. He is also the founder and current executive director of The New Steinbeck Society of America.

Dr. George has edited or co-edited three other books—*John Steinbeck: A Centennial Tribute, John Steinbeck's Sense of Place*, and *Ethics, Literature, and Theory: An Introductory Reader*—and published more than thirty articles, reviews, prefaces, notes, and encyclopedia entries on Steinbeck, including "John Steinbeck" in *The Oxford Encyclopedia of American Literature*. He was recently presented with the 2003/2004 Richard W. and Dorothy Burkhardt Award for outstanding Steinbeck scholarship. The present volume evidences his lifelong interest in the interdisciplinary connections between literature and philosophy.